ALSO BY ANDREW MARANISS

Strong Inside

Games of Deception

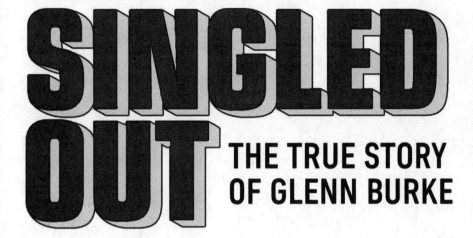

SINGLED OUT

THE TRUE STORY OF GLENN BURKE

ANDREW MARANISS

PHILOMEL BOOKS

PHILOMEL BOOKS

An imprint of Penguin Random House LLC, New York

First published in the United States of America by Philomel,
an imprint of Penguin Random House LLC, 2021

Copyright © 2021 by Andrew Maraniss

Visit us online at penguinrandomhouse.com.

Library of Congress Cataloging-in-Publication Data is available.

Printed in the United States of America

ISBN 9780593116722

1 3 5 7 9 10 8 6 4 2

Edited by Kelsey Murphy

Design by Monique Sterling

Text set in Legacy Serif

With love and high fives for Alison, Eliza, and Charlie

CONTENTS

CHAPTER 1

JOY AND PAIN

obby Haskell had learned not to be surprised by anything he encountered on the blustery streets and alleys of San Francisco's Tenderloin district.

In the early 1990s it was his job to scour these places, looking for the people most of society preferred to ignore, the drug addicts, sex workers, and runaways, the sick and the dying. As a therapist and homeless advocate for the Tom Waddell Clinic, Haskell's mission was to find these men and women, to earn their trust, and to educate them on the health care services available to them through the clinic, to offer a human connection in a world in which they felt all alone.

Haskell has never forgotten the day he walked into one of the many cheap hotels in the seedy Tenderloin in search of a homeless man his boss had asked him to track down. To call these places hotels was a stretch; they weren't national chains that offered free breakfast, a pool, and cable TV. Instead they were the kinds of dingy hostels that locked the fire escapes to keep people from skipping out on their bills. A bar of soap was a luxury. But for the men and women who could scrape together enough money (typically less than $10 a night), a room here was a step up from living on the street, even if just for a month, a week, or a day.

Haskell[1] found the room he was looking for and knocked on the door. Even by the dismal standards of the Tenderloin, this was the barest room he'd ever seen. No furniture; just a mattress in the corner. And on that mattress was a Black man, curled up in the fetal position, wearing nothing but a pair of shorts. The man was sobbing and soaked in sweat, crying tears Haskell recognized from years on the streets: tears of hopelessness, fear, and drugs.

Haskell sat cross-legged on the floor, not preaching, not judging, only offering conversation and information about his clinic's social and medical services. Gradually the man stopped crying. There was a spark in his eyes and the hint of a muscular, athletic body. In this godforsaken place, he still exuded charm and charisma.

The man on the mattress spoke with the ease of someone accustomed to meeting new people. He began to share the story of his life, telling tales of athletic feats on the playgrounds of Berkeley, California, of a professional baseball career that had carried him to the game's highest peak, of the brief but joyful days of freedom and light when he was one of the most popular men in town.

Bobby Haskell had heard all kinds of bizarre stories from people on the streets. One man had insisted that the FBI had planted radios in his thumbs; another claimed to be a Vietnam veteran suffering from PTSD, though he was far too young to have served in that war.

But Haskell was savvy enough to know the difference between lies and schizophrenia and the strange but true.

So when the man sitting across from him said he had once played for the Los Angeles Dodgers, had started in center field in Game 1 of the 1977 World Series, and had even invented the high five, Bobby believed him.

The man on the mattress?

His name was Glenn Burke.

CHAPTER 2

TOP OF THE HEAP

On October 11, 1977, Glenn Burke stood in the heart of the sports universe, patrolling center field at Yankee Stadium for the Los Angeles Dodgers in Game 1 of the World Series.

After spending six seasons working his way up through the Dodgers' Minor League farm system, Burke had arrived in the Bronx prepared for this moment in the spotlight.

He was an uncommonly talented athlete, even among other big leaguers, with so much potential that Dodger first-base coach Jim Gilliam had compared him to one of the game's all-time greats, Willie Mays. Dodger manager Tommy Lasorda had enough confidence in his rookie to write Burke's name in the starting lineup in the biggest game of either man's career. Teammates loved his enthusiasm and

Glenn Burke started in center field for the Los Angeles Dodgers in Game 1 of the 1977 World Series. His sixth-inning single should have scored Steve Garvey, but home plate umpire Nestor Chylak missed the call, robbing Burke of a World Series RBI. (ABC Sports)

gap-toothed grin, the laughter he brought to the locker room, the funky music blasting from his boom box.

Burke cut an imposing figure in his gray-and-blue Dodger uniform. With his broad chest, muscular legs, and seventeen-inch biceps, other players marveled at his strength and physique. He had an energy and toughness to match, never backing away from a fight. And he needed that attitude in New York. When the visiting Dodgers arrived at Yankee Stadium for a workout the day before Game 1, raucous young Yankee fans were there to greet them, rocking the team bus and shouting slurs at the players. As Game 1 unfolded, fans targeted Dodger players with rolls of toilet paper, stink bombs, whiskey bottles, and hard rubber balls.

None of this flustered Burke. Not the big city, not the Yankee–Dodger rivalry, not the stakes of the game, not the projectiles flying out of the bleachers. He had said so the day before, when he granted a sportswriter a phone interview while relaxing in his room at the Dodgers' luxurious New York hotel, the Waldorf Astoria.

"I don't get nervous no more," he confessed. "The pressure hasn't hit me yet. When everybody was grabbing and hugging and pouring champagne over my head [after the Dodgers beat the Philadelphia Phillies to advance to the World Series] I thought to myself how lucky I was to be in the big leagues . . . Everything is happening so fast. It's hard to analyze what I'm going through, but I don't want the music to stop."

The reporter asked Burke for his thoughts on playing in Yankee Stadium, a venue that was not only famous, but one of the most difficult ballparks in which to play center field. The expanse of green grass between the foul poles was enormous, with the left-center-field fence standing 430 feet from home plate, dead center 417. Just beyond the wall were reminders of the Yankees' dominant past, shrines to Hall of Famers including Babe Ruth and Lou Gehrig.

"Those monuments are real cool. I never thought anybody had stuff like that," Burke said. "Maybe they'll have one for me someday."

But there is no monument to Glenn Burke today at any Major League ballpark. He cherished his good fortune in life when he granted the interview on October 10, 1977, but he'd never start another World Series game after October 11. He'd be run out of baseball for good by 1980, and his life would unravel altogether a few years after that.

What happened?

To arrive at the answer, you need to know something about the Dodgers' fun-loving center fielder, a secret he kept from the public in 1977.

Glenn Burke was gay.

And as people learned this about him in the late 1970s, it was their homophobia, an irrational fear and hatred of gay people, that starved him of opportunity and launched him into a tailspin from the bright lights of the World Series to the dark alleys of the Tenderloin.

Burke died less than a year after Bobby Haskell found him on that mattress. But even in those final months, he held out hope that lessons learned from his struggles as a gay Black man in Major League Baseball would someday make life better for other people. That in his brief time on earth, forty-two years that coincided with an unprecedented period of gay liberation, he had made a lasting difference.

CHAPTER 3
HEART'S DESIRE

The day Alice Burke left her husband in 1952, she fixed him one last dinner.

Life had once been good for Alice and Luther Burke. He worked at the Oakland shipyards, she was a nurse's aide, and they had started a family together. Before Glenn came along, there were the four girls, Beverly, Lutha, Joyce, and Elona.

But Luther drank too much, and sometimes at night, after he closed the bedroom door, the girls could hear the commotion, fighting, and abuse. Luther had been a boxer in the navy; Alice was a sweet woman who worked hard and loved her children. She stood no chance against a drunk and violent man.

And then one day, when Alice was pregnant with Glenn, her oldest daughter, Beverly, summoned the courage to pose a question. "Why are you staying with Dad," she asked, "when he hurts you all the time?"

It was a simple question, but leaving an abuser is never easy. And for a pregnant African American mother of four in 1952 with little money and the rest of her family thousands of miles away, leaving was far more complicated than Beverly could have imagined. The next day, Alice made Luther's breakfast and made his lunch as usual. But the minute he was out the door, she started packing. When Luther came home from work that night, his wife and children were gone, and so was all but one piece of furniture. Alice had left Luther dinner on the kitchen table.

She took the kids to Louisiana to stay with her parents for a few months, saved some money, and proved a point to Luther: she would not tolerate his abuse. She and the girls ultimately moved back in with Luther in Oakland, and Glenn was born there on November 16, 1952. Alice's strength and courage revealed Luther's weakness; he wanted nothing to do with a family he couldn't control through fear. By the time Glenn was eleven months old, Luther moved out. Though he occasionally came back to visit, he eventually started a new life with a new family, far away in Alaska.

With or without their father, this was a family that was emblematic of the East Bay in the mid-twentieth century. During World War II, thousands of Black sharecroppers moved to Oakland from the Deep South to build ships. By the war's end, the city's African American population had quadrupled. But after the war, the shipbuilding and other manufacturing jobs disappeared. With jobs scarce, more affluent white residents left town—one hundred thousand of them between 1950 and 1960 alone. The people left behind faced mounting economic and social pressures: fewer jobs, freeway construction and urban renewal projects that decimated businesses and neighborhoods, and eroding city services. And when Black citizens called for justice, the response from the white establishment was to tighten its grip. Poor Southern whites who had also moved to the Bay Area for wartime jobs were recruited to join the police force. They brought their racial attitudes with them from Dixie, and often used their state-sanctioned power to abuse Black citizens.

It was in the midst of this tension that Alice Burke raised her family, moving between homes in North Oakland and South Berkeley. Berkeley, home of the University of California, was emerging as its own hotbed of conflict in the 1960s as administrators cracked down on student protests against the war in Vietnam and racism at home. For a young Glenn Burke, the political and social changes in Oakland and Berkeley (the "East Bay" across from San Francisco) were not yet much of a concern. He felt the strength and love of his mother, the protection of his older sisters, and the friendship of a mix of Black, white, Asian, and Latinx friends on the block. The home was constantly filled with people: the sisters and their schoolmates, their boyfriends, and extended family. Alice loved to cook, and the smells from the kitchen were a reminder of her Louisiana roots: gumbo, yams, mac and cheese, potato salad—all made from scratch.

Glenn was a "pretty good kid for a boy," his sister Lutha recalled, and even when he did get into trouble, it was "usually something laughable," she said. He and his buddies would stand on the street and break into applause whenever a car drove by. The driver would look around and wonder what was happening, and while Lutha could never understand the appeal, Glenn and his friends got the biggest kick out of it. Other times, they'd jump out of the bushes and throw water balloons at passersby, hiding just in time not to be seen (or so they thought).

If this was a home mostly filled with love and laughter, there was one occasional interruption: Luther's infrequent visits. Alice and her ex remained on speaking terms, and sometimes he'd come by the house. Lutha wanted nothing to do with her father. One time he showed up on the doorstep, suitcase in his hand and coat on his arm. She slammed the door in his face and said dryly to her mom, "Your husband is on the porch."

The drop-in dad would attempt to "toughen up" the boy who lived with all these women, picking on Glenn, roughhousing with too much force. Just trying to make the boy hard like him, he'd say. As much as Luther's visits made Glenn anxious and uncomfortable, he still found pockets of peace: at the playground, in church, drawing pictures, listening to music, singing. He had a beautiful voice. And it was that voice that led to one of two formative experiences in the life of a young Glenn Burke, his first taste of the spotlight.

In December of 1961, just after his ninth birthday, a white folk-music trio known as the Limeliters announced they were looking for talented schoolchildren to sing along with them as they recorded a live album. Glenn, then a student at Lincoln Elementary, was one of fifty Berkeley kids handpicked to participate in two live concerts recorded for the album. Dressed in a gold sweater, Glenn joined a multiracial group of children singing along with the professionals, belting out tunes such as "Lollipop Tree," "Stay on the Sunny Side," and "America the Beautiful."

The album appeared in stores early the next year. *Through Children's Eyes: Little-Folk Songs for Adults*, sold for $4.98 and was a hit with review-ers. "Kids Steal the Show" read a headline in Des Moines, Iowa. Years later, Lutha said the experience provided Glenn a window to a larger world. "He grinned the whole time. It was just a wonderful opportunity for him to connect with kids and adults of all races," she said. "At that time, there were not many opportunities for something like that. It probably set the tone for his life."

Around the same time, Glenn experienced another glimpse of fame. On Saturday mornings, he and his sisters loved to watch *The King Norman Show*, a local children's television program. With his wife and French poodle as sidekicks, host Norman Rosenberg donned a royal gown (actually his bathrobe) and jeweled crown and turned the televi-sion studio into a magical world known as Happy Bedlam, which he ruled with "kindness and gifts." Recorded in front of a live studio audi-ence of children and moms, the show was, according to one newspaper description, "a pasteboard empire of popcorn and candy, toys and talent." The program featured pogo stick races, guessing games, and tal-ent shows, and there was one segment designed to make even the most sugar-high kid sit at attention, perhaps even shed a tear. Each week, a child who had written a heartwarming letter asking for a present for themselves or a friend was invited to sit in the Heart's Desire booth.

Glenn's oldest sister, Beverly, decided to write a letter to King Norman. She was shocked to receive a phone call from the television station with the news that her letter had been selected. So the next Saturday, Beverly dressed up and everyone went down to the studio. The time came for the segment, and Beverly took her place in the booth. King Norman read her letter out loud. "All the little boys in the neighborhood like to ride their bikes, but my mom can't afford to buy Glenn one. My heart's desire is that Glenn could have his own bike so he can play with the other boys in the neighborhood."

As the studio audience cheered with delight, King Norman asked Glenn to come down to the stage, where he presented him with a brand-new red bicycle.

"What are you going to do for your sister to thank her for writing in?" Norman asked.

"I'm going to let her ride the bike when we get home," Glenn replied.

But that promise didn't last.

"He wouldn't let nobody ride that bike," Lutha recalled decades later. "We'd ask him, 'What about what you said when you were at the TV station?' He'd just look at us and grin."

As far as young Glenn Burke was concerned, he had now starred on television and recorded a live album. He knew what it felt like to stand apart from the crowd. And there was one other way in which he felt special back then, an aspect of his being that would come to define his self-worth, for better or worse, for the rest of his life.

At his core, Glenn Burke was an athlete—one of the best anyone had ever seen.

CHAPTER 4
BUSHROD KING

Lutha was home babysitting her younger sisters one day in the early 1960s when Glenn, then ten or eleven years old, came home from Bushrod Park, tears running down his cheeks.

Bushrod was Glenn's sanctuary, where he discovered his love for baseball and basketball and where his talents became legendary. But that wouldn't happen for a few years. For now, he was just one of the young kids hanging around the park, hoping to get picked to play by the older guys, learning a little about the ways of the world in the process.

Lutha asked Glenn why he was crying. The bigger boys had been teasing him, he said, calling him short.

If there was one thing Lutha would not tolerate, it was someone disrespecting her family. She was the protector. She told her siblings to stay put, and bolted out of the house on her way to Bushrod to confront the punk bullying her brother.

But as she crossed Telegraph Avenue, she turned around to see her sisters, the ones she was supposed to be watching, following her. "Here comes Joyce, here comes Elona, I look up and here comes five-year-old Carol running across that busy street," she recalled. "Lord have mercy."

The kids reminded Lutha of a flock of baby quail following their mother through the woods. All she could think about was how she would get everyone home safely without her mom finding out what had happened. Otherwise, Alice would kill her for putting the children in danger.

But they all made it to Bushrod, the youngsters curious how their sister was going to handle this problem. Lutha found the boy who'd been picking on Glenn, and with the fierceness of an older sister that no boy was going to mess with, she stared him down and scolded him. Mission complete, she led everyone back home, undetected by their mom, and nobody at Bushrod Park messed with Glenn Burke ever again.

Freed from the bullying, Burke thrived as an athlete, spending long hours at the park, playing in pickup games, joining teams. Anything but football; his mother worried he'd get hurt and forbade him from playing. When one game ended in the morning, he'd move on to another in the afternoon, spending so much time in his uniforms they practically become a second skin, Alice peeling a sweat-soaked jersey off his body before bed.

In middle school, one of Glenn's favorite pastimes was a game called strikeout, a two-man playground version of baseball. A chalk square on a brick wall marked the strike zone; Glenn and his friends took turns pitching a tennis ball to one another. One of his favorite opponents was Vince Trahan.

"I don't think Glenn ever lost," Trahan recalled. "He threw the ball so hard. And when he was batting, he was always hitting it over the fence." Another opponent was Jon Nikcevich. "He'd bet me a quarter that he could take me deep on individual pitches," Nikcevich remembered. "We lost a lot of tennis balls there." And Nikcevich lost a lot of quarters.

Basketball, however, was Glenn's favorite sport, then and always. He developed his skills on the lower-height hoops at the school playgrounds around town, where his leaping ability and body control were far ahead of his peers.

"We'd all be trying to do aerial acrobatics," Trahan recalled, "but the difference was that where we'd be somewhat above the rim when we dunked it, Glenn was damn near touching the top of the backboard. He was so muscular and always two or three steps ahead of everybody. It just came natural to him."

Located in North Oakland near the border with Berkeley, Bushrod Park was the battleground where the top players from each city met to see who was the king of the East Bay. "It was like two heavyweight champions ending up in the ring, and the ring was Bushrod," said Trahan. "No fights, no guns, just athletic respect. The competition was intense."

So intense that if your team lost a game, it was unlikely that you'd ever get back on the court. Choosing sides was critical.

And this, in his teen years, is where Burke demonstrated his athletic supremacy and his empathy. What made him special, friends say, was not just the fact that he'd dominate those games. He'd do it alongside guys nobody else would ever pick to be on their teams, the kids who otherwise would have spent a long day on the sidelines. He'd see those boys standing there, the ones who were out of shape or too short or who couldn't jump or shoot, and he'd take them on his team. And he'd win. And win again. And again. It was an act of compassion, yes, but also the ultimate badassery: *I'll take these rejects and still beat you.*

The confidence Burke gained on the playing fields and courts of Oakland and Berkeley extended to other areas of his life. He was the funniest kid in his circle of friends, not only adept at perfectly mimicking the popular Black comedians of the day, but also cutting his buddies to shreds with improvised freestyle riffs. They called it the "hoorah," and Glenn was the hoorah champion. He'd bust on your clothes, on the way you walked or talked, on your mama. "He was a great improviser, no written material, just spontaneous," Trahan recalled. "He never lost a hoorah battle."

One time, his basketball prowess and his sense of humor came together. Kids at the park asked how he could jump so high and hang in the air so long.

"Potatoes," he deadpanned.

He was just messing with everybody, but all of a sudden, the other boys at Bushrod started eating a lot more spuds.

CHAPTER 5
HOT STUFF

John Lambert played seven years of pro basketball with the world's best players in the NBA, and Glenn Burke never played a down of organized football, but Lambert says one of the most athletic feats he ever witnessed involved Burke and a pigskin after school one day when they were students at Berkeley High.

As Burke and Lambert cut across the football field on the way to Glenn's house, an errant football landed by Burke's feet. He leaned over, picked it up, and flicked it over the head of the field-goal kicker.

Sixty-five yards away.

Ask anyone who hung around Glenn Burke in high school and they'll tell you stories about his astonishing athleticism. How he'd stand flat-footed underneath a basketball hoop, jump in the air, triple pump, and dunk the ball behind his head. How he once hit a baseball so hard it ripped through a chain-link fence more than three hundred feet away. How he never lifted weights, but was still the strongest kid anyone had ever seen.

Glenn Burke was hardly the first great athlete to ascend from the playgrounds of Oakland and Berkeley. But with a lethal combination of speed, strength, leaping ability, confidence, and competitiveness, many of his contemporaries considered Burke the best athlete of all, a double threat in basketball and baseball.

Glenn Burke (back row, far left) as a student at Berkeley High School. One of the most progressive schools in the country, BHS was the first high school to implement a Black Studies program. Students frequently protested the war in Vietnam and the mistreatment of Black citizens by the Oakland police. (Berkeley High School)

Burke's basketball prowess was legendary at Bushrod Park, but that wasn't the only place he played ball. Glenn and his friends roamed the entire Bay Area, sharpening their skills. Lambert recalls the times they arrived at Cal's Harmon Gym, home of the Bears basketball team, well after midnight. The janitor would let the guys in, they'd turn on the lights, and they'd have the court all to themselves as the rest of Berkeley slept. Other times they'd show up at a gym just before it was set to close, hide in bathroom stalls until the doors were locked, and then hit the court. They'd play fast and hard, pushing the ball, always pushing, running, and dunking. And sometimes they'd take off their shoes and slide around in their long white socks, improving their body control and ballhandling.

After a hoops session, Glenn and the boys would head over to one of their parents' homes to raid the refrigerators and watch sports on TV. His teammate Jon Nikcevich loved spending time with Glenn's mom and sisters—Glenn's house was so much more fun and full of music, life, and laughter than his own.

Glenn kept his friends smiling, no matter the time or place. Pete Padgett, son of the basketball coach at Cal, played on a summer league baseball team with Glenn, spending nine innings crying with laughter. Game after game, Glenn unleashed a running commentary of sarcasm directed at opponents and teammates alike, mocking the way they walked or talked or swung the bat. Nikcevich recalled the times Glenn came to his house to shoot hoops in the backyard. They'd come inside

to cool off and listen to Richard Pryor's comedy albums or play some music, Glenn alternating between spot-on imitations of Pryor and the Godfather of Soul, James Brown.

Glenn Burke was one of several Berkeley High School athletes to reach the professional ranks in the 1970s, joined by baseball players Ruppert Jones and Claudell Washington and basketball players Phil Chenier and John Lambert. (Berkeley High School)

But even as Burke blossomed as an athlete and gained a legion of friends and admirers, the seeds of his eventual fall hid in plain sight. Glenn and Nikcevich spent many an afternoon getting high. And outside of sports, Glenn was aimless, showing little interest in school.

But those signs of danger existed well beneath the surface; it was Burke's phenomenal athleticism that everyone admired. And who questions excellence? For now, Glenn Burke was the charismatic star of the best basketball team in Northern California.

Coach Spike Hensley's Berkeley High School Yellowjackets were loaded with talent; Hensley's gift was knowing how to manage his players, allowing them to showcase their unique skills within a team structure. There was John Lambert, the big man who could block shots, rebound, and run the floor. There was Marvin Buckley, automatic with his outside jump shot. There was Dan Palley, the steady and dependable guard who always knew where to feed the ball; speedy Larry Green,[1] who could steal the ball, snake his way down the court, and finish at the hoop; Jon Nikcevich, dazzling with his floppy socks and sharp passes, a

Glenn Burke's first love was basketball. A tremendous leaper and rebounder despite his small size, Burke led the Berkeley High School Yellowjackets to an undefeated season as a senior in 1970, culminating with a title in the Tournament of Champions. (Berkeley High School)

clone of the college star Pistol Pete Maravich. Glenn had nicknames for everybody—Pete Carlson was Petey Wheatstraw, the Devil's Son-in-Law; long and lanky John Grant was Earthworm; Marvin Buckley was Cupcake, after the way he shaped his Afro.

Hensley's practices were one long session in pressure defense. First team against second, running, moving the ball, traps, double-teams—everybody could handle the ball, everybody could run. After practice, Burke and Nikcevich loved to steam up the showers in the cold locker room, covering the drains with towels to stop the hot water and let it pool to their knees—until the janitor came running in screaming for them to cut it out.

Glenn viewed games as his time to put on a show, his time in the spotlight, like he was back on King Norman's set or singing with the Limeliters. Even in pregame warm-ups he brought the crowd to its feet, driving down the lane, tossing the ball high off the glass, catching it with one hand and slamming it through. Glenn was a good player in practice, but he was a great one in games. He stood less than six feet tall, but he played forward, not guard, and dominated much taller players, out-leaping six-foot-six defenders for rebounds. With the ball in his hands, Burke was slippery and unpredictable, freelancing his way to jaw-dropping buckets. "He could shake and bake his body around and contort into different positions," recalled Pete Carlson. "He'd spin in midair and come around the other side of the basket. Nobody did that back then." Burke's leaping ability was so unworldly, it appeared he could simply levitate. He'd jump toward the basket, a defender would jump with him, and as that defender fell back to earth, Glenn would still be up there, now with a clear path to the basket. "Glenn could just jump out of the gym and stay up there until everybody went home," Coach Hensley marveled.

The Yellowjackets started the 1970 season hot and never let up, winning their first ten games, then twenty. The only close game came against rival Kennedy High School from nearby Richmond. Berkeley trailed by thirteen points with less than three minutes left, but Burke took control of the game, scoring fifteen points down the stretch. "He single-handedly won the game for us," Carlson recalled.

By season's end, Hensley's fast-break offense and pressure defense had overwhelmed every single opponent, and Berkeley High School won the Tournament of Champions, the ultimate prize for teams from Northern California. Helix High School down in Southern California also put together an undefeated season, led by future college and NBA star Bill Walton, but there was no overall state championship back then. In a perfect 32–0 season for Berkeley, it was Burke who shined the brightest, named Northern California Player of the Year after averaging 23.5 points and an astonishing 11.5 rebounds per game.

Glenn Burke

Glenn Burke graduated from Berkeley High School in 1970; other famous graduates of the school before and after include authors Thornton Wilder and Ursula K. Le Guin; actors Daveed Diggs, Rebecca Romijn, and Andy Samberg; Black Panthers co-founder Bobby Seale; basketball pioneer Don Barksdale; rapper G-Eazy; e-sports commentator Sam Hartman-Kenzler; and Grateful Dead guitarist Phil Lesh. (Berkeley High School)

For the players and the Berkeley community, this team represented more than just perfection on the basketball court. As a war raged in Vietnam, as the nation continued to mourn the assassinations of Martin Luther King Jr. and Robert F. Kennedy, as African Americans forcefully confronted racism in the Bay Area, and as police violently subdued student protestors, the Berkeley High School Yellowjackets represented unity triumphing over division. Hensley had been criticized by some white parents for adding so many Black players to his team, but his only goal was to let the best guys play. And here was a vivid illustration of the promise of diversity and equity—Black guys and white guys becoming friends, standing up for one another, enjoying one another's company, achieving perfection on the basketball court. "People watched us work together and said this is the way the world ought to be," recalled Lambert. "Everybody working together for a common goal. It was a model for what things should have been like."

At a time when young people rebelled against their parents and the social norms of the past, here was Glenn Burke, achieving all the conventional markers of teenage masculinity. He was the strongest, the fastest, the funniest, and the most charismatic and popular kid in town.

Glenn Burke was the teen idol every other boy aspired to be.

CHAPTER 6
MONEY TALKS

Gary "Burger" Warren, a close friend of Burke's at Berkeley High School, had seen the way kids marveled at Glenn's exploits at Bushrod Park, and how spectators in the cramped Berkeley High School gym jumped to their feet when he soared to the basket.

But he had never seen anything quite like this. It was a year after Glenn had graduated from high school, and Burger and Glenn had been invited to a fraternity party on the campus of Cal Berkeley.

While pretty sorority girls congregated in one room, the frat boys gathered in another, plying Burke and Burger with shots of hard liquor. Glenn was on a roll, boasting of his athletic feats, telling jokes, and imitating Richard Pryor. After an hour or so, many of the girls left the house, tired of being ignored. But the boys couldn't get enough of Glenn's stories. "I couldn't believe he had all of those guys so mesmerized," Warren recalled. "It was like they viewed him as a god or something. Those white guys were completely infatuated with him."

Eventually Warren had enough, too, and decided to go home. But Glenn stayed, and as Burger walked out the front door, he could still hear the white boys laughing at Glenn's jokes.

Doug Goldman, a Cal student, long remembered the first time he met Burke at another party near campus. He recognized Glenn from the pickup games at Harmon Gym, where Doug enjoyed watching the regular noontime game featuring Cal players and other talented hoopers from the area. Even with players such as future NBA star Phil Chenier on the court, it was Burke who commanded attention. When most guys stood around waiting to choose sides, Burke would lope down the court, pick up speed as he neared the basket, leap in the air, tuck the ball behind his neck, and slam it through the hoop. "I was just in awe," Goldman recalled. Goldman also noticed a small peace medallion hanging around Burke's neck, glistening against his broad chest.

Goldman recognized the medallion when he ran into Burke at the party, and the two struck up a conversation about basketball, R&B music, and playing the drums. Burke also discovered that Goldman owned a car, and he soon began bumming rides off him whenever he visited the Cal campus to play ball or party. Sometimes they would end up at Doug's parents' house, where they'd sit in the rec room listening to music and telling jokes.

Goldman and Burke couldn't have come from more disparate

backgrounds, and yet they developed a lifelong friendship. Burke, the poor, fatherless kid from Berkeley; Goldman, the Jewish kid from swanky Atherton, whose family lineage made him fabulously wealthy. You may have heard of his great-great-uncle Levi Strauss, of blue jeans fame.

Goldman grew up with an awareness that many of the people who seemed interested in him were just after his money. But with Glenn, the friendship was genuine. "We enjoyed one another's company. I wasn't looking for anything from him other than friendship," Goldman recalled. "He wasn't looking for anything from me other than I could give him rides."

Two years removed from his senior year at Berkeley High School and the undefeated state championship basketball season, Burke was still figuring out what to do with his life. He remained a legend at the playgrounds and parks of the East Bay, and he gained a following at Cal, too, both in the pickup games at Harmon Gym and the parties on campus, where he was always dancing in the middle of the room, always laughing, always the center of attention.

He had given college basketball a shot at the University of Denver, but quickly grew homesick, didn't care for the cold weather, and moved back home before ever playing a game. He enrolled briefly at the College of Alameda but quit when he realized how bad the team was there. Then it was on to Laney College, where he briefly joined his former high school teammate Pete Carlson.

In preseason conditioning drills, the coach had his players run around nearby Lake Merritt. Carlson and his teammates returned from the grueling run ready to pass out, but the coach ordered them to run sprints. Only then, when the guys were gasping for air and covered in sweat, was it time for practice to start. But one guy was missing. "Where's Glenn?" someone asked. Finally, Burke came strolling into the gym carrying a boom box on his shoulder. He'd slowly run the whole lake listening to music. "At that point," Carlson recalled, "Glenn was not that serious about what he was doing with us. He was a great ballplayer, but he was still trying to find himself." He didn't last long at Laney.

A restless Burke found comfort in familiar environments, places where his past accomplishments were more important than his uncertain future. He hung around the basketball team at Berkeley High School, enjoying the company of coaches and players who admired his heroics during the unblemished season of 1970. And at Bushrod Park, he played the role of protector. As a kid, Burke had been bullied by the bigger boys. Now he kept youngsters out of trouble with the older kids. "We knew if we had problems in the neighborhood, we could go to Glenn and he'd straighten things out," recalled Shooty Babitt, an East Bay athletic phenom who went on to play in the major leagues. "He was kind of like the big brother in the 'hood."

Finally, Burke enrolled at Merritt College[1] in Oakland, his fourth attempt at higher education. Truth be told, school wasn't really Glenn's thing, and his grades had likely prevented him from receiving scholarship offers from many universities.

But Glenn thrived as a two-sport star at Merritt. Although basketball was his first love, Burke had always been adept at making the transition from hoops to baseball when the calendar turned to spring. After winning the Tournament of Champions as a senior at BHS, he turned around three days later and collected five hits in his first Yellowjackets baseball game, including a grand slam and two other homers. The pattern continued at Merritt, where Burke's basketball abilities caught the eye of Al Attles, coach of the NBA's Golden State Warriors, and his baseball production attracted the attention of Major League scouts. In his second year at Merritt, Burke blasted a 480-foot homer to straightaway center field against rival Laney, snapping the school's 43-game conference losing streak. Coach Stan Korich knew he had something special in Burke, who ran the 100 in 9.7 seconds and bench pressed 350 pounds. "Glenn Burke," he told the local press, "has definite superstar potential for the Major Leagues."

Over the course of the 1972 season, Burke hit .282 with 4 homers and 12 RBI in 21 games, earning second-team all-conference honors. Those weren't superstar statistics, but they were good enough for scouts from the Phillies, Giants, and Reds to come watch him practice at Bushrod and play games at San Leandro Ball Park, the same fields where big league stars Vada Pinson, Frank Robinson, Willie Stargell, and Joe Morgan had once learned the game.

And then on June 11, 1972, Burke was shooting hoops at Bushrod when Lutha rode up on her bicycle. "Mama says you've got to come home," she said. "The Dodgers are there to see you."

"I don't want to play for the Dodgers," Glenn said, clutching his basketball. He was a Giants fan, and that meant hating the Dodgers, a rivalry that began before both teams had moved to California from New York City in 1958. "Leave me alone."

Lutha cycled home. And then back to the park.

"If you don't come home, Mama's going to come here and get you!"

"I don't care," Glenn replied. "I ain't playing with no Dodgers. I don't like the Dodgers."

So Lutha made the round trip home and back again, this time returning with their mother, Alice.

Finally, Glenn listened. He came home to find Dodgers scout Ray Perry waiting in the living room. Perry told Burke that the Dodgers had drafted him in the seventeenth round, and they'd like to offer him a $5,000 bonus to sign with the team and join their Minor League ball club in Ogden, Utah. Burke was still holding out hope that Attles and the Warriors would offer him a tryout, or he'd have another shot to play major college basketball, but the guaranteed cash from the Dodgers was too much to resist.

He signed the contract and, at age nineteen, accepted a new mission in life: to become a Major League baseball player.

CHAPTER 7

GOD'S GIFT TO BASEBALL

t would have been nearly impossible for Burke to begin his professional baseball career in a town more different from where he had grown up than Ogden, Utah. From the Pacific Ocean to the Wasatch Mountains. From an ethnic melting pot to a virtually all-white community. From a hotbed of liberal activism to a center of religious conservatism.

In Ogden, the Black players stuck together, with Burke moving into the historic but decaying Ben Lomond Hotel to share a suite of rooms with Marvin Webb and Cleo Smith, two African American players who also had grown up in the Bay Area. For Burke and his Black and Latino teammates beginning their careers in the lowest rung of the minor leagues, a daunting journey to the majors was made all the more difficult by the circumstances in which the trek began, an alien and hostile environment far from friends, family, or anyone who looked like them.

One time, Burke, Webb, and Smith were walking around downtown when they encountered a Mormon man passing out religious pamphlets on a street corner. The Mormon religion considered African Americans to be inferior people, so the guys had no interest in the literature.

"Thanks but no thanks," Burke said.

"I'm good," Webb added.

Their lack of interest upset the man, and he lashed out.

"You're the reason for all the problems in the world!" he yelled at Webb.

"If you don't get that paper out of my face, there's going to be another problem," Webb replied. Glenn lunged forward, ready to "kick the guy's ass," but Marvin and Cleo held him back.

Another time, Burke walked into a small café for a bite to eat. The restaurant was nearly empty, but still the waitress kept Glenn, the only Black customer, waiting for nearly a half hour before she took his order. It was an embarrassing and dehumanizing ordeal for Burke, who told the waitress he deserved the same service as any of the white customers. Surprised to be called out for her bigotry, the waitress offered a weak apology, telling Burke she hadn't realized he was a ballplayer. That made a bad situation worse, implying Burke only deserved to be treated fairly because he was a local celebrity. He left the woman a thirteen-cent tip.

Just two weeks after signing his contract, Burke played in his first professional baseball game on June 26, 1972, when the Ogden Dodgers, decked out in their replica Dodger uniforms with an *O* on the cap instead of the big league club's interlocking *L* and *A*, took on the Idaho Falls Angels. Fifteen minutes before the first pitch, members of the Ogden City Council and the Weber County Commission entertained the crowd with a quick one-inning game. Then it was time for the real thing, with Smith running out to third base, Webb to second, and Burke to left field. He was officially a professional baseball player.

Burke's stay in the Pioneer League was brief and unremarkable. He played eleven games in the outfield and pinch-hit in three more,

Glenn Burke's first stop in pro baseball was Ogden, Utah, home of the Dodgers' Pioneer League team. When he wasn't on the field playing ball, Glenn could often be found listening to and singing along with music. Burke's professional baseball career would also end in Ogden, when he played 14 games there for the Oakland A's Triple-A affiliate in 1980. (Doug Harris)

collecting nine hits in forty-five at-bats for a lowly .200 batting average with no doubles, triples, home runs, or stolen bases. He performed no better in the field, committing three errors in just twenty chances. It was an inauspicious start in a cutthroat business.

Nevertheless, the Dodgers promoted him to their farm team in Spokane, Washington, a member of the short-season Northwest League. The Spokane Indians' season had already started, and players milled about the field the day Burke arrived. All eyes were on the newcomer. Jim Cody stood on the dugout steps as Glenn walked across the field toward the clubhouse, stunned by Burke's obvious physical strength—broad chest, defined calves, thick thighs. "I looked at him and I couldn't believe it," Cody recalled. "He was such a finely tuned athlete. It was amazing, just amazing." Burke made his way to manager Bill Berrier's office, where teammate John Snider was struck by the soft-spoken way in which Glenn introduced himself. "It was interesting because he was real quiet," Snider recalled. "I think that was the only time he was quiet in the next three years."

Burke wasted no time making friends; he and pitcher Ed Carroll Jr. discovered they shared the same birthday, November 16, just a year apart. Glenn loved showing off his athleticism, challenging teammates to footraces in the outfield, sprinting from foul line to foul line. Other times he'd walk up to a guy and throw a few phantom jabs, mimicking the great heavyweight Muhammad Ali—float like a butterfly, sting like a bee. "He wasn't going to hit you," Carroll recalled. "But he wanted to prove that he could if he wanted to." On long bus trips, Burke blasted his portable radio, singing along to the music. "I'd never met anybody who was that much of an extrovert," Cody said. "And he always used to brag about how he played for the Berkeley High Yellowjackets and how good of a basketball player he was."

Glenn never missed an opportunity to show off his leaping ability. On a road trip to Lewiston, Idaho, as Burke, Cody, and other teammates walked around town after a game, someone dared the guys to jump up and touch a sign hanging overhead. Cody took a running start, jumped, and barely touched the bottom of the sign. Burke leaped up and scraped his elbow on the top of it.

On another road trip, Glenn and pitchers Bob Lesslie and Larry Corrigan were sitting around bored in a hotel when they noticed a basketball hoop in the parking lot. Glenn went down to the front desk and asked for a basketball. "He would take the ball and do a complete 360-degree spin and reverse stuff it behind his head," Lesslie recalled. "Then he'd start firing it up from three."

Berrier, the team's highly respected manager, recognized his young outfielder's cockiness. Burke, he said, considered himself "God's gift to baseball." That didn't bother Berrier much; if anything, Burke reminded him of himself. A former small college All-American football player, Berrier admired an athlete with confidence and grit; the tougher the better.

Still, Berrier looked for opportunities to bring Burke's ego down to earth; he had a lot to learn if he was going to fulfill his potential as a professional athlete. On one trip, Berrier spotted the same hotel basketball hoop where Burke had dazzled his teammates with his acrobatic slam dunks. He challenged Glenn to a simple game of H-O-R-S-E. In a classic case of the cagey old veteran outwitting the brash young phenom, Berrier pulled out an array of old-fashioned hook shots and two-hand set shots. Burke couldn't keep up, and Berrier beat him. "He went on and on about my crazy hook shot," Berrier said decades later.

Another night, during a rain delay in Seattle, Burke sat next to Berrier in the bleachers waiting for the field to dry. Burke complimented Berrier on his fashionable checkered blazer. Burke was the most stylish player on the team, shining his $40 patent-leather shoes when the other guys laced up $10 Chuck Taylors. "I think I ought to take that right off your back," he said. Berrier was up to the challenge, removing the coat and placing it on the bleachers as he glanced at his watch. "I'll tell you what," he told Burke. "You have one hour to try to get it. Come get it if you want it." Burke took one step toward his manager, thought better of it, and walked away. "We got to be good friends," Berrier recalled. "He knew I said what I meant, and I wouldn't put up with any crap. He respected that."

Though he coached at one of the lowest levels of professional baseball, Berrier understood the importance of his role: teaching ballplayers the Dodger Way, stressing fundamentals and identifying Major League prospects. As a former Minor League ballplayer himself, he'd seen other players sabotage their careers through a simple lack of hustle and was determined not to let that happen to any of the men under his command. "I made my guys run out every ground ball and fly ball every time. No loafing," he recalled. "I once had a roommate in Albuquerque who was hitting .320. One game he hit a ball back to the pitcher, took one step toward first base and ran back to the dugout. He lost his Major League opportunity because of that. They gave up on him and traded him. So with my guys, I had my stopwatch and if they didn't run out a ball within two-tenths of a second of their best time, I would fine them."

Berrier understood the importance of sleep to high performance. He also knew his players were far more likely to stay out carousing than to get to bed by curfew. On one road trip to Portland, Oregon, he came up with an ingenious way to see which players stayed out late without having to wait up for them himself.

As curfew approached, he struck up a conversation with the hotel's elevator operator. "I hear there's a baseball team in town," Berrier said, concealing the fact he was the team's manager. "Would you be willing to get autographs on this baseball from any of the ballplayers you see tonight?" The hotel employee was glad to oblige, collecting six autographs after midnight and delivering the ball to Berrier before breakfast. At the ballpark that night, Berrier stood in front of his players as they stretched before the game, casually flipping the telltale baseball from hand to hand. "I understand there were a few guys who stayed out after curfew last night." All the players denied it. *Nope, not us.* "Then how

The 1972 Spokane Indians, Glenn's second stop on the way to the big leagues. Glenn (middle row, second from right) hit .340 with two homers and eight stolen bases in forty-one games. Note that he signed this picture "Eddie McElroy" after the character he played for laughs in the clubhouse. (Bob Lesslie)

did your names get on here?" Berrier replied, reading the signatures of the six players who had unwittingly confessed to their transgression with their late-night autographs. He fined the players $25 apiece, a hefty sum at a time when minor leaguers received just $3 a day in meal money. At the end of the season, Berrier used all the money he collected in fines to throw a party for his players.

When Burke first arrived in Spokane, he brushed off most of Berrier's advice, telling the skipper he already knew how to play the game. But Berrier was no pushover. "They're paying me to be the boss," he reminded Burke. "So if you want to do it your way, you better buy out my contract and get rid of me." As the season progressed, teacher and student grew closer together. Burke listened as Berrier taught him the finer points of the game: how to back away from the plate on a hit-and-run, how to steal third base, how to be more selective at the plate. Burke's speed in the outfield gave his pitchers confidence that any fly ball would be caught; his right arm was as powerful as a cannon. When Glenn struggled, it was typically at the plate, when pitchers fed him off-speed pitches. "He could hit a fastball," Berrier recalled, "but he'd be a sucker for a slider or a breaking ball. That's where his bullheadedness came in. He wouldn't make the adjustment and hit the ball the other way [to right field]. He was always trying to pull it." Burke wanted to succeed, wanted to please his manager. When he failed, everyone knew how much it bothered him.

Berrier was impressed with his young outfielder's skills, production, and competitive spirit. By season's end, Burke led the team with a .340 batting average. One of Berrier's year-end responsibilities was to prepare a report for Dodger management with an assessment of every player's performance. If he believed a player had the tools to advance to Triple-A or the majors, he was required to fill out a special form. "I did that for Glenn," Berrier recalled. "He had Major League potential because of his hands, the power in his swing, and he could run very good."

What Berrier didn't know, and what Burke would only recognize in retrospect, was that there was a hidden reason why he threw himself so fully into the game.

"I knew I was different," Burke wrote in his autobiography. "I wasn't dating women or men." Instead, the nineteen-year-old spent all his energy on baseball. Focusing on hitting and running and catching and throwing allowed him to avoid looking inward. That breakthrough would come soon enough. But for now, he convinced himself that avoiding any sort of romantic relationships made him a better player, and would fuel his journey to the major leagues.

CHAPTER 8
TRUTH OR DARE

By 1973, the Los Angeles Dodgers had held their annual spring training exercises in Vero Beach, Florida, for twenty-five years. The old navy barracks at Dodgertown were showing their age. Players slept on cots in tiny rooms with leaky plumbing and huge cockroaches scurrying around the floors at night.

This was the year that several talented young Dodger prospects advanced to the major leagues, forming the nucleus of a team that would contend for National League titles for more than a decade.

At age twenty, Glenn Burke was too young and too raw to have a shot at the big league club, but his first spring training was a big deal nonetheless. It was a chance to show off his skills to the Dodger brass and a chance to get to know other players at all stages of the organization, from minor leaguers fresh from high school to veteran ballplayers on the big league roster.

It didn't take long for Burke to draw attention, but not because of anything he did on the field. One night, Burke's roommate had been startled awake by Glenn screeching at the top of his lungs. His roommate flipped on the lights. "What the hell happened?" he asked. Burke lay flat on his back, a giant spider perched atop his chest, staring right back at him. Burke screamed again and jumped out of bed. "How did you know it was on you in the dark?" his teammate asked. "I," Burke stammered, "could hear it breathing."

Word spread around camp—"Glenn Burke says he could hear a spider breathing"—the start of a period in his fledgling career when his teammates weren't sure what to make of him. Burke became louder, looser, and more unpredictable. He'd have his teammates rolling on the floor in laughter one minute and dodging a punch the next. A tension and frustration lay just beneath the surface, and no one was quite sure when it would erupt. And most puzzling—to teammates who paid attention—was Burke's complete lack of interest in girls.

Coming out of spring training, Burke was assigned to the Dodgers' Florida State League team in Daytona Beach. In the clubhouse, he loved to assume the fictional personality of Eddie McElroy, a raunchy and slick ladies' man character invented by a popular Black comedian named Rudy Ray Moore.[1] "My name is Eddie McElroy," Burke would declare as he sauntered through the locker room. "I bring all the women joy!"

Burke's white teammates loved the act so much they began to call Burke "Eddie," never Glenn. But Marvin Webb, a Black teammate from the Bay Area and one of Burke's closest friends on the team, grew suspicious. "I ain't never seen him with no women," he recalled.

One time, Webb had two girls over to his hotel room and Burke told him he wasn't interested in hanging out. "Well, he's just a funny guy," Webb explained to the women. "Just a funny kind of a guy." Another time, Webb, Burke, and two women were playing truth or dare. Just when the sexual innuendo began to get intense, Burke got up and declared that he needed to go shopping. "It's eleven thirty at night!" Webb shouted. "Where are you going shopping?"

Before one game, a beautiful young Black pageant winner, "Miss Daytona," visited with the players down by the dugout. She clearly had her eyes on Burke. "God, Glenn, she's interested in you!" teammate Jim Cody told his buddy, but Burke wanted nothing to do with her. Webb was perplexed. "What the heck is the matter with him?" he asked himself. "What is wrong?"

Webb never forced the issue or asked Burke directly why he had no interest in women. And the truth was Burke still didn't really know the answer. "Perhaps [Marvin] knew I was gay before I realized it," he later surmised.

Daytona Beach Dodgers, 1973. Glenn (top row, third from left) led the team with 10 homers, 57 RBI, and 42 stolen bases. His buddy Marvin Webb sits in the first row, third from right. (Bob Lesslie)

Burke could not reconcile the questions he had about himself and the assumptions he and everyone around him held about the unquestioned heterosexuality of a professional athlete. There had never been an openly gay Major League baseball player. Burke wasn't quite sure what it meant to be gay; he just knew he was different from his teammates. With no one to talk to about his feelings, his frustration began to show in ever more violent ways.

On the team bus after a game in Lakeland, Burke noticed that somebody had snatched a beer from his equipment bag. "Who went in my bag?" he demanded. Webb silently nodded in the direction of the culprit. *Pow!* Burke punched his teammate. "Don't ever go in my bag again." Everyone scrambled out of their seats, some guys holding Burke back, other guys wrestling with the beer stealer. Manager Bart Shirley had enough. "Okay, okay," he shouted, "take it easy!" Burke shot back, "I'm tired of you telling us to take it easy!" Shirley, a nonconfrontational man, was no match for Burke. On another bus ride, Burke and a couple other players smoked marijuana in the back. Shirley told them to cut it out. "Go back to the front of the bus and leave us alone!" Burke demanded. Shirley complied.

The tensions between Burke and Shirley spilled over onto the field. In one game, Burke stole third base with two outs in the inning, a baseball no-no. Shirley told Glenn if he ever tried a stunt like that again, he'd pull him out of the game. "Yeah, and if you do," Burke replied, "I'll kick your ass."

One night, the Montreal Expos' farm team from West Palm Beach came to Daytona, boasting a roster of future major leaguers including teenage stars Ellis Valentine and Larry Parrish. Burke hit a hard liner into the outfield gap and sped around the bases for a triple, sliding into the third base bag manned by Parrish. Parrish took exception to Burke's hard slide, claiming that Burke spit on him. Burke said he didn't spit, but the arguing continued, back and forth, until both teams came running out of their dugouts, ready to fight. Burke faked like he was going to swing at Parrish, and the Expo jumped backward. As Valentine came running in from the outfield to protect his teammate, Burke ripped off his jersey in a show of strength, with shirt buttons flying all over the infield grass. "See, I'm a big man, too!" he yelled. Players from both teams milled around, but no punches were thrown, and the game resumed. But once again, Burke sent a message to friend and foe alike: *Don't mess with me.*

Whatever respect he earned from his teammates for his tough-guy attitude was enhanced by his spectacular play on the field. In 110 games with Daytona Beach, Burke stood out as the team's most talented player, leading the club with 68 runs, 12 doubles, 10 homers, 57 RBI, 24 stolen bases, and a .309 batting average. And he routinely showed off his rocket of a right arm, throwing out a team-high 14 runners on the bases from the outfield.

Burke's performance earned him a promotion to Bakersfield of the California League, 113 miles from Los Angeles but still light-years from the big leagues. Road trips in the California League required long, hot, and stuffy bus rides up and down the Pacific coast. To beat the heat and try to get some rest, some of the smaller players would strip down to their underwear and climb up to the luggage racks, where they could stretch out and sleep. One time the bus caught fire in the middle of the night, with half-naked ballplayers jumping out of windows to safety.

By season's end, even as Burke wrestled with questions about his own sexuality and anxieties that bubbled to the surface in spontaneous displays of aggression, there were two things about which his Dodger teammates were certain: First, he could flat-out play ball. This kid had Major League potential. Second, despite his occasional temper, he was as extroverted, charismatic, well-liked, and outwardly confident as anyone in the entire Dodger organization. Wherever those long, lonely bus rides took them, when the guys stepped off in a new town, they didn't arrive as just a Dodgers farm team. "We were," teammate Larry Corrigan recalled, "Glenn Burke's team."

CHAPTER 9
BAD BLOOD

It was the early spring of 1974, and Burke was set to begin his third season of Minor League baseball, joining the Dodgers' Eastern League team in Waterbury, Connecticut.

The ballplayers would be the guests of honor at a dinner that town leaders had planned for them. It wasn't often that Minor League baseball players felt the need to dress up, but Burke and several of his teammates wanted to look good for the occasion.

Ed Carroll Jr., a left-handed pitcher from California, had no doubts the twenty-one-year-old Burke was the most fashionable member of the team. "If there were forty people walking down the street dressed up nice," he recalled, "Glenn was dressed flamboyantly nice. You'd know the difference."

When Burke changed clothes in the clubhouse, teammates noticed he wore colorful Speedo-style underwear while the rest of them wore plain white boxer shorts or jockstraps. Burke always had a stylish cap, tight pants, wide-collared shirts; on occasion he even broke out platform shoes with live goldfish swimming in the clear heels. He was fly, and he knew it. So when Burke invited Carroll to go shopping for sports coats for the team dinner, the pitcher tagged along. Next thing he knew, Burke had convinced him to purchase a gaudy green, yellow, and beige jacket. "It wasn't me," Carroll recalled, "but he talked me into it."

Burke's influence on his teammates extended beyond their fashion choices. In a tradition-bound game where any display of emotion was taboo, Burke rebelled against the unwritten rules of baseball. When a teammate homered or returned to the dugout after scoring a run, Burke was there to congratulate him in a style he brought from the playgrounds of the East Bay. In an era when simple handshakes or a slap on the butt were the only expressions of joy on the field, Burke shook things up.

"We used to practice this dance where you'd clap your hands up and down, the hand jive," teammate Marvin Webb said. "We used to do that before games. Nowadays, players have all these elaborate routines they do before games. Glenn and I used to do that back in 1973 and 1974."

Around the same time as the team dinner, players began splitting into small groups to find houses and apartments to rent for the season. Carroll joined Burke and Cleo Smith in an old Victorian home with "pointy corners" that reminded Carroll of an upside-down ice cream cone. Smith did most of the cooking, winning raves for his fried chicken recipe.

On road trips, Burke and several teammates smoked pot constantly, ignoring team rules against it. On one trip to Canada, the team's floor at the Hôtel Gouverneur in Quebec City began to reek of marijuana as Glenn and others lit up. As smoke began to fill their room, Webb poked his head out the door when he heard voices on the floor. It was the team trainer, trying to find the source of the telltale odor. Burke and Webb bolted, heading off to a nightclub. When they returned, they noticed all their remaining marijuana was missing. The trainer gathered all the guys who had been staying at that end of the floor, demanding to know who'd been smoking pot.

"I didn't do it. It wasn't mine," Webb said. "You ain't sending me home because of this."

"I never did that stuff in my life," said the next player as Webb stifled a laugh—his teammate looked high even as he denied it.

Then the trainer asked Glenn.

"Yep, that's my weed," Burke said without a hint of regret or embarrassment. "That's my weed and I want it back, too."

Burke faced no immediate consequences, but his candor shocked his teammates. It was hard enough advancing through the Dodgers' highly competitive Minor League system to the big leagues without giving the organization a reason to question your character. Most Dodger minor leaguers fully bought into the franchise's culture and the expectations on and off the field, what was known as the Dodger Way. "We were made to feel proud of our organization, how we were taught to play, that we did things the right way," teammate Joe Simpson recalled. "We believed we were part of a model organization."

So, while other players toed the line, it was Burke's occasional confrontations with authority figures that marked him as an outlier, not his latent sexuality, which he did not yet acknowledge or completely comprehend. His on-field production drew the attention of Dodger executives, but so, too, did his rebelliousness and his ambivalence toward the Dodger Way. This was a big concern for a franchise that liked to portray a squeaky-clean image to the public.

Not that Glenn Burke gave a damn about that. No one could stop him from doing his own thing.

Most of the time, that meant displaying his incredible athleticism on the field. Pitcher Jim Cody remembered the time he gave up a deep fly ball to the outfield ("the hitter just creamed a shot off me," he recalled) and Cody sprinted behind third base, ready to back up a throw from the outfield on what he assumed would be an easy triple. But when he looked up, Glenn had caught the ball. "I was shocked," Cody said. "I had never seen anybody cover ground like that."

Another time, Burke led off an inning and scored a run before the next batter completed his at-bat. Burke had doubled in his first two at-bats of the game, and the opposing pitcher retaliated his third time up by plunking him with a fastball to the hip. Burke rolled around in the dirt in apparent agony, twisting and turning, screaming out in pain. The team trainer came out and asked him to try to walk it off, but Burke took two steps and fell back to the ground. The crowd gasped. Slowly, he dusted himself off and limped to first base. He then proceeded to steal second and third base on the next two pitches. Now standing on third, he darted back and forth, rattling the pitcher, who committed a balk, and the umpire awarded Burke home plate. He'd been faking the injury the whole time, and he relished fooling his opponent to the point of humiliation. "That's how he could take over a game," teammate Larry Corrigan recalled. "When he felt like playing, he was explosive."

But other times, Burke frustrated his teammates with a stubborn indifference. Corrigan remembered a road trip to Bedford, Quebec, a cold, "godforsaken place" where players dressed in dingy trailers, grass refused to grow in the infield—and Burke declined to move in the outfield. As they stood around shagging fly balls during a chilly batting practice session, Burke turned to Corrigan. "This has been a horrible road trip," he said. "I don't even feel like playing." "Well, you have to play," Corrigan pleaded. "I'm pitching tonight."

Corrigan got his wish; Burke started the game in right field. Meaning, at least he stood there. Corrigan gave up a single to lead off the game, and then the next batter followed with a hit-and-run single that rolled into the outfield a few feet to Burke's right, slowly bouncing past him. "He never moved an inch toward the ball," Corrigan recalled. "Not an inch. That was Glenn."

And then there was The Brawl. Ask any member of the 1974 Waterbury Dodgers about that otherwise unremarkable season, and they'll all ask if you've heard about the fight. Some of those players advanced to the major leagues, fulfilling boyhood dreams. Others never progressed any further in the minors, Waterbury once and forever the high-water mark of their pro baseball careers. But regardless of the trajectory of their lives in baseball, The Brawl in Quebec City stands alone as a bizarre, violent, and comic illustration of the machismo, competitiveness, and unrefined nature of Minor League baseball and Glenn Burke's place in that world.

There was bad blood between the Dodger and Expo minor leaguers dating back to the standoff a year earlier in Daytona Beach, when Burke and Larry Parrish argued at third base over the spitting accusation. Players on both teams brought that baggage with them to their Eastern League teams in Waterbury and Quebec City in '74; both sides prepared to resume the fight at the slightest provocation.

Placing Glenn Burke anywhere near a powder keg was the surest way to provoke an explosion, and that's just what happened in this early April game under sleeting skies in Quebec.

John Snider, playing third base for Waterbury, was due to lead off the top of the seventh inning in the Dodgers' batting order. After Quebec made the third out to end the sixth, Snider ran into the dugout to put on his helmet and grab a bat from the rack. As he fastened his batting glove, he looked out at the field and saw Burke standing on top of the pitcher's mound, the last place he should've been at that moment, staring and screaming into the Quebec Carnavals' dugout along the first-base line.

Given the tensions already crackling in the frigid air that night, Snider knew this episode would not end well. The Quebec pitcher had thrown a fastball near Burke's head to lead off the game, sending an unmistakable message that his team was ready to fight. As Burke had patrolled right field throughout the game, Carnaval players peppered him with insults. After playing catch with the Dodger center fielder before the bottom of the sixth inning to keep his arm loose, Burke was supposed to throw the ball across the diamond back into the Dodger dugout, as was custom. Instead, he rifled it straight into the Carnavals' dugout along the first-base line, startling his heckling opponents and igniting a new round of taunts. And now there he was, standing on the pitcher's mound trading verbal crossfire with the home team.

"Why don't you come out here if you want to do something about it?!" Burke screamed, and the Carnavals took him up on the offer, sprinting out of the dugout. Before Burke's teammates could make it out to the field to join the fisticuffs, Burke had already decked the Quebec pitcher, knocking him straight to the frozen infield like falling timber. By then, Burke's teammates had rushed the field, some players throwing punches, others trying to break up the fight. Dodger pitcher Ed Carroll Jr. and manager Don LeJohn tried to calm things down, standing between an enraged Burke and the Carnavals, but Burke simply reached over them and smacked a Quebec player right in the face, sending him tumbling to earth.

Next, Carroll made his way over toward the Dodger dugout, where another fight had broken out. Dodger Cleo Smith had stepped down into the dugout to grab a bat, and Larry Parrish stood outside, daring him to come out and fight with just fists, no bats. Smith obliged, and Parrish threw a punch as Smith ascended the dugout stairs. Smith, a former teen boxer, ducked just in time, popped back up, and responded with a right hook to Parrish's jaw, sending Parrish sprawling over a three-foot railing into the stands. "And don't you come back out here!" Smith yelled.

By this point, mini skirmishes had broken out all over the field, like brushfires on the plain, and Quebec fans had joined the action, screaming French epithets the Waterbury players didn't understand and dumping beer on the players battling near the grandstand. Dodger players responded by hurling bats at the fans. Meanwhile, Carnaval outfielder Ellis Valentine socked Dodger catcher Dennis Haren in the face, opening up a cut from the side of his mouth clear to his other ear. Haren felt a gash between his nose and upper lip, and pulled a tooth out of it. Dodger pitcher Bob Lesslie saw Haren writhing on the ground and ran over to pick him up, but just as he arrived, Quebec's Tony Scott yelled, "You want some, too?" and hit Lesslie with an uppercut to the face, knocking out his two front teeth.

Finally, all the players were either knocked nearly unconscious or exhausted from all the punching. LeJohn considered it the biggest fight he'd ever seen in twenty-one years in pro baseball.[1]

Glenn Burke, the guy who had started it all, stood triumphantly in the center of the mayhem, like the last pro wrestler standing after a battle royal, having punched two guys out cold and suffering not a scratch.

CHAPTER 10
UNFORGETTABLE

Standing tall in the aftermath of The Brawl, Glenn Burke was the very image of ideal American manhood: strong, athletic, tough, fearless, and victorious.

In other words, in 1974 he was the last man any straight person would have guessed was gay.

The stereotypical gay man of the era was considered by straight people to be unathletic, frail, effeminate, and timid, and suspicious at best, but more likely criminal, perverted, and sinful. Gay kids were bullied and beaten; gay adults were beaten, too, fired from their jobs, arrested, discharged from the military, and disowned by families. American psychiatrists had considered homosexuality a mental illness until 1973, and gay sex was still a criminal offense in most states.

People enjoyed the contributions of gay and bisexual men (both out and closeted) to everyday life—even as they simultaneously denied and punished their existence. People sang "Rocket Man" and "We Are the Champions"; they watched *The Brady Bunch*, *Star Trek*, and *Frankenstein*; they wore Christian Dior, Versace, and Yves Saint Laurent; they read *Leaves of Grass*, *Notes of a Native Son*, and *In Cold Blood*; they admired the *Mona Lisa*, *The Nutcracker* ballet, and the ceiling of the Sistine Chapel; they subscribed to *Forbes* magazine, and they marched on Washington.[1]

And yet, as of 1974, the idea of an openly gay politician or television character would have been unthinkably controversial. Not only were there no openly gay athletes in Major League Baseball, the National Football League, or the National Basketball Association, but most Americans would have found the notion far-fetched: a gay man could not possibly be athletic enough to play pro sports. Few of the gay symbols of pride and solidarity yet existed: there was no rainbow flag, no alliance between gays and lesbians, and no LGBTQIA+ initialism. Gay men typically lived two separate lives, disconnected from any larger gay social, political, or economic network, remaining "in the closet" to hide their sexuality from family, employers, and straight friends. Gay love, joy, and achievement were there all along, but straight Americans demanded they be hidden, convincing themselves such things didn't— and shouldn't—exist.

As the 1974 season progressed, Glenn Burke's talents on the baseball diamond were undeniable. And as he continued to mature from boy to man, Burke also understood another undeniable truth: he was gay, he was sexually attracted to men, and he was ready to act on it.

With baseball season winding down in late summer, Burke knew he'd soon be heading home to the Bay Area for the winter. And though his religious upbringing told him that sex outside of marriage—let alone a gay relationship—was wrong, there was one man, a gay white high school teacher more than twice his age, whom he wanted to see when he got back to Oakland. This would be the man to whom he'd reveal his sexuality. Burke valued his advice as an experienced gay man, and exchanged phone calls with him, making plans to get together when he returned to California.[2]

Finally the day came that changed Glenn Burke's life forever. Back home in Oakland after baseball season had ended, he visited his former teacher's house for dinner. They talked for hours, sharing a mutual attraction and admiration, eventually settling on the floor beside a crackling fireplace. They embraced, became intimate, and spent the night in each other's arms. Glenn went home in the morning, walked into the bathroom, and sobbed to the point of hyperventilating. These were not tears of sadness or regret; they were tears of relief. For the first time, he later wrote, he acknowledged his sexuality and felt the rush of falling in love. "This was who I was," he recalled, "the whole me at last."

A week later, Burke went out with some straight friends in San Francisco. One of them noticed a beautiful girl across the bar. "Look at that fox," the friend said. *Look at her boyfriend*, Burke thought to himself. Burke and his buddies struck up a conversation with the good-looking couple, asking if they knew of any clubs nearby where there was dancing. "Try the Cabaret," the girl offered, "but watch out—gays go there, too." For the first time, it dawned on Burke that there was another world about which he knew very little. There were other gay men, and there were places where they hung out. San Francisco, in fact, was the US capital of gay culture. There was so much to learn and to explore, just across the Bay Bridge from where he grew up.

First, however, Burke had another interest to pursue, this one two hundred miles in the other direction. Basketball, not baseball, had always been his first love. The long days at Bushrod Park, the late-night pickup games at Harmon Gym, the state championship run at Berkeley High School—these were the highlights of Burke's athletic life. He may have just been coming to terms with the fact that he was gay, but he had never had any doubts that as an athlete, his identity was first as a basketball player. So when the National Collegiate Athletic Association announced in January of 1974 that it had changed its rules to allow athletes who played professionally in one sport to compete collegiately in another, Burke saw an opportunity to give college basketball another shot.

He reconnected with his old friend Pete Padgett, whose father, Jim, had been the head basketball coach at Cal Berkeley and was now coaching at the University of Nevada, Reno, where Pete was a junior and star of the team.[3] The elder Padgett's departure from Cal had been ugly. Some white fans complained that he recruited "too many" Black players, going as far as to mail death threats that had Padgett checking underneath his car for explosives.

But in building the basketball program at Reno, which had just begun playing at the Division I level, Padgett felt no such bigoted pressures, and he was thrilled to welcome a player of Glenn Burke's talent, even if it had been years since the twenty-two-year-old Burke had last played competitive basketball. Burke arrived on the Reno campus and made an immediate, positive impression on his teammates. Senior guard Chalmer Dillard loved Burke's charismatic and confident demeanor, and the way any room lit up when he walked in cracking jokes and blasting music from his boom box, dressed in a stylish red hat, black jacket, and shined shoes. Even as the new guy on campus, he was the life of every party.

On the basketball court, his athleticism was as impressive as ever. Dillard marveled at Burke's perfectly sculpted physique, dumbfounded as to how he developed it without ever seriously lifting weights. Glenn was quick and strong; he could run the floor, he could twist and turn and drive to the basket, he could dish the ball to open teammates, and he could nail a midrange jump shot.

In his first game, after not having played competitive ball for more than two years, he scored 53 points and led Reno to victory against Stephen F. Austin, repeatedly driving between two towering Lumberjack defenders to score at the rim. Three games later, matched up against future NBA guard Gus Williams and former BHS teammate John Lambert, Burke tallied 22 points in a close loss to Southern California. Through the season's first six games, Burke was the team's most productive player, averaging 16 points, 5 assists, and 4 rebounds per game.

And yet things never felt quite right. After three years living independently in pro baseball, Burke chafed at the idea of a nightly curfew. After three years away from school in pursuit of a Major League Baseball career, he had no real interest in going to class or doing homework. Achieving success with a freelancing style of play that had always served him well, Burke resented Coach Padgett's insistence that he work within his system. Further, Burke felt that Padgett favored his son over the other players. And unbeknownst to his Wolf Pack teammates, there was the matter of Burke's newfound acceptance of his sexuality. Here he was, one of the few Black students, and one of what he assumed were the few closeted gay students, living in an unfamiliar city and dealing with curfews and class assignments when the new life he wanted to experience was back in San Francisco. "It just seemed to get to the point where he just wasn't enjoying it anymore," Pete Padgett recalled. "I don't think he wanted to continue on in that environment."

Burke played the first half of Nevada's game against North Dakota State, but never came off the bench in the second half. After the game, he was the first to leave the locker room, and Padgett announced to players and newspaper reporters that Glenn was no longer a member of the team. Frustrations boiled over. "I think the problem is that Burke couldn't adjust to the college way of life and way of playing basketball," Coach Padgett said after the game. "He lacks the discipline." An excuse was also given that Burke had injured a knee; it was in his best interests to shut down his basketball career so as not to ruin his prospects in pro baseball.

Burke's sudden departure was devastating to the friends he'd made in just four months on campus, just six basketball games in late November and early December, a testament to the power of his personality. "Glenn is one of those people in your life you'll never forget," Dillard recalled decades later, "no matter how short a time you spent with them."

CHAPTER 11
LIVING IN A CLOSET

In 1975, *The Advocate* magazine ran national advertisements in mainstream publications showing straight readers that gay people were a part of their lives even if they didn't realize it. Depicting a group of ordinary-looking men and women standing side by side, the ad was simple but provocative for the time: "Meet the chairman of the board, your clergyman, the mechanic, your favorite actress and maybe your son or daughter. They all live in a closet."

Even *The Advocate*, a gay magazine founded in 1967, didn't go so far as to suggest that someone's favorite Major League ballplayer might be gay.

Which is not to say the thought hadn't crossed the editors' minds. A year earlier, the magazine had mailed letters to Major League teams requesting interviews with players "living a gay lifestyle." The request was meant to jolt the baseball establishment into acknowledging that there were indeed gay men playing the game. Editors were stunned by the hostility of the few replies they received, especially one from long-time Minnesota Twins public relations director Tom Mee.

"The cop-out, immoral lifestyle of the tragic misfits espoused by your publication," Mee wrote, "has no place in organized athletics at any level. Your colossal gall in attempting to extend your perversion to an area of total manhood is just simply unthinkable."

Mee's rant was featured in a landmark 1975 series of articles, "Homosexuals in Sports" by Lynn Rosellini of the *Washington Star*. "Mee is not the only one who loathes any suggestion of homosexuality in sports," she wrote. "For hundreds like him in the image-conscious athletic establishment, homosexuality remains a fearsome, hateful aberration."

This was the context in which Burke returned to the Dodgers' Class AA team in Waterbury for the 1975 season. All that separated him from the major leagues was the Dodgers' Triple-A team in Albuquerque. But while his teammates understood that it was their ability to hit the curveball or to throw strikes consistently that would determine their fates, Glenn Burke knew that as a closeted gay man, his challenges extended well beyond the basepaths. In the spring and summer of 1975, he'd be a gay man in baseball, living a double life, keeping a secret from the profession that provided a livelihood while at the same time discovering a new world where he could be himself, fully and without shame.

As a twenty-two-year-old big fish in a small, decaying town, this would not be easy.

Once a center of commerce in colonial America, Waterbury had become world-famous for manufacturing clocks and everything brass—buttons, buckles, cowbells, lamps. But after World War II, the city entered a decades-long decline as automation reduced jobs, consumers chose plastic over brass, and out-of-town factory owners moved jobs elsewhere. When a 1955 flood killed twenty-four people and wiped out 187 businesses, the road to rock bottom had been fully paved. By the time Burke arrived in the mid-seventies, people were unemployed, downtown businesses were shuttered, and streets were empty.

The town had a long baseball history, with more than a dozen Minor League teams—the Spuds, the Authors, the Invincibles—entertaining fans there dating back to the late 1800s. But the stadium where Burke and the Dodgers played was a joke. Some ballpark quirks add character: the towering Green Monster at Fenway, the ivy-covered walls at Wrigley, the fountains in Kansas City. But the unusual feature in Waterbury added nothing but danger. A running track extended through foul territory along the first base line before cutting across the outfield grass behind second base and shortstop. The fact that a track dissected the field was bad enough; what made it worse were the elevated curbs on either side of the running lanes, posing a threat to ground balls and infielders alike.

Dodger farmhands considered Waterbury cold, wet, and boring; for John Snider and his wife, Jane, fun consisted of driving out into the country to admire old rock walls. In this environment, whatever enjoyment was to be had came when the players hung out together at the apartments they shared, in the clubhouse, or at bars. And while Burke remained the most outgoing player in the clubhouse, keeping everyone loose with his jokes and music, he began to carefully remove himself from social situations with his teammates, and instead sought clandestine relationships with gay men in town. Most important, and most confusing to his teammates, he decided not to share a house with any of them in '75, renting a small room at the Waterbury YMCA.

Three years before the Village People released their hit song extolling the virtues of gay life at the Y ("They have everything for young men to enjoy / You can hang out with all the boys"), Burke was already onto the notion. When his friends on the team questioned the decision, Burke told them he loved to play basketball, and living at the Y allowed him to shoot hoops every morning before he went to the ballpark.

His teammates thought this was odd, but Burke was a different kind of dude, so they didn't make too much of it. But one day, Marvin Webb came to the Y to play basketball with Glenn. After they shot around for a while, Burke invited him to check out his room. Webb was surprised by how small it was, maybe six feet across and twelve feet deep, and dumbfounded when Burke introduced him to an out-of-town guest, his lover from California.

Webb looked around the room and saw just one small cot. "Where," Webb asked, "is he going to stay?"

Glenn didn't respond, but the answer was obvious.

An unspoken drama was unfolding in this small room at the Waterbury Y, at once simple and profound. Burke was in love and wanted to share this most basic of human emotions with his buddy, Webb. But disclosing his sexuality to his teammate required enormous courage. If Webb reacted with hostility or even whispered nonjudgmentally in the clubhouse, Burke's career could be over. And though Webb walked out of the YMCA uncertain about how he felt about the revelation, within days he affirmed Burke's trust, telling Burke not to worry; they'd always be friends.

When Burke's partner returned home to the Bay Area, Glenn ventured into nearby New Haven, home of Yale University. There, he met a white professor, a man who was fully his type—older and scholarly. Burke and the professor established a routine, with Glenn riding a bus twenty-three miles every morning so they could meet for a leisurely lunch on the fabled New Haven Green, an expansive and historic downtown park.

At night after home games, Burke made up various excuses when his teammates invited him out to chase women, sometimes having one quick drink and leaving, other times saying he needed to get back to the Y for a late game of basketball. Instead, he'd go to the town's gay bar, the Road House Café, always looking over his shoulder to be sure no one saw him walking in. But one night, Burke walked out of the bar just as a member of the team's administrative staff walked in. Neither man said a word, but Burke gave him a knowing look, as if to say, *Neither one of us will speak a word about this*. And neither did.

The encounter caused Burke to think more seriously about the implications of being found out by other members of the baseball establishment. The best protection from his bosses' likely homophobia, Burke decided, was his performance on the field. "I'm just going to have to hit .300 and lead the league in steals," he concluded. "Then nobody can say shit to me."

Burke fell short on batting average, hitting .270 in 1975, but he slugged a career-high 12 homers and set an Eastern League record with 48 stolen bases.

At season's end, Burke couldn't wait to get back to San Francisco, where he could surround himself with other gay men and not have to put on an act every day. Ever since his appearance on *The King Norman Show*, he had enjoyed the spotlight and relished being the center of attention in any gathering of people. But increasingly, he found it difficult to reconcile his sexuality with the hetero culture of professional baseball. No longer did he want to provide the spark at his teammates' gatherings. Now, he told a friend, he wanted to "leave his teammates behind and slip away to his own party." Fortunately for him, in the midseventies Black people and gay men were changing the way Americans partied in an exhilarating new way.

Disco Fever was spreading, and Glenn Burke caught it.

CHAPTER 12
GLISTENING

Outside the club, standing under the night sky, John Duran could hear the seductive *thump-thump-thump-thump* of the bass. He flashed the bouncer a fake ID with the name Carlos Ramirez. Duran was underage, just seventeen, but nothing was going to keep him from checking out Studio One, the hottest discotheque in Los Angeles.[1]

There were familiar faces at the bar, Hollywood celebrities he recognized from TV and the movies, men he had not known were gay, but there they were, smoking, drinking, and flirting with other men. Duran continued on through a pair of double doors, and it was there, on the dance floor, that he "first found heaven." Suspended from the ceiling, silver disco balls reflected prisms of light on shirtless men moving to the music, an aroma of sweat, alcohol, and cologne filling the air as the

DJ kept the beat going all night long, seamlessly mixing one song into the next.

To walk into a disco in 1976, wrote Jack Slater in the *Los Angeles Times*, was to step into "a giant jukebox: America's ultimate adult amusement park." At Studio One in Los Angeles, Studio 54 in New York City, Artemis in Philadelphia, Dugan's Bistro in Chicago, or the thousands of other discos across the country, whether the clientele was gay or straight, the scenes were similar: the relentless beat of high-decibel music; strobe lights, whiskey, and polyester; a mass of bodies writhing on the dance floor, radiating heat, moving in unison, becoming one with each other and with the music in a state of collective euphoria.

At the disco, it didn't matter if you had a dead-end job or bills to pay or a horrible boss; if your parents wouldn't speak to you anymore after you came out as gay; if you felt invisible at school. The dance floor was an escape from all that, a fantasyland where the best dancers earned attention and admiration by performing the hustle, the bus stop, or the bump.

To be a young gay man at a disco in the mid-seventies was to experience an exhilarating sense of freedom. Gay men of previous generations had congregated mostly under cloaks of secrecy, slipping through unmarked entrances in dark alleys that led to windowless bars. Far too often, the police stormed into these places, busting down doors and cracking heads, arresting men for drinking or dancing or kissing or holding hands. Laws prevented gay men from enjoying the simplest elements of a date that straight men and women took for granted. Convictions on these "crimes" labeled these men as sex offenders—which often meant getting fired from a job and evicted from an apartment. Lives were turned upside down over expressions of love.

The bigotry, harassment, and paranoia were frustrating, demoralizing, and constant, and yet, gay people fought back. In 1959, police entered Los Angeles's Cooper Do-nuts, a late-night bakery popular with gay and transgender people, demanding identification; a law at the time dictated arrest for anyone whose gender presentation did not match the one shown on their ID. When the police began making arrests, other customers tossed coffee cups and trash at the cops, eventually taking the small-scale riot into the streets until police backup arrived. Seven years later, on New Year's Eve, cops descended on the Black Cat, a popular new gay bar in the Silver Lake neighborhood of Los Angeles. Just as joyful partygoers, surrounded by colorful balloons and sparkling Christmas trees, counted down the seconds to midnight, police stormed into the bar and began beating the customers and arresting men who had kissed in celebration of the arrival of 1967. A little over a month later, more than two hundred gay Angelenos marched in protest of the violence and arrests.

Two years later, in June 1969, New Yorkers staged the most

On February 11, 1967, hundreds of people protested the violence inflicted by police on gay patrons of the Black Cat Tavern in Los Angeles. (ONE National Gay and Lesbian Archives at the USC Libraries)

legendary act of gay resistance in American history. Cops raided the Stonewall Inn bar in Greenwich Village, arresting gay, lesbian, and transgender people—but patrons and onlookers resisted, violently, sparking a six-day street battle with cops that eventually attracted thousands of participants. The courage and startling bravery of the people who stood up to the police inspired a turning point in gay rights in this country. The "Stonewall riots" attracted national media attention and marked the moment when many gay people first recognized the power of a "gay community," a call to action to come out from the shadows, acknowledge their existence, and demand equal protection under the law.

The rise of disco and the movement toward gay liberation took place simultaneously, linked so closely that it was often hard to discern where one trend's energy ended and the other's began. In her book on the social significance of disco, *Hot Stuff*, author Alice Echols states that as women, minorities, and gays in the 1970s rewrote the traditional scripts that had confined their existence for generations, disco played a central role, "broaden[ing] the contours" of what it meant to be a woman, a racial minority, or homosexual. "As for gay men," she wrote, "they became newly visible, largely through the dissemination of disco culture."

Tired of harassment by the police, gay men with disposable income organized house parties and rented private clubs for DJs to spin records late into the night. Elaborate lighting, professional sound systems, and attention to wardrobe were as essential as the dancing, all elements previously found only on Broadway. But while Broadway musicals traditionally championed "a steely persistence and cheery denial of suffering," Echols claimed, disco was not about a melancholy longing but "a superabundant spectacle."

The spectacle was so alluring that by the summer of 1976, more than ten thousand discos in the US earned combined revenues of over $4 billion. Stores rolled out entire lines of clothes to suit the tastes of the disco-crazed, a book of disco dance moves reached number one on the *New York Times* bestseller list, and artists such as Donna Summer, Gloria Gaynor, Chic, KC and the Sunshine Band, the Bee Gees, Sylvester, and the Village People ruled the radio.

As Americans discovered the fun, escape, and sex appeal of the disco scene, gay men achieved corresponding new levels of visibility in other areas of society. In the fall of 1976, two network television shows featured gay characters, a first in American TV history; straight men began to take fashion and grooming cues from their gay brothers; and gay people from intolerant families and towns flocked to big cities to carve out their own neighborhoods, amassing economic and political clout that could not be ignored. In San Francisco's Castro District, just across the bay from the neighborhood where Glenn Burke grew up, gay men by the thousands renovated old homes; opened their own restaurants, flower shops, and camera stores; created their own softball teams; and ran for public office.[2]

All told, it appeared that Burke was reaching adulthood at just the right moment in history. Here was a gay Black man who loved to live his life out loud, stealing bases, slamming dunks, and swinging fists; singing and disco dancing and making others laugh; always dressed to impress; never backing down; always the center of attention. He was so well suited for the 1970s that when a documentarian asked former major leaguer Tito Fuentes to define Burke's electric personality, Fuentes compared him to the iconic symbol of the decade. "I would describe Glenn," he said, "as like a glistening mirror ball at a discotheque when the light hits it and all of these different reflections and colors flash all over the room."

The problem for Burke was that his magnetic personality and superior athletic talents were leading him down a path deep into the heart of homophobia. There were no quarters of American society more hostile to gay people than the locker rooms, stadiums, and fan bases of the sports world. As other gay men discovered a new freedom in the mid-seventies, and as Burke experienced a taste of it in San Francisco each winter, he spent each baseball season locked in a culture that resisted these social changes. Worse yet, he had to pretend to like it that way, keeping his secret and living a lie in the woman-chasing, homophobic world of pro ball. It was a repressive existence that could have crippled him with fear, anxiety, and self-doubt.

Glenn Burke's teammates marveled at his fun-loving skills on the dance floor, where he always attracted a crowd of admirers. Here he dances with his sister Joyce at their sister Paula's wedding. (Family photo via Doug Harris)

But Glenn Burke had excelled to such a degree that as Dodger spring training opened in February 1976, some members of the organization believed he might earn a spot on the Major League roster. To the extent that baseball is a mental game, where self-confidence and clarity of thought fuel success, Burke's rise through the Dodger ranks had already been a far greater accomplishment than anyone could have guessed.

He might not live the Dodger Way, but Glenn Burke was close to becoming a Dodger.

CHAPTER 13

CUP OF COFFEE

By the spring of 1976, the dormitories at the Dodgers' spring training complex in Vero Beach had been renovated, and the entire site felt more like an all-inclusive Florida resort than a former military barracks.

Players, team executives, and their families lived comfortably in Spanish-style villas nestled on tree-lined streets named after Jackie Robinson, Roy Campanella, and other legends from the team's Brooklyn days. Dodgertown boasted such luxuries as an Olympic-sized swimming pool; two golf courses; tennis, shuffleboard, and basketball courts; a private pond for bass fishing; a horseshoe pit; and a game room stocked with a huge TV and plenty of ping-pong and pool tables. The team played its spring training games at five-thousand-seat Holman

Stadium, and the grounds included three other full-sized fields for workouts, along with batting cages and pitching machines. There were so many orange groves and palm trees that *Sports Illustrated* dubbed Dodgertown "a baseball training facility disguised as an arboretum."

Dodger families enjoyed a Christmas in March theme night with a gift-giving Santa, and a Western Night featuring country crooners, grilled steaks, and BBQ ribs. No other team offered anything like this, bolstering the Dodgers' reputation as the game's model franchise. But that didn't negate the cold reality that Dodgertown was also the place where some players' Major League dreams would die, where they'd be assigned to Minor League outposts or cut altogether.

On the evening of April 8, 1976, Glenn Burke relaxed in air-conditioned comfort in the Dodgertown movie theater. Players on the Major League roster had already departed on the team's private plane, bound for the regular season opener in San Francisco. Minor leaguers stayed behind for a few more weeks of workouts.

Burke had turned heads at Dodgertown, playing so well that he had been named the top rookie player in spring training. "He's going to be a major league superstar," a Dodger exec told one reporter. "I've never seen anyone get a better jump on a fly ball in centerfield." But the big league roster was loaded with veteran players, and Burke was set to begin the year gaining more seasoning at Triple-A Albuquerque, New Mexico.

But suddenly, the movie stopped playing and the theater's bright lights came on. Someone called out Glenn's name, demanding he report to the press room. Burke's heart raced as he left the theater on his bicycle. Had he actually been cut? Was this the end?

It was just the beginning. A team executive gave him the news any kid who's ever swung a bat dreams of hearing. He was headed to the major leagues. The Dodgers were calling him up to replace injured second baseman Davey Lopes on the roster. He needed to fly across the country to meet the team in San Francisco for the season opener against the Giants the next day.

After working his way up through the Dodger farm system, with stops in Utah, Washington, Florida, Connecticut, California, and New Mexico, Glenn Burke made his Major League debut back home in the Bay Area against the San Francisco Giants on April 9, 1976. (National Baseball Hall of Fame)

There could not have been a more appropriate city for Burke to make his Major League debut. The Bay Area was home; his mom and sisters could simply drive across the Bay Bridge to see him play. And San Francisco was the capital of gay America, the Castro District thriving just eight miles from the Giants' Candlestick Park.

Still, if Burke's sexuality hadn't been a secret, it would have shocked the fans at Candlestick and the hundreds of thousands watching on KTTV channel 11 back in LA. In Lynn Rosellini's landmark series on gay athletes in the *Washington Star* a year earlier, a New York doctor offered a theory on why homosexuality was "unknown" in Major League Baseball. "There is a fear of getting hurt by the ball," he claimed, "particularly in the genitals." The doctor's statement was patently absurd, and nobody proved that more than Glenn Burke. Not only was he the toughest guy on the team, afraid of no man or baseball, he never even wore a protective cup.

The Dodger-Giant matchup marked the first time the teams had faced off in a season opener since they both had moved from New York in 1958. East Coast or West, there was no fiercer rivalry in baseball, and Giant fans relished heckling the visiting Dodgers. Still, as he walked across the infield grass toward the Dodger dugout prior to the game, Burke was startled by the ferociousness of the Giant fans' jeering. "Why are they booing me?" he asked relief pitcher Mike Marshall. "Glenn," Marshall replied, "they're booing *me*. They don't even know who you are."

On a veteran Dodger team, Burke was indeed the biggest unknown on the roster, which made him a subject of interest to newspaper reporters. Davey Lopes, the injured second baseman, told one writer that Burke had "unlimited potential," while Dodger coach Jim Gilliam compared him to one of the game's all-time greats, a future Hall of Famer familiar to Giants fans. "Once we get him cooled down a little bit," Gilliam declared, "we think he's going to be another Willie Mays."

Burke watched most of the game from the Dodger bench, alone with his thoughts, pondering what lay before him as a Major League player. Part of him wanted to hit .300 and become a superstar, as Lopes and Gilliam predicted, so that if his secret ever got out, he could tell the haters to "go to hell." But another part of him—unlike anyone else on the roster—yearned for mediocrity; if he hit .250, he could remain relatively anonymous and guard his privacy.

In the top of the ninth inning, with the Dodgers trailing 4–2, two outs, and runners on first and second, Burke got the call from manager Walter Alston. Brought in as a pinch hitter representing the go-ahead run, Burke stepped into the batter's box against Giants reliever Gary Lavelle and ripped a hard ground ball up the middle. But San Francisco had shortstop Chris Speier positioned perfectly; he snatched the ball, tossed it to second baseman Rich Auerbach for the force-out, and the game was over. "Our scouting report on Burke was that he was a tough hitter and that he hit balls hard up the middle," Giants manager Bill Rigney told reporters in the victorious Giants clubhouse. "So with my brains, I told Chris to play toward the middle."

In the Dodger clubhouse, Alston presented Burke with a wristwatch in honor of his big league debut, and the team's radio crew interviewed him on the postgame show. "I was called up because of my speed," Burke told listeners. "I run from home plate to first base at 3.8 to 4 seconds, and that's one of the fastest on the team."

As he showered and dressed, Burke reflected on all that had transpired on his first day as a Major League player and the way he'd been treated by his teammates and manager. "What a great day," he later recalled thinking. "And what a class organization the Dodgers are."

Over the next three weeks, Burke tasted the fruits of the Major League life, flying on the Dodgers' team plane to Atlanta and Houston, collecting big league meal money, staying at plush hotels. But he hardly ever played. Finally, on April 29, after right fielder Bill Buckner sprained his ankle, Alston approached Burke during batting practice at Dodger Stadium: he would bat leadoff and play left field that night against St. Louis, his first Major League start.

In the third inning, Burke collected his first big league hit when he beat out a slow roller off Cardinal pitcher Pete Falcone. Two innings later, he flashed the speed that made him such an electric prospect. Burke's single to center drove in a run; when Cardinal center fielder Bake McBride briefly bobbled the ball, Burke scrambled to second base. Then, taking a long lead off second, Burke rattled Falcone to the point that he balked. An ordinary player would have still been on first; Burke's uncommon speed and daring had carried him all the way to third.

After the game, a 5–0 Dodger victory, Burke told reporters that he had been prepared for the moment. "I may be a rookie," he said, "but I didn't want to act like a rookie. I've been waiting for a chance, and I got it. I've always felt I could play in the Major Leagues." And yet, Burke's ambivalence also came through in the same interview. "I still like to play basketball and if I get another chance—and I can't make it in baseball—I'll give it a try," he said. "But baseball offered me the money."

Burke met lofty expectations in his first start, but less than a week later, when Davey Lopes's rib injury healed, he was sent down to the Dodgers' Triple-A team in Albuquerque. Having hit .444 in nine games with the Dodgers, Glenn Burke's first Major League stint, the proverbial "cup of coffee," had been a big success.[1] There was no guarantee he'd ever be called back up, but if he played well in Albuquerque, the odds were in his favor.

Before his first game with the Albuquerque Dukes, Burke spoke confidently to a local sportswriter about his goals for the season. "I was the ringleader at Waterbury and I'm going to be the ringleader here," he said. "I don't predict. I just talk about what I've already done. I'm not an easy out and I don't give up. I'm going to play like Albuquerque's in the big leagues. All I want to do is play ball and have fun and please the fans. I want to be one of the main attractions around here."

At first, Burke tried too hard to impress, and the results were disastrous. In his first nine games, he hit just .184 with only one RBI. So, before he reported to the ballpark for a game against Tucson on May 16, he took a moment to breathe. As a child, his faith had grounded him, provided a sense of peace in times of stress. And so on this Sunday morning, he stood in his apartment's kitchen and prayed to God. He gave thanks for simply being alive, for being healthy. He prayed for safe travels on an upcoming road trip to Sacramento and Honolulu.

With a renewed sense of calm and purpose, Burke arrived at Albuquerque Sports Stadium, where the grandstands popped with the colors of youth ballplayers dressed in uniform. Burke dominated the game like he had as a Berkeley Little Leaguer, collecting three hits, blasting his first homer of the season, driving in four runs, and stealing two bases in a 12–7 victory.

The spectacular performance turned Glenn's season around, propelling him to a run of remarkable success. In one game, he rapped four doubles, stole third base, and threw a runner out at home plate. In another, he broke up a no-hitter with a ninth-inning single and drove in the winning run in the tenth. In one stretch, he collected hits in twelve straight games; in another, he stole thirty-three bases in just forty-eight games. By season's end, he'd set a Pacific Coast League record with sixty-three steals.

And yet, even as he built a rock-solid case for a return to Los Angeles, Burke further cemented his reputation as an unpredictable hothead. He lost a chance to extend his hitting streak when an umpire ejected him from a game for arguing, and he constantly tested the patience of mild-mannered Albuquerque manager Stan Wasiak, earning the nickname "Bad Boy" in the process. "Glenn played with a chip on his shoulder," teammate Joe Simpson said. "Sometimes that chip would weigh him down."

Wasiak would make a suggestion; Burke wouldn't listen. Wasiak would ask Glenn to do something; Burke refused. Glenn developed such a reputation as a renegade that Dodger general manager Al Campanis demanded that Wasiak keep him posted on the young prospect's antics. "And then one day in Phoenix," Dodger Minor League pitcher Larry Corrigan recalled, "Glenn pulled some bullshit in center field. As he was walking back into the dugout, Wasiak says, 'I'll call Campanis on you!'" Rather than submit to this display of authority, Burke fired back. "Fuck you! I'll call Campanis on *you*!" For the rest of the season, Corrigan kept a close eye on Burke, considering him to be "a ticking time bomb waiting to go off at any minute."

Still, Corrigan and his wife, Laurie, considered Burke a good friend. On more than one occasion, as they drove from their apartment to the ballpark, they saw Burke walking down the highway, shirtless in denim bib overalls. They'd offer Glenn a ride, and he'd accept.

One time, Glenn invited Larry and Laurie over to his apartment for a party. Laurie considered Glenn to be a "gorgeous man with the body of an Adonis. He had muscles everywhere." And at Glenn's party, she noticed, all the guests were good-looking guys, too. "Where are all the girls?" she wondered. "After that party, it kind of dawned on us," Larry recalled. "My radar was up at that point. He hadn't come out yet, but he was dealing with a lot of heavy issues that at that time weren't really spoken about."

On September 1, the Dodgers, like every other Major League team, had the opportunity to expand their roster for the remainder of the season, and Burke was called back up to LA. He joined a team in transition, one that would ultimately finish a disappointing ten games behind the first-place Cincinnati Reds in what would be the last of Walter Alston's twenty-three seasons as manager. Where Alston appeared to be losing his edge, energetic third-base coach Tommy Lasorda dove headfirst into opportunity, giving pregame pep talks, slapping players' backs, marching toward the spotlight, and making it clear he wanted Alston's job. Three months after the season ended, he got it.[2]

Glenn Burke's future was now in Lasorda's hands. When spring training came around in February, he would resume his quest to become an everyday player as a closeted gay man, but he wouldn't do so in a vacuum.

Sports pages were full of stories about Dave Kopay, a recently retired professional football player who had made the shocking revelation that he was gay.

Front pages were full of stories about Anita Bryant, a popular singer and former Miss America runner-up who had launched a nationwide anti-gay-rights campaign.

As he had inched closer to a permanent home in the major leagues, Glenn Burke wondered how he'd be treated if straight members of the public learned he was gay.

Turned out, all he had to do was open a newspaper to see the answer. A lot of people would hate him.

CHAPTER 14
ON FIRE

With her long, tan legs and stylish red hair, Anita Bryant was talented, beautiful, and famous. Born in a small town in Oklahoma, she learned to sing as a toddler, and by the time she was six she was one of those precocious, cute kids wowing television audiences with her voice and charm. At age nineteen, she won the Miss Oklahoma pageant and came in second runner-up for Miss America. She recorded a string of hit songs, traveled overseas to entertain American soldiers, and performed at Republican and Democratic national conventions, the Super Bowl, and the funeral of former president Lyndon B. Johnson.

Her wholesome, patriotic, and devout image appealed to white middle-American sensibilities, and she became a television

A former Miss America contestant from Oklahoma, Anita Bryant used her platform as a popular singer to speak out against equal protection for gay citizens. In response to her high-profile bigotry, scores of gay men and women across the country became more politically active. (AP Photo)

spokesperson for popular brands including Coca-Cola, Holiday Inn, Tupperware, and Kraft. Everybody knew her catchphrase for Florida citrus: "Breakfast without orange juice," she told TV viewers, "is like a day without sunshine."

In 1977, at age thirty-seven, Bryant became the face and voice of another campaign in Florida, one that dramatically changed the course of her career and the gay rights movement. She used her position of privilege not to lift up vulnerable people, but to persecute them.

In January 1977, Dade County, Florida, commissioners passed an ordinance that protected gay citizens from discrimination in employment, housing, and public services. Notably, gay people in Miami could no longer be fired simply because of their sexuality. But within weeks, homophobic opponents launched a public campaign to overturn the law, naming their movement Save Our Children. They couched their bigotry in pro-family rhetoric, focusing on the supposed danger of gay public school teachers by portraying them as deviant sexual predators, ignoring study after study that disproved that claim. In the months leading up to a June 1977 countywide vote whether to roll back the anti-discrimination ordinance, Bryant devoted her life to the anti-gay cause, headlining numerous events in Miami and making inflammatory statements to the national media.

"I would give my life if necessary to protect my children," she told a reporter in February 1977. "I'm concerned with giving them the right food and clothes to wear and if I let up on the spiritual and physical thing, what good is it? If they're exposed to [homosexuality] I might as well feed them garbage."

While Bryant led her crusade in South Florida, 140 miles up the road in Vero Beach, Glenn Burke returned from California for another spring training.

For baseball fans, the very words *spring training* evoked feelings of hope and renewal, a time and place where the weather was warm, the regular season yet to begin, anything and everything still a possibility. All those sensations were magnified in Dodgertown with portly and loquacious new manager Tommy Lasorda at the helm. When the forty-nine-year-old Lasorda wasn't eating, he was boasting about his players' abilities and the team's World Series destiny. When he wasn't boasting about his players' abilities and the team's World Series destiny, he was eating. Over the course of the upcoming season, he would put on thirty-five pounds.

Lasorda had grown up in a large, working-class Italian family outside of Philadelphia, the second of Sabatino and Carmella Lasorda's five sons. His father drove a truck at a local quarry, and his mother kept

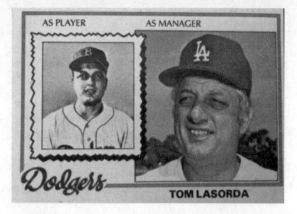

Tommy Lasorda spent twenty seasons as Dodger manager (1977–96), compiling an overall record of 1,599–1,439 and winning World Series titles in 1981 and '88. He was elected to the National Baseball Hall of Fame in 1997. (Topps)

AS PLAYER   AS MANAGER

Dodgers   TOM LASORDA

their home full of guests, food, laughter, and singing. Tommy had a way with words from an early age, once winning a school spelling bee. He loved playing baseball and listening to Major League games on the radio, and he never missed an opportunity to drop his glove and brawl. As a left-handed pitcher, his talents propelled him to brief stints in the major leagues, but it was as a Dodger Minor League manager and big league third-base coach where he shined. Every day, he thanked the Big Dodger in the Sky for the opportunity to work for the organization he loved so deeply. When the Dodgers named him manager, he told reporters the thrill was "like being presented the Hope Diamond."

Depending on one's perspective, Lasorda spent the spring blowing smoke or expertly building the self-confidence of his players. He told Bill Russell he was the best shortstop in baseball, outfielder Dusty Baker that he would bounce back strong from an off year in '76, first baseman Steve Garvey that he'd hit thirty homers, second baseman Davey Lopes that he was the unquestioned leader of the team. He slapped butts, devoured pasta and egg rolls, hugged home-run hitters, cracked jokes, and showered the national sportswriters visiting Vero Beach with tales of Dodger greatness to come.

In his first meeting with his players at Dodgertown, Lasorda made his lofty expectations clear. No longer would they roll over and accept the dominance of the rival Cincinnati Reds. "Guys, I'm going to tell you right now. We've got a good ball club and we're going to win," he said. "We're going to win because we're gonna play together. You may hate the guy next to you. Off the field, fine. I don't care. But when you come in here and put that uniform on, it's got 'Dodgers' on the front of it. If a guy gets in a fight on the field, I want to see everybody out there backing him up. We're gonna win together and lose together, laugh together and cry together. But we'll do it as a team."

But for Glenn Burke, rejoining the Dodgers for spring training was more complicated than that. It meant leaving the comfortable cocoon of gay San Francisco, where he was accepted and could live free, for the unyielding confines of professional baseball. He was forced to live a lie every second of every day, denying one of the most basic elements of his humanity just to make other people comfortable, while at the same time attempting to reach his full potential as a ballplayer. Adding to the unease was the presence of newcomer Rick Monday, a talented veteran white center fielder the Dodgers had acquired from the Chicago Cubs over the winter. Where Burke had developed a reputation as a loose cannon, the "Bad Boy," Monday lived out the tenets of the Dodger Way even before he joined the team. He had been a favorite of Lasorda's ever since his high school days in Southern California, and cemented his All-American Boy credentials as a Cub when he sprinted across the outfield in a game against the Dodgers to prevent two protestors from setting fire to an American flag. All told, it would be no easy task for Burke to gain playing time over the veteran Monday.

When spring training concluded, the Dodgers assigned Burke to Triple-A Albuquerque, rather than Los Angeles, a discouraging turn of events. He didn't hide his feelings after arriving in New Mexico, complaining to sportswriter Bart Ripp with such regularity that Ripp regarded Burke's grumbling as much a part of the game-day routine as batting practice. "Man, I can play this game," Burke would tell him. "The Dodgers are holding me back. If they don't take me up [to Los Angeles], I want out of this place." If he wasn't called up soon, he threatened, he might give basketball another shot, even if that meant playing in a European league.

Burke channeled his anger into aggression and success on the baseball field. He hit safely in thirteen straight games in early May, impressing fans with an uncommon combination of speed and power. On May 22, he single-handedly dismantled the visiting Tacoma Twins, going 4-for-4 with 3 runs scored, 2 RBI, 2 two stolen bases. Laughing in the locker room after the game, dressed in a red T-shirt emblazoned with Las Vegas showgirls, Burke explained to Ripp how he escaped a fifth-inning rundown. When he attempted to steal second, the pitcher stepped off the mound and threw to first; Burke was caught in a pickle. As Burke darted back and forth between first and second, the ball went from pitcher to first baseman to second baseman to first baseman to pitcher to shortstop before first baseman Randy Bass launched an errant throw into left field that allowed Burke to slide safely into third. "I used a juke step," he told Ripp. "I learned it from Johnnie Rogers [the 1972 Heisman Trophy–winning Nebraska running back] on television."

In Miami, Florida, Anita Bryant continued to deliver outrageous speeches that attracted national attention in proportion to their hate. "I'm not only aflame, I'm on fire" with righteousness, she declared as she warned members of the Dade County Commission they'd "burn in hell" if the ordinance preventing discrimination against gay people remained in place. "Homosexuality is an abomination to the Lord," she declared.

Bryant's scare tactics inspired her followers to violence and intimidation. They firebombed the cars of two gay activists, beat another pair of gay men as they passed out literature, and smashed out the apartment windows of yet another gay man. Bryant refused to take responsibility for the vicious acts her campaign had inspired, going as far as to offer the baseless theory that gay people were attacking themselves to generate publicity. But just a few weeks later, that claim was sadly exposed for the lie that it was when Robert Hillsborough, a gay San Francisco gardener, walked down the sidewalk with his roommate after a night of disco dancing. Four teenage boys approached and began beating them, then chased them down in a car when they tried to escape. "F——, f——!" they yelled as they stabbed Hillsborough to death with fifteen cuts of a knife. "Here's one for Anita!"

With Rick Monday nursing an aching back, Burke's electric play in Albuquerque was too much for the Dodgers to ignore. On June 2, he was finally called back up to Los Angeles. But not before antagonizing his Minor League manager one last time.

In his final game with the Dukes, Burke knew he was headed to the Dodgers the next day. With two outs in the top of the ninth, Burke stood in center field as Albuquerque clung to a one-run lead—one more out and he was headed to the big leagues. The visitors had the tying run standing on third and the go-ahead run at first when the batter hit a towering fly ball to center field. Burke camped under the ball, ready to make a routine catch, when he suddenly took off his mitt, casually switching it from left hand to right before snatching the game-winning out with the wrong hand. As Glenn ran back to the dugout, smiling from ear to ear, manager Jimmy Williams chewed him out. "If you ever do that again . . ." he started, before Burke interrupted. "I'm leaving, skip," he replied. "Now you'll have something to talk about when I'm gone."

Some of his Triple-A teammates resented Burke's promotion, claiming fellow outfielder Joe Simpson, leading the Pacific Coast League with a .374 batting average, should have gotten the call. "Nobody said anything," pitcher Rick Nitz told Ripp, "but you know Glenn didn't deserve to go up. Joe Simpson is just as good a player and he's got a better attitude." Years later, Burke made a credible claim that the Dodgers gave him a raw deal after they learned he was gay. But here in the spring of 1977, before his sexuality became an issue, at least some of his teammates felt the Dodgers gave him a preferential leg up after he threatened to play professional basketball.

Burke joined a team that had jumped out to one of the best starts in Major League history. By the end of April, the Dodgers already led the second-place Reds by a whopping 7.5 games, a record lead for the first month of a season. The Dodgers won thirty of their first forty games, and all of Lasorda's spring training predictions were coming true. The power hitters were crushing homers, the base stealers were swiping bags, and nobody could hit the pitchers.

"If Tommy Lasorda broke a rack of pool balls," third baseman Ron Cey marveled, "all fifteen of 'em would go in." In classic Lasorda humor, the manager said the season was unfolding just as he planned, despite the doubters. "I'm not surprised at our lead," he said. "I feel like the hypochondriac who died and had it written on his tombstone, 'They wouldn't believe me.'"

Joining a red-hot team in mid-season came with its own set of pressures; Burke knew he better not mess up a good thing. He told a Los Angeles sportswriter that he understood the expectations. "A lot of guys in the minors are saying they can play in the Big Leagues," he said. "But when they get there, when they get that chance, they'd better produce."

He got off to a solid start at the plate, hitting safely in 3 of his first 10 at-bats, going 5-for-17 with 2 stolen bases in his first 5 starts. But it was his charismatic presence in the clubhouse that made the biggest impression on his teammates. At first glance, it seemed so improbable. Here was a team full of veterans playing extremely well; why would they allow a rookie to come in and become the life of the clubhouse? But it turned out Glenn Burke was just what the Dodgers needed, a seemingly carefree and self-confident man loosening things up when the team's steady march toward the playoffs threatened to generate ever-increasing levels of pressure and anxiety.

From the moment he arrived in the Dodgers' clubhouse, Burke adopted the space as his own. He brought in a boom box, blasting disco tunes from the tape deck before every game and dancing to the music. He freestyled his own rhymes; some teammates called it poetry—today we'd call it an early form of rap. He'd arrive and depart the ballpark in style, changing in and out of his Dodger uniform from a variety of eccentric outfits, including black pinstripe suits with red carnations and more than a dozen stylish hats. He cracked jokes in the clubhouse, cut up in the dugout, and mocked teammates and coaches just like the hoorah battles of his childhood.

Tommy Lasorda was a frequent target of his jokes. Burke would stuff a pillow under his jersey and strut around the clubhouse, bowlegged, spouting platitudes and profanities just like the manager. During games, he observed Lasorda's love for attention, the way he perched himself on the top step of the dugout to give celebratory bear hugs to Dodger players returning to the bench after hitting homers. So Burke messed with the manager, sprinting to the top step before Lasorda could get there and sharing an overexuberant hug with the home-run hitter, leaving the manager hanging. Lasorda could take the jokes; the team was winning. And he could also dish it back. When Burke showed up for a road trip carrying a briefcase as if he had important paperwork to deal with, Lasorda ribbed him mercilessly.

On bus rides and long flights, he befriended everybody on the team. He talked football with Steve Garvey, the first baseman who had played quarterback at Michigan State. Don Sutton, the star pitcher, nicknamed Burke "Toby" after a character in the popular TV miniseries on slavery *Roots*. The moniker was insensitive at best, but even in its cringeworthiness it came with a measure of affection; to white and Black players alike, Burke was one of the guys. Sutton, in fact, was the first Dodger player to invite Glenn to join the veteran players for drinks after a game. "He was the most lively personality I ever covered in forty-five years in sports," journalist Lyle Spencer recalled decades later. "It's hard to even compare him with anybody. He was this electric personality." Second baseman Davey Lopes said Burke's antics were an invaluable part of the Dodgers' clubhouse culture. "If a few laughs have cleared the worry out of your mind before you go out to hit a baseball," he said, "you concentrate better."

There was another aspect to Burke's personality the players appreciated more than anyone on the outside could know. To the outside world, the Dodger organization billed itself as squeaky clean. Don Merry of the *Los Angeles Times* described the franchise as "extremely professional, slightly conservative, authoritarian and dedicated to doing things correctly and in first-class style. They radiate a slight aura of superiority. It is doubtful that even a high-powered Madison Avenue firm could have concocted a more favorable image." Dodger players knew there was a heavy dose of bullshit in that portrayal. They were no saints: guys cheated on their wives, drank, and smoked; Lasorda dropped so many f-bombs behind closed doors that players began counting them; teammates resented one another's success; occasionally they threw punches. In that context, Glenn Burke appeared to be the realest of the real, unashamed to carry the swagger of the East Bay into the Dodger clubhouse. In truth, Burke was as concerned about his image as the rest of them, cultivating a macho and fun-loving facade to distract attention from the kind of scrutiny that might reveal his true self.

On June 6, Dade County voters went to the polls and soundly over-turned the gay rights ordinance by a margin of more than two to one: 202,319 people voted to repeal the protections for gay citizens, while only 89,562 voted to retain them. Standing among admirers at a Miami Beach hotel, Anita Bryant celebrated victory. "Tonight the laws of God and the cultural values of man have been vindicated," she claimed. "With God's continued help we will prevail in our fight to repeal similar laws throughout the nation which attempt to legitimize a lifestyle that is both perverse and dangerous to our survival as one nation under God."

What Bryant didn't realize at that moment of triumph was that she had unleashed forces that would undermine her career and accelerate the gay rights movement into a powerful new gear.

Gay Americans emerged from the defeat more united and vocal than ever before. And fair-minded observers couldn't help but notice the hypocrisy and hate inherent in Bryant's campaign. It also turned out that for someone as image-conscious as Bryant, stoking the fires of bigotry eventually proved bad business. At the height of the Miami campaign, she lived in a twenty-seven-room mansion and earned more than $500,000 annually for her religious books, record albums, and appearances. But the national brands that paid her to represent their products grew weary of her controversial politics and dropped her as a spokesperson. Even a planned television series was canceled by a network concerned about backlash. Gay citizens were now considered a "community," and one that flexed some power. There were more small victories to come for Bryant—she was voted Most Admired Woman by the readers of *Good Housekeeping* magazine—but the overall trajectory of her career plummeted. She became the butt of jokes on national television and never had another major hit record; her businesses went bankrupt. Within three years, she revealed that her marriage had been a sham all along, marked by infidelity, drug abuse, and thoughts of suicide. When she filed for divorce from her controlling husband, the same Christians who had backed her campaign in Miami turned on her, claiming she would go to hell for rejecting morality and embarrassing Jesus.

Just a day after the Miami vote, Jean O'Leary and Bruce Voeller, the co-directors of the National Gay Task Force, could already sense that their defeat had created a new opportunity for long-term progress.

"Anita Bryant and her Save Our Children Inc. are doing the 20 million lesbians and gay men in America an enormous favor," they wrote in the *New York Times*. "They are focusing for the public the nature of the prejudice and discrimination we face."

In their column, the authors pushed back against the bigoted opinions Bryant and fellow homophobes had passed off as truth. Gay teachers weren't hurting kids, they argued; intolerant extremists were.

"It took many of us a long time to realize that these stereotypes were lies, and that there were so many healthy, happy, productive, responsible human beings in this world who had refused to deny or repress their capacity to love members of their own sex," they wrote. "For some of us this realization had to wait until we were well into adulthood, and we suffered because we, too, believed the lies that we were sinful, criminal, sick."

O'Leary and Voeller disputed the notion that their very existence was immoral. Rather, they said, it was Bryant and her followers who acted unethically by peddling ugly stereotypes, denying the humanity of gay men and women, and ignoring the unique vibrancy of gay culture.

"We believe it is immoral to lie to children. We believe that it is immoral to teach them to hate people for whom they choose to love. We think it is immoral to foster prejudice and discrimination by pretending to children that there are no real people who are gay."

Two weeks later, a gay man wrote a letter to the *Chicago Tribune*, explaining why one idea, often floated by people who claimed to be tolerant, was so offensive: the belief that homosexuality was acceptable as long as gay people didn't "flaunt it," but kept it hidden.

"Why should we have to?" he wrote. "We have a right to live open lives, being honest with ourselves, our families, our friends, and our employers."

Glenn Burke understood that while he deserved to live an open life as a human being created in the image of God and as a citizen of a nation that proclaimed all men were created equal, such high-minded ideals had little relevance in the world of professional athletics. Gay activists could say whatever they wanted, but the truth was his sexuality threatened his existence as a Major League baseball player.

As the stakes grew higher for the Dodgers throughout the summer and into the fall, with a National League pennant and World Series berth in sight, the pressure mounted on Burke every day, both to perform at the highest level and to pretend to be something he wasn't.

CHAPTER 15
OPEN SECRET

Dusty Baker loved road trips to Houston. The Astros were a talented team, but it wasn't the rivalry that made the Dodgers' star left fielder look forward to Texas. It was the food. Several of his wife's friends and relatives lived in the area, and the "aunties" loved to cook. Whenever the Dodgers came to town, Baker rounded up a few teammates and took them out for home-cooked meals before games at the Astrodome. The soul food always hit the spot.

On one trip to Houston in 1977, Baker invited Burke to come to a friend's house for lunch. As the group sat down to eat, Glenn excused himself to use the bathroom. One of Baker's wife's best friends, a lesbian, turned to Dusty.

"Do you have any gays in baseball?" she asked.

"No, not that I know of," Baker replied.

"You got any on your team?" she inquired.

Baker gave her a look. "If there aren't any in baseball that I know of, how are there going to be any on my team?"

"That boy in the bathroom is gay," she said matter-of-factly.

Baker was skeptical. The woman had just met Glenn a few minutes earlier.

"You don't know what you're talking about!"

"Yes, I do," she insisted.

Baker thought back to a similar conversation, when a woman in Los Angeles saw a photo of Glenn in the newspaper and told him she thought Burke was gay.

The more Baker thought about it, the more it added up. When the team came back to Los Angeles late at night after road trips, Glenn

As a young player with the Atlanta Braves, Dusty Baker appreciated the mentorship of veteran players such as Henry Aaron. After he was traded to the Dodgers, Baker took many young players under his wing, including Glenn Burke. (National Baseball Hall of Fame)

would always say he had a friend picking him up. He'd walk way down to the end of the airport terminal and never let a teammate give him a ride home.

Baker thought about the times he'd tried to set up Glenn with one of his wife's cousins. "They were *fine*, and they all liked Glenn," Baker recalled. "Glenn would say, 'She's too fat,' or 'She's too ugly.' Something was always wrong with them. I was like, 'Come on, man. You can tell me something else. I know what cute is. And I know what pretty is. And I know what fine is. And they were fine, cute *and* pretty."

He thought back to the nights the Dodger players went out partying at discos in National League cities.[1] The ballplayers who were single, Baker said, "had their choice of girls," one of the perks of being fit, famous, and well paid. And the Dodger the women wanted most was Glenn Burke. "He was the life of the party," Baker recalled. "He was the most fun-loving dude, and he could dance like James Brown or Michael Jackson. He was so light on his feet. The girls would flock to him and ask him to dance. But at the end of the night, he'd go home by himself every time."

In retrospect, the signs were obvious. But the notion of a gay teammate was initially unfathomable to most of the Dodgers. Gay men, they believed, simply did not play Major League Baseball. But as the Dodgers inched closer to the 1977 National League West title, guys started to figure out Glenn Burke's secret. Second baseman Davey Lopes remembered hearing about it from another player over dinner. "My fork dropped out of my mouth," Lopes recalled. "I said, 'You shouldn't be saying things like that unless you're 100 percent sure. You've got to be careful. A rumor like that could end a guy's career.' He said, 'Davey, I'm telling you, Glenn is gay.' I started thinking about it, and I said, 'You know what? If he is, I don't give a shit.' He was an integral part of the ball club as far as I was concerned. He added a lot to the chemistry of the team, the way he could make you laugh."

Davey Lopes was a mainstay in the Dodger infield from 1973 to 1981. He loved the energy and laughter Glenn Burke brought to the clubhouse. (*Los Angeles Times* Archives / UCLA Special Collections)

Late in the season, the Dodgers traveled to San Francisco for a series against the Giants. "I bet you're glad to be home to eat some of Mama's cooking," Baker said to Burke. "Oh, yeah, Johnnie B," Burke replied, "I'm loving seeing Mama." After the game, Baker ran into Burke's mom outside the Dodger locker room. "I bet you you're glad to have Glenn home," he said. Alice's reply shocked him. "I haven't seen Glenn," she said. "He's been hanging with his friends in San Francisco."[2]

Glenn's lie about seeing his mother was the tipping point for Baker. He knew that two of Glenn's old friends from the Bay Area and the minor leagues, Marvin Webb and Cleo Smith, were staying in Glenn's vacant room at the Hyatt Regency, the Dodgers' hotel. Baker had assumed Glenn didn't need the room because he was staying at his mom's house. Baker and Dodger right fielder Reggie Smith knocked on the hotel room door; Webb answered.

"Is Glenn gay?" Baker asked.

"I'll tell you what," Webb replied. "You probably need to ask him. All I can say is I ain't never seen him with no women all the years I've been with him."

For Burke, the facade he'd created, the double life he'd been living, was beginning to fall apart. He knew of other gay players in the Major Leagues, men who married women and started families and lived miserable lives, unwilling to risk their reputations and careers by being honest with themselves. Burke had never been willing to deny his sexuality to that degree. Yes, he'd try to keep it a secret, but he was still going to go out, have fun, and pursue relationships, just like every other Dodger.

So he had developed little tricks, ways to escape social situations that made him uncomfortable, to break free from his teammates, to avoid being caught. If someone asked him to meet a woman, he'd show up, meet the woman, and leave. *Hey, you asked me to meet her. I met her.* After games, when all the other guys went out one door to waiting girlfriends and wives, Burke left through another exit on the other side of the stadium. After road games, when players returned to the team hotel briefly before heading out to a disco, Burke would often say he was just going to stay in his room, or go for a walk alone. He'd look in the phone book for gay bars, or call a gay friend and ask for recommendations. Then he'd take a cab to a bar, getting out a couple of blocks beyond it so it wouldn't be obvious where he was headed, walking back to his destination with his face turned away from passersby. Once inside, he kept one eye on the action and the other on the door, always watching to make sure nobody he recognized walked in.

Even with the precautions, Burke sensed that the Dodgers had someone following him, tracking his whereabouts. And he was probably right. "Back in those days, we know for a fact that we were being followed when we'd go out because there were rumors flying around about guys using drugs," Baker recalled. "There were times when I'd come in to the clubhouse and Tommy [Lasorda] would tell me, 'I heard you were at the Red Onion' [a popular Mexican restaurant with a lively bar scene]. So, if they were following me, they were following Glenn."

The whole secretive routine was stressful and tiresome for Burke, adding another layer of anxiety for a young player already dealing with the pressures of a rookie season in the middle of a high-stakes pennant race. "Straight people," Burke said, "cannot know what it's like to feel one way and pretend to be another. To watch what you say, how you act, and who you're checking out." And yet, being human, Burke complicated the situation even further—by becoming friends with another young gay man associated with the team: manager Tommy Lasorda's nineteen-year-old son.

Everybody had called Tommy Lasorda Jr. "Spunky" since before he was even born; he earned the nickname by constantly kicking while he was in his mother Jo's womb. As a kid, the only time he saw his father was when he hung around the ballpark. Jo placed a photo of her husband on the dinner table so the family could pretend to eat together every night.

Spunky was a left-hander like his dad, and while he had some skill as a teenage ballplayer, baseball was never his passion. Instead, he lived for fashion, photography, modeling, and being seen. While his dad waddled around ballparks in Dodger polyester, Spunky strutted down the streets of West Hollywood in designer clothes, his long blond hair so full and bouncy he looked like a walking shampoo commercial. He hardly ever ate, and spent hours in front of mirrors applying makeup. One night he showed up at a gay club wearing a cape, his hair pulled back in a ponytail, his slender, tan fingers clutching a long cigarette holder. As a student at Sunny Hills High School in Fullerton, California, his friends weren't the jocks but the most beautiful, fashionable girls in school. One classmate later described Spunky's startling feminine good looks, saying, "Tommy's bones were carved, gently, from glass."

All the Dodger players knew Spunky—they saw him at Vero Beach and in the clubhouse at Dodger Stadium. One time Lasorda Sr. showed players a home movie in Dodgertown—some guys were amused by a shot of Spunky lounging around in tiny jean shorts. Spunky knew clothes, working variously at a shoe store and a tailor's shop, and he knew music, especially the sound of disco and emerging Black women artists. When Spunky accompanied his dad on road trips, he'd often sit next to Dusty Baker, another music aficionado, and the two would talk disco. Spunky loved Diana Ross, Thelma Houston, Linda Clifford, and Patti LaBelle.

Most players assumed Spunky was gay, but out of deference to their manager, they never made an issue of it. Lasorda Sr., for his part, maintained a relationship with his son throughout his life, and by all accounts it was a loving bond. They met for an Italian dinner every Sunday night when the Dodgers were in town. But Lasorda never acknowledged his son's sexuality. When journalist Peter Richmond asked him about it for a feature in *GQ* magazine, Lasorda vehemently, and profanely, denied it. When Spunky died of AIDS in 1991, Lasorda refused to publicly acknowledge the disease as the cause of death, insisting that his son had died of an unrelated case of pneumonia.[3]

Burke admired Spunky's flair for fashion, and asked him to tailor his suits. They enjoyed visiting clubs around Los Angeles together, developing a close and carefree relationship that Burke later described as like two "teasing sisters." Whether Burke and Spunky were ever more than friends is unknown. Burke was asked about it numerous times after his playing days and always maintained it was none of anyone's business. Some friends and teammates insist they were lovers; others claim Burke told them he wasn't interested in someone as "flamboyant" as Spunky.

Regardless of the extent of their relationship, Spunky and Glenn both understood that Lasorda Sr. wouldn't approve if he knew about it. Glenn confessed to Spunky that he thought he was being treated differently; he wondered if Spunky's dad knew he was gay. One night, they decided to give the manager the shock of his life. The plan called for Glenn and Spunky to show up at Lasorda's house for dinner as if on a date, Spunky dressed in pigtails and women's clothing. They chickened out and didn't follow through on the prank, but Burke relished the very thought of it. "Tommy would have shot us in the head," he recalled. "Then he would have had a heart attack and died."

An irony of Glenn Burke's semi-closeted existence in such a homo-phobic environment as Major League Baseball was the amount of everyday behavior that might have been considered homoerotic in different circumstances. Yes, Burke's teammates made jokes with slurs that Glenn chose to ignore. But they often did so while walking around naked in the clubhouse. Men showered together, dressed and undressed in close confines. They slapped one another on the butt, hugged after homers, shared rooms, and went out together nearly every night. They laughed, cried, fought, and bonded on long cross-country flights. All this touching, nudity, and emotion was considered acceptable because of the unspoken assumption that everyone was straight. The dynamic changed as rumors about Glenn began to spread. Guys started wearing towels around the clubhouse more frequently and made offensive jokes out of earshot: "Don't bend over in the shower. Here comes Glenn."

Dodger executives considered Glenn Burke one of the team's top young prospects due to his powerful body, dazzling speed, and Minor League production. When Rick Monday suffered a back injury, Burke got his shot to play consistently in the outfield. (National Baseball Hall of Fame)

Still, for all the presumed resistance to a gay teammate, nobody directly confronted Glenn about it. Much of the tone was set by the reaction of team leaders such as Lopes and Baker. Baker saw a lot of his younger self in Burke; they were both from California, both loved basketball, music, nice clothes, and laughter. Baker considered it his responsibility to look after the team's young Black players, just as legendary slugger Henry Aaron had done for him as a rookie in Atlanta. He took the young guys out for drinks, taught some of them how to fish, cooked them dinner. In Baker's mind, there were two kinds of rookies: the obnoxious punk the veterans hated, and the fun kid who gave everyone a good laugh. That was Glenn. As a ballplayer, Burke had plenty of potential, Baker believed. He could run, he could throw, and he was improving as a hitter. He had trouble with breaking balls and high fastballs, but he was a quick learner. He was determined, and he didn't appear to let a lot bother him, which Baker considered rare for a rookie. For Lopes, Burke's contributions on the field were secondary; he considered him an essential member of the team, "a catalyst for promoting unity on the ball club," regardless of how well or how much he played. Where others thought only of themselves, Lopes admired the way Burke cheered on his teammates, always the first player to congratulate another on a good play. That sort of togetherness was going to be important in the playoffs.

But first, there was one more series to play against the Houston Astros at Dodger Stadium to close out the regular season. And this is when so many of the undercurrents in Glenn Burke's life converged. His uncommon enthusiasm, his support for his teammates, his African American East Bay hip-factor, his appreciation for a supportive mentor, his spot in the Dodger lineup, his willingness to share joy with another man—it all came together in one glorious moment in time that echoes to this day.

CHAPTER 16

HANDS UP

The Los Angeles Dodgers were on the verge of making history. Steve Brener, the team's publicity director, and Rich Kee, the photographer, wanted to be prepared when it happened.

Heading into the 1977 season's final series, a four-game set at Dodger Stadium against the Houston Astros, three Dodgers had slugged thirty or more home runs: first baseman Steve Garvey (thirty-three), right fielder Reggie Smith (thirty-two), and third baseman Ron Cey (thirty). Left fielder Dusty Baker had smacked nine homers in September but had been stuck on a season total of twenty-nine for nearly a week. If he could knock just one ball over the fence against the Astros, the Dodgers would become the first team in Major League history to have four players hit thirty or more home runs in the same season.

Brener and Kee came up with an idea to stage a photo of the four sluggers during batting practice before the first game of the Astros series. That way, if Baker homered in any of the four games, Brener would already have the photo in hand and could immediately share it with the national media, a delicious publicity opportunity for the Dodgers. Kee came up with the ideal setup: he would position the players on the infield grass, each in full uniform, each holding a bat, with the amber lights of the black Dodger Stadium scoreboard displaying a giant number 30 behind them.

Everything was set—until Baker told Kee he had concerns about the photo shoot. It was bound to jinx him, and it would be awfully embarrassing if he didn't hit 30 and the photo leaked out.

"Look, Dusty," Kee responded, "I'll shoot the picture quickly, hand it over to Steve, and if you don't hit your thirtieth by Sunday, nobody will ever see this image. Fair enough?"

"Okay, Rich," Baker replied, reluctantly. Kee had been around the team all year, and Baker trusted him. "I'll do it."

In less than ten seconds, the scoreboard operator posted the huge number 30, Baker and Cey knelt on one knee with Garvey and Smith standing behind them, and Kee snapped a few photos with his Nikon. Baker breathed a sigh of relief—it didn't appear anyone else had seen what had just happened.

But soon after the Dodgers returned to their clubhouse following batting practice, there was another potential jinx. Reggie Smith called up the Astros' locker room and asked to speak to J. R. Richard, Houston's flame-throwing pitcher who was scheduled to pitch the season finale on Sunday afternoon. Richard picked up and Smith began taunting him,

Dodgers PR man Steve Brener and team photographer Rich Kee posed the four Dodger sluggers (standing: Steve Garvey, left, and Reggie Smith, right; kneeling: Dusty Baker, left, and Ron Cey, right) for a publicity shot even before Baker hit his record-breaking thirtieth home run. Had Baker not homered in the season finale against J. R. Richard, this photo would never have been seen. (Los Angeles Dodgers)

declaring that Baker was going to hit his thirtieth homer off him on Sunday. Baker couldn't believe what he was hearing, shaking his head, waving his hands, and mouthing *No, no!* in Smith's direction.

All this extra pressure was the last thing Baker needed. The Dodgers had clinched a playoff berth on September 20, and while Lasorda gave most of his starters some days off during the season's final week, he kept Baker in the lineup so he could try to slug his thirtieth homer. "You're gonna hit it, you're gonna hit it," Lasorda kept telling him. "God isn't going to let you hit twenty-nine homers and not thirty."

But Baker didn't homer on Thursday, Friday, or Saturday. So now it would all come down to the last game of the regular season against the pitcher Baker considered his biggest nemesis, J. R. Richard, a six-foot-eight, 222-pound right-hander who could fire the ball 100 miles per hour and had given up just one homer in 27.2 innings pitched against the Dodgers all season.[1] With his size and blazing fastball, Richard was considered by Dodger outfielder Joe Simpson to be "one of the scariest dudes in baseball." Baker was all but resigned to the fact that it just wasn't meant to be; he would end the season stuck on twenty-nine. He decided to quit swinging for the fences and revert to his normal line-drive swing against Richard. He wanted to be sharp for the playoffs. Winning the World Series was more important than the record, anyway.

Hard-throwing Houston Astros right-hander James Rodney (J. R.) Richard was one of the most feared pitchers in all of Major League Baseball in 1977. For the Dodgers to make baseball history, Dusty Baker would have to hit a home run off Richard in the final game of the season. (Topps)

Before stepping up to the plate for his first at-bat against Richard, Baker noticed a couple of Black men sitting in the front row above the Dodgers' dugout, handling cash. After he singled to left field, Baker looked over and saw one of the men giving the other guy some money. *Those [jerks]*, Baker thought to himself. *They're gambling to see if I'm going to hit this home run or not.*

His next time up, Baker struck out. Walking back to the dugout, he saw one of the men laughing, slamming down more cash.

Richard overpowered the entire Dodger lineup. After five innings, the Astros led 2–0, and the only base hit the Dodgers had managed was Baker's first-inning single.

Heading into the bottom of the sixth, the Dodgers were due to send thirty-nine-year-old pinch hitter Manny Mota out to the plate to lead off the inning. Mota, a classic slap hitter, hadn't homered in more than five years, but in the previous night's game he had come close, lofting a fly ball deep to right field. Dodger pitcher Tommy John kidded Mota about his rare flash of power, daring him to hit one as far as he could if he got another at-bat.[2] And now here he was striding to the plate, everybody on the team knowing what was on his mind. Standing on the top step of the dugout, Lasorda turned to Davey Lopes. "Wouldn't it be great if he hit a homer?" "If he does," Lopes replied, "I'll buy everyone on the team a steak dinner."

Mota smacked Richard's second pitch over the left-field fence into the Dodger bullpen, his first home run since 1972 and what would turn out to be the final homer of his career. Over in the dugout, Lopes pretended to faint.

Richard settled down and retired the next two batters. Now it was time for Baker to hit again in what would likely be his next to last at-bat of the game. Just two more chances to make history. Before he stepped out of the dugout, Baker muttered to Lasorda, "Man, I just don't think I'm going to get it." Lasorda responded with yet another grandiose pep talk, yammering on about Moses parting the Red Sea and other biblical miracles. *Just believe, Dusty; just believe!* As Baker strode to the plate, Glenn Burke cheered him on from the on-deck circle. Burke had entered the game in the top of the fifth inning as a defensive replacement, and he'd bat behind Baker. And from the front row, the guy who had been wagering on Baker all day shouted out, "Come on, baby, you can do it! Come on, man!"

But J. R. Richard quickly got ahead in the count; after throwing one ball and two strikes to Baker, he was just one strike away from getting out of the inning. On the fourth pitch, he fired a fastball low and outside. Baker was concentrating so hard it appeared the ball simply stopped in mid-flight. He uncorked a powerful swing, made contact on the sweet spot of the bat, and watched as the ball sailed over the left-center-field fence at the 395-foot mark. The crowd cheered wildly as Baker circled the bases. At that moment, he said later, he felt "like the happiest man in the world."

As he rounded second base, Baker looked toward the Dodger dugout, and the first people he saw were the "brothers on top of the dugout," one of them throwing a pile of cash at the other. "I was just as happy to shut those guys up, and Lasorda, as anything," he recalled decades later.

As Baker crossed home plate, forty-six thousand Dodger fans screamed in delight, and the first Dodger teammate to greet him was a jubilant Glenn Burke.

The manner in which Burke chose to congratulate Dusty Baker changed history. Not in the way presidents or popes or kings change history, or earthquakes or floods or famines. Not in a way that any distinguished scholar would deem significant, but in a more ordinary and fundamentally human kind of way that changed the manner in which people all over the world, to this day, express joy for the achievements of others. Glenn Burke didn't shake Dusty Baker's hand or give him a hug or pat him on the butt. Overcome with emotion, proud that Baker had finally done it, that his teammates had entered the record books, feeling the energy of the tens of thousands of men and women cheering from Dodger Stadium's five decks above him, Burke shouted out, "Way to go! Way to go!" and held his right hand over his head, inviting Baker to slap it, which he did, with gusto.

Glenn Burke had just invented the high five.[3]

CHAPTER 17

BIG BLUE WRECKING CREW

Bill Frishette paced the aisles of Dodger Stadium, hawking malted ice cream, when Dusty Baker socked his historic home run. He watched as Baker rounded the bases to thunderous applause, and listened to the cheers as the crowd summoned Baker from the dugout for a curtain call. And then he stopped in his tracks as his buddy Glenn Burke stepped up to the plate.

Frishette, twenty-seven, had struck up an unlikely friendship with Glenn. A lifelong Dodger fan, he had worked part time as a roving food vendor at the stadium ever since he was sixteen years old, a clever way to get paid to watch games. Usually he sold malts, which was better than getting stuck selling soda; it was no fun lugging around a heavy wooden crate holding twenty-four glass bottles of Coke.

Before he ran all of Nike's business with Major League Baseball, Bill Frishette managed a Nike store in Santa Monica and sold concessions at Dodger Stadium. His friendship with Glenn Burke set Nike on a path that led it to becoming the official uniform and footwear supplier of MLB in 2020. (Bill Frishette)

One Sunday morning, as Frishette roamed the stadium before a game, Burke took a seat at a card table in the concourse, ready to sign autographs for fans, a Sunday tradition at Dodger Stadium. When no one immediately lined up to meet Burke, Frishette walked over and introduced himself. He told Burke that he had been working Dodger games for more than a decade, and had recently taken another job in Santa Monica managing a shoe store called the Athletic Department. Frishette wasn't sure if the owner of the store, a guy named Phil Knight, would sell enough shoes to keep the paychecks coming much longer, so he kept his side gig at Dodger Stadium. He told Burke about the shoes he sold, a brand called Nike that was popular with runners and beginning to make inroads in basketball. Burke told Frishette he knew all about Nike; he'd been to the Athletic Department store in Berkeley, next to the Indian restaurant on Addison Street. Frishette invited Burke to visit his store in the Westwood area of Los Angeles near UCLA; he'd hook him up with some free shoes.

Burke took him up on the offer. He was especially interested in the Astrograbbers, lightweight football shoes designed for artificial turf. Nike didn't make any baseball cleats yet, but Burke thought the shoes might work well when the Dodgers played road games on plastic grass in places like the Astrodome or Veterans Stadium in Philadelphia. He took a pair, grabbed some basketball shoes as well, and invited Frishette to join him at UCLA for a pickup basketball game with some of the Bruins. Frishette's jaw dropped watching the Dodger outfielder shake and bake and slam dunk on some of the best players in college basketball. Burke invited Frishette to come visit him in the clubhouse before a game, where he introduced him to the other players. Soon, several Dodgers stopped by the Westwood store to pick up free shoes. Nike was still five years away from its first TV commercial; just having pro athletes wear their shoes off the field was huge for business.

While the crowd continued to cheer Baker's record-setting homer, Frishette was more interested to see what Burke would do in his first at-bat now that the Dodgers had tied the game 2–2.

With his first pitch, Richard fired another fastball. Burke half expected to be drilled in the ribs, retaliation for the two Dodger homers in the inning, but the pitch sailed high for a ball. Confident he wasn't going to get beaned, Burke dug in and sent Richard's second pitch high into the afternoon sky; it landed on the other side of the blue fence, Glenn's first Major League homer and the Dodgers' third longball of the inning. When he returned to a jubilant Dodger dugout, Dusty Baker greeted him with a high five. A cultural phenomenon had begun.

Richard retired the next batter to end the Dodger sixth, wrapping up a bizarre and historic inning. The big right-hander had never before given up three home runs in a game, let alone one inning. Manny Mota smacked the only home run he would hit during the decade between 1972 and the end of his career in 1982. Baker had set a Major League record with his homer, and Burke had clubbed his only home run as a Dodger and one of just two he'd ever hit as a major leaguer, while also inventing the high five. And in true baseball fashion, all this turned out to be irrelevant in the outcome of the game itself: Houston scored four runs in its next at-bat, Richard never gave up another hit, and the Astros won 6–3.

The loss mattered little to the Dodgers. As champions of the National League West, they were headed to the playoffs to take on the Eastern Division champion Philadelphia Phillies in a best-of-five series to determine who would represent the NL in the World Series. With veteran left-handed pitcher Steve Carlton set to start Game 1 for the Phillies and Dodger outfielder Rick Monday still battling back spasms, Lasorda announced that Burke would start in center field. When a surprised sportswriter asked the manager why he'd start the rookie in this situation, Lasorda pulled a notebook filled with statistics out of his desk drawer. "Glenn Burke," he said, "had four hits in six at-bats against Carlton this year with two RBI and a double."

The manager's decision intrigued Jack Stevenson, a reporter for the Associated Press, so he set out to learn more about Burke. He watched him take batting practice—Burke wore batting gloves on both hands, tucked his Dodger cap underneath his blue helmet, pressed his chin tight against his left shoulder, held his hands at nose level, bat angled back over his head—and then chatted with him after he'd taken his cuts.

Burke told Stevenson that his first Major League home run had been a thrill he'd been waiting for, that he didn't feel nervous about his first postseason game. He fondly remembered the Tournament

Glenn Burke takes batting practice prior to the Dodgers' National League Championship Series game against the Philadelphia Phillies. Manager Tommy Lasorda put the rookie in the starting lineup due to his success against Phillies starting pitcher Steve Carlton. (AP Photo)

of Champions, when he'd led Berkeley High School to a Northern California basketball championship. "I like to play before big crowds," he said. "I think I do better when I hear that roar."

Fifty-five thousand, nine-hundred and sixty-eight fans turned out for Game 1, and there was indeed quite a roar at Dodger Stadium, but Burke went hitless in three at-bats, stranding five base runners. Burke wasn't the only Dodger who struggled; the Phillies jumped out to a 4–0 lead and held on to win 7–5.

Back in the Dodger clubhouse after the game, Lasorda held court in his spacious office, seemingly unbothered by the defeat. Where the Dodgers' previous manager, Walter Alston, worked out of a spartan, closet-sized office, Lasorda had transformed a former training room into a comfortable, blue-carpeted lounge where he adorned the walls with photos of celebrities (including one wall devoted entirely to Frank Sinatra), stocked two refrigerators with food and wine, and welcomed everyone from ballplayers to the Hollywood elite to hang out and chat.

Even after the loss to the Phillies, actor James Darren, like Lasorda an Italian American from Philadelphia, ventured into Lasorda's office with his starstruck thirteen-year-old son, Anthony, in tow. Lasorda understood that at that moment, he had an opportunity to create an unforgettable memory for the young man, to show his players he wasn't obsessing over the loss, and to make a good impression on the reporters gathered around. He handed Anthony a Dodgers cap and called over to shortstop Bill Russell to bring over a bat. Soon, Anthony was clutching a Dodgers jacket and a pair of shoes, and half the team had come over to say hello. "The kid, no matter how successful he ever gets or how big he becomes," Lasorda said, "will always remember this night as the greatest night of his life."[1]

The next day, Lasorda welcomed another celebrity into the clubhouse twenty-five minutes before the first pitch. This time it was his buddy Don Rickles, a comedian known for dishing out insults. The intent was to take the players' minds off the pressure of a must-win game. "Hello, fellas," Rickles began, "and thanks, Tommy Lasorda. Look at him. Look at that stomach. You think he's worried about you guys? No way. If you lose, he's gonna tie a cord around his neck and get work as a balloon." Rickles glanced around the room, directing barbs at the players—stars and benchwarmers alike. He trained his eyes on light-hitting backup infielder Ed Goodson. "You're going to love being traded to Atlanta. Tell Goodson what you told me, Lasorda—that you're fed up with him!"

Apparently, the laughter worked: the Dodgers exploded for seven runs and Don Sutton pitched a complete game, scattering nine hits and allowing just one run. The highlight came in the fourth inning, when Dusty Baker slugged a grand slam to give the Dodgers a 5–1 lead. Once again, Burke was the first to congratulate his teammate, jumping out of the dugout with his cap on backward and wearing teammate Davey Lopes's blue warm-up jacket to give Baker another high five. *Los Angeles Times* photographer Andy Hayt, stationed next to the Dodger dugout, captured a photo of the scene, Burke's hand coming forward, Baker leaning back, looking a bit surprised. In the decades to follow, the picture has circulated widely, often mistaken to be a shot of the first high five.

Now deadlocked at a game apiece, the rest of the series would be

When Dusty Baker hit a grand slam in Game 2 of the NLCS vs. the Phillies, Glenn Burke leaped off the bench and greeted him with another high five. This photo has often been mistaken as a shot of the first high five against the Astros, but Burke was on deck in that game and wouldn't have been wearing a jacket with his hat on backward. (Andy Hayt / *Los Angeles Times*)

played in Philadelphia; Lasorda would advance to the World Series or experience heartbreak in his hometown. In Game 3, the Dodgers erupted for three runs in the top of the ninth inning off Phillies closer Gene Garber to steal a 6–5 win. From a pop-culture perspective, however, the most significant aspect of that game went virtually unnoticed by anyone other than Bill Frishette. Burke and a handful of his teammates had dyed their white Astrograbber shoes blue and worn them in the game for the first time, gaining better traction on the Veterans Stadium turf. They were the first major leaguers ever to wear Nikes on the field. Thanks in part to his friendship with Burke and the connections he helped him build, Frishette went on to a long and distinguished career with Nike, rising to become the director of the company's baseball business. In 2020, Nike became the official supplier of Major League

Baseball uniforms. Every single player wore a Nike swoosh on his chest, a development that traces its roots back to Glenn Burke's 1977 conversation with a frozen malt vendor at Dodger Stadium.

The weather for Game 4 was cold and rainy. With the Dodgers one win away from the World Series, Lasorda again started Burke in center field against Philly ace Steve Carlton. As players dressed in the visitors' clubhouse, Burke broke the tension, putting on a winter coat and hat and hamming it up—guys were doubled over with laughter. Once again, it was Baker who broke the game open, walloping a two-run homer in the second inning to give the Dodgers the only runs they'd need, as pitcher Tommy John limited the Phillies to just one run in a 4–1 series-clinching Dodger victory.

The scene in the victorious Dodger clubhouse was pure bedlam, all smiles, shouts, back slaps, handshakes, hugs, and high fives. The guys were soaking wet from the rain and the bottles of champagne they sprayed around the locker room. In one corner, Reggie Smith stood facing a group of four players—Lee Lacy, Rick Rhoden, Lance Rautzhan, and Glenn Burke—leading a call-and-response directed not at the Phillies, but their NL West nemesis, the Cincinnati Reds. For the first time in three years, it would be the Dodgers in the World Series, not Cincinnati.

"Tell me about the Reds!" Smith shouted.

"The who?" the guys yelled back.

"The Reds!"

Dodger outfielder Reggie Smith signs autographs for young fans. The Dodgers led the Major Leagues in attendance in 1977, drawing 2,955,087 fans to Dodger Stadium. (*Los Angeles Times* Archives / UCLA Special Collections)

"The Reds who?"

"The Red Machine!"

"What Red Machine?"

"The big, mean Red Machine!"

"No, tell me about the Crew!"

"The who?"

"The Blue Crew!"

"What Blue Crew?"

"The Big Blue Wrecking Crew!"

"Wahoo!"

Burke stepped out from the scrum, waving an empty bottle of bubbly like a conductor's baton and leading the group in a reprise of the cheer. The party continued into the wee hours of the morning, Lasorda hosting the gang at his family's Italian restaurant just outside the city. Burke had played in every game in the series, starting Games 1 and 4 against Carlton and appearing as a defensive replacement for Rick Monday late in Games 2 and 3. Though he struggled at the plate, going hitless in seven at-bats, he had been a vitally important part of the team's pennant run, and his teammates knew it. Players on winning teams talk about chemistry, clubhouse culture, and unity. No one on the team had inspired more of those feelings than Glenn Burke.

"He could take any moment in time and make it fun," Rick Monday said many years later. "There was no better guy in the clubhouse, I'll tell you that. There was no one who didn't love having Glenn around."

Monday understood that baseball was inherently a game of disappointment. Twenty-six teams started spring training in February of 1977, and only one would end the season happy in October. Even the best teams lose at least sixty games a year. Great hitters get a base hit only 30 percent of the time. Players spend long stretches on the road, away from family, under constant scrutiny from media and fans. At any moment, they could be traded to another city, demoted to the minors, or released altogether. "We all have different mechanisms to deal with life," Monday said. "Baseball, quite frankly, has a lot of deniability. You're denying the fact that you've played one hundred and forty-two games and you're physically and mentally tired and you have twenty games to go. Yet, Glenn had a levity that compensated for that."

Burke's profound impact on the team was all the more impressive considering he was a rookie, an African American in a predominantly white sport, and gay. And what his teammates didn't realize, even the ones who suspected he was gay, was the stress Burke was experiencing in his personal life. Since 1975, he had been dating a Harvard grad named Michael Smith, a man who fit Burke's profile in the sense that he was older, highly educated, and white. But Smith was also controlling, temperamental, and condescending. "One minute Michael would make me feel like the most wonderful person in the world," Burke recalled, "then he would turn on me and become very critical and vicious." Burke's friends and family couldn't stand Smith, and some people called him the "Wicked Witch of the West."

Burke's toxic relationship with Smith was on-again, off-again, full of passionate arguments and makeups. After one bitter argument, Smith gathered all of Burke's possessions in the Castro apartment they shared and threw them out onto the street. When things were working, Burke appreciated Smith's charm, his good looks, his intelligence, and his encouragement. "He was the one guy," Burke said, "who gave me the incentive to play baseball, to say, 'No matter what, you are what you are, and don't let nobody put you down for it if you want to play baseball.'" But more often, Burke sensed that Smith was using him, showing off his strong, handsome, famous Black boyfriend to friends even as he mocked his intelligence. As an aspiring activist for gay rights, Smith saw an opportunity for Burke to make headlines by publicly coming out as gay during the World Series against the Yankees. Burke had no interest in creating that kind of sideshow during the Series, let alone jeopardizing his career. He sensed that Smith had little appreciation for the tightrope he walked every day as a closeted gay man in baseball—or at least didn't care.

During the introduction of the players before Game 3 of the World Series, Burke had earned a lusty ovation from the Dodger Stadium crowd by hugging former Dodger catcher Roy Campanella, the paralyzed Hall of Famer in a wheelchair, before taking his place along the base line. Sensing an opportunity to publicly attach himself to the man drawing cheers, Smith started speaking very loudly about his relationship with

Burke from his seat near home plate. Finally, one of Burke's other gay friends, Wes Jackson, got up from his seat and demanded that Smith shut his mouth. Smith complied, but only until Game 4, when he again started shouting about his relationship with Glenn, drawing turned heads and stares from the fans around him.

Burke had started Game 1 in New York, figuring in the most controversial play of the entire World Series. With the Dodgers leading 2–1 and Steve Garvey on first after a bunt base hit, Burke stepped to the plate. Lasorda called a hit-and-run, and Burke executed perfectly, bouncing a soft single to right center field as Garvey streaked toward second. Third-base coach Preston Gómez noticed that Yankee right fielder Reggie Jackson was letting weak-armed center fielder Mickey Rivers get the ball, and he waved his arms for Garvey to continue around third base and run for home. Rivers's bouncing throw pulled Yankee catcher Thurman Munson a few steps up the first base line, forcing him to lunge back toward the plate to tag the sliding Garvey. Home plate umpire Nestor Chylak called Garvey out, denying Burke a moment of World Series glory and the Dodgers a bigger lead. In the television booth, color commentator Tom Seaver went ballistic as producers rolled a replay that showed Garvey had beaten the tag. "The umpire is out of position! The umpire is down the line! He's not even in the picture! Where is he?!" The bad call was costly, as the Yankees ended up winning the game 4–3 in twelve innings.

While Burke's presence in the Dodger clubhouse kept the team loose, Yankee players were constantly at one another's throats—and at manager Billy Martin's. The team's quarrels played out publicly, and nobody denied the tensions. Then again, many of the squabbles would have been impossible to hide, such as when a feuding Reggie Jackson and Martin had to be separated in the dugout during a nationally televised game at Boston's Fenway Park. "We have controversy all the time," said outfielder Lou Piniella. "We're used to it—although it does get sickening."

Even with players asking to be traded when they weren't sniping at one another, the Yankees' dysfunction worked: they won a hundred games in the regular season (two more than the Dodgers) and led the World Series three games to two heading into Game 6 at Yankee Stadium.

The 56,407 fans at Yankee Stadium and millions watching on television were treated to one of the most electrifying individual performances in World Series history that night, as Yankee right fielder Reggie Jackson put on an unparalleled display of power.

In the fourth inning, Jackson blasted a two-run homer to right field on the first pitch from Dodger starter Burt Hooton, giving the Yankees a 4–3 lead. In his next at-bat, in the fifth inning, Jackson pummeled another two-run homer, this time on the first pitch from reliever Elias Sosa, giving the Yankees a 7–3 lead. When Jackson walked to the plate in the bottom of the eighth inning, Yankee fans rose to their feet, chanting, "REG-GIE, REG-GIE, REG-GIE!" He connected on the first pitch from knuckleballer Charlie Hough, sending yet another homer soaring over the center-field fence. Three pitches, three gargantuan home runs. Even the Dodger players, knowing their World Series hopes were dashed, paid their respects. As Jackson ran past first base, Garvey clapped his bare hand against his glove. In the dugout, tears fell from Burke's eyes, each drop a sign of respect for a player he had admired when Jackson played for his hometown Oakland A's from 1968 to 1975. "I cried because I was happy for him," Burke said. "Reggie was an all right guy and that was a tremendous individual feat."

Reggie Jackson earned the nickname Mr. October with an incredible performance in Game 6 of the 1977 World Series, bashing three home runs on three straight pitches to clinch the pennant for the Yankees. As Jackson circled the bases following his last homer, an admiring Glenn Burke shed a tear in the Dodger dugout. (Topps)

The 1977 regular season had concluded with Glenn Burke celebrating Dusty Baker's achievement with a high five. The postseason ended with him crying tears of joy for a victorious opponent.

The Dodgers had a special man in Glenn Burke, and his teammates knew it.

Despite all the challenges, he had reached the apex of the game.

Maybe things would work out after all.

CHAPTER 18
INDECENT PROPOSAL

The pain was overwhelming and Glenn Burke wished it would stop. But the tattoo artist on Cahuenga Boulevard had already created half a scorpion, Burke's astrological sign, on his forearm. He'd have to let him finish.

With that marker of independence complete, Burke was ready to take another plunge. He bought a brand-new Volkswagen just down the road at Bob Smith's VW, the first car he ever owned.

Burke had made decent money with the Dodgers, and he knew a World Series share was on its way, a hefty bonus of more than $20,000.

He'd spend the off-season splitting time between Los Angeles and San Francisco, enjoying the fruits of the Dodgers' success even as he discovered that fame came with a price. On his first visit back to the

Castro District in San Francisco after the World Series, Burke had been told one of the neighborhood's many bars was throwing a party in his honor. But as quickly as he walked in, he walked out. "They weren't my friends there," he recalled. "They were mostly people just making a big deal because I was a gay baseball player." The scene revealed an unease Burke had felt for some time. In the baseball world, he worried he'd be shunned because he was gay. In the gay world, he resented that his fame was the only reason some men cared about him—otherwise he'd just be another gay Black man facing two layers of discrimination. This was more than a minor annoyance. For the first time, Burke later admitted, the thought of quitting the game entered his mind. Removed from baseball, he could just be Glenn Burke, not Glenn Burke: Gay Major Leaguer.

In November, Burke returned to Los Angeles, in large part to suit up for the Dodgers' winter basketball team, a chance to bond with his teammates and play the game he loved. Though Dodger management hated the idea of its ballplayers risking injury on the basketball court, the players relished everything about it. A local publicity agent had contacted catcher Steve Yeager with the idea. The Dodger team played twenty charity games against teachers from schools in Southern California to raise money for the schools' athletic programs. The owners of Josephine's, a popular restaurant in the San Fernando Valley, put up $2,000 to cover the cost of uniforms and warm-up suits. The Dodgers traveled in luxury—renting a well-stocked RV for a game in Whittier, chartering a fifty-five-foot yacht for a game on Catalina Island, and flying a private jet to a game in China Lake.

"I imagine the Dodgers don't like it too much, but I have to think that every guy, sooner or later, gets into some kind of pickup basketball game," Yeager told a reporter covering the team's first game. "This way, at least, we're organized, we're staying in shape, we're having some fun and we're helping out some schools."

At the very least, for Yeager, Burke, Garvey, Lopes, Cey, Monday, Sutton, and the other Dodger hoopers, it beat the alternatives: short-stop Bill Russell spent the off-season farming pecans in Oklahoma, Doug Rau and Jerry Grote ranching in Texas, and Mike Garman digging potatoes in Idaho.

Television actor Ron Masak, a frequent guest of Lasorda's in the Dodger clubhouse, traveled with the team and served as public address announcer, while former LA Laker Tommy Hawkins coached with assistance from Dusty Baker and Reggie Smith. "Coaching" was a loose term: "We have one basic play," Garvey admitted. "Shoot."

In the first game, Hawkins started Monday over Burke, a move that drew catcalls from the sportswriters who knew of Burke's basketball prowess. "Always the second-stringer," Burke sighed in jest, loud enough for everyone to hear him.

When Hawkins summoned Burke from the bench, Masak introduced him to the crowd as "Meadowlark," a reference to the Harlem Globetrotters' most popular star, Meadowlark Lemon. Burke dazzled the crowd from the moment he took the court, whipping behind-the-back passes and skying for powerful slam dunks. The game was a rout—shockingly, a team of professional athletes lambasted a bunch of teachers—and Hawkins urged his guys to take it easy at the end. Plus, he could sense that the 1,500 fans were preparing to storm the court at the buzzer to collect autographs. He yelled out at his guys to keep the ball at the end of the court closest to the exits so they could make a quick getaway when time expired, but Burke wouldn't stop shooting (he ended up leading the team with twenty-six points). And some fans didn't wait for the game to end—at one point, four girls climbed down from the bleachers to give Garvey a kiss. "I think we've created a monster," he said.

When Burke returned to San Francisco for the remainder of the winter, he immersed himself in a Castro District in the midst of social and political movements unlike anything ever seen in the US. At the heart of the action was Harvey Milk, a forty-seven-year-old entrepreneur and activist. A veteran of the navy and a former stock analyst, Milk had grown up in New York before coming out of the closet and starting a new life in San Francisco. He moved there in 1972, opening a camera shop at 575 Castro Street. As president of the Castro Village Association, a coalition of gay business owners, Milk gained clout in

One of the most significant gay politicians in American history, Harvey Milk encouraged gay people in San Francisco to come out of the closet, speak out on social issues, patronize gay-owned businesses, and elect gay public servants. (San Francisco Public Library)

the neighborhood by calling on gays to "buy gay." Milk had unsuc-cessfully run for San Francisco Board of Supervisors seats in 1973 and 1975, but was elected in November 1977, becoming the first openly gay man elected to public office in California, and one of the first anywhere.

Milk's rise to prominence came at the same time right-wing activ-ists such as Anita Bryant pushed for anti-gay measures across the coun-try. While some gays were demoralized to be portrayed as degenerate criminals, Milk didn't shy away from the fight. He welcomed it. As Cleve Jones, another prominent gay activist, later wrote, Milk believed that every movement needed something to push against. And what better opponent than a self-righteous Miss America type like Anita Bryant? Milk understood that Bryant's campaign only energized his support-ers, causing many gay men and women to become politically active for the first time. "The idea of gay rights had taken root," Jones wrote, "and the thought of playing the victim, whether individually or collectively, was repellent."

Just as Black Power activists had advocated in the Bay Area during Glenn Burke's youth, Milk's message to gay people in San Francisco was all about self-determination. Gays should not pin their hopes on sympathetic liberals, Milk argued, but elect gays themselves. His busi-ness message had evolved into a political one, transforming from "gay buy gay" to "gay vote gay." He believed that meaningful social progress would not be made if gay men continued to treat the Castro only as a social gathering place and sexual playground. He urged people to get "out of the bars and into the streets," demanding equal protec-tion under the law. Further, he believed that gay rights could only be achieved if more gays publicly proclaimed their sexuality.

"Gay people will not win our rights by staying quietly in our closets," he said. "We are coming out to fight the lies, the myths, the distortions. We are coming out to tell the truths about gays, for I am tired of the conspiracy of silence. So I'm going to talk about it. And I want you to talk about it. You must come out."

Milk's pronouncements carried an urgency in California, as a state senator from Orange County named John Briggs had introduced a proposition, known as the Briggs Initiative, that not only mandated the firing of gay public school teachers, but also any public school employees who supported gay rights.

California voters would decide the issue the following November, a decision that was viewed by supporters and opponents alike as the ultimate test of the anti-gay-rights movement that had begun in Miami. Milk would spend most of 1978 publicly debating Briggs, giving a strong, unapologetic, and reasoned voice to gay citizens unlike anything anyone had ever witnessed. "I am just one person," Milk said, "but I have power. I remember who I am."

It was in the midst of this rancorous public debate over the rights of gay citizens in California, and in American society more broadly, that Glenn Burke received a call from Al Campanis, the Dodgers' general manager, asking for a meeting. As GM, Campanis drafted players, assembled the team's roster, and negotiated players' contracts (a one-sided affair in the days before free agency). Campanis had been born in Greece in 1916; his family moved to New York when he was a kid, and he fell in love with baseball. Signed by the Dodgers in 1940, Campanis had been a roommate and friend of Jackie Robinson's when they played for the Montreal Royals in 1946, a year before Robinson became the first African American player in Major League Baseball. Burke had always felt an affinity for Campanis. When Burke first came up to the Dodgers from Albuquerque, Campanis had bought him a new suit. Even when the GM had asked Minor League managers to keep an eye on Burke, or Reggie Smith to share a room with him to keep him under control, Burke sensed that Campanis only kept a watchful eye on him because he believed in his potential. Joe Simpson, another young outfielder in the Dodger system, said Campanis's affection for Burke was clear. "I think he was very fond of Glenn," he said. "If Al had any favorites, I would say Glenn was one of them, ultimately to my detriment and any other outfield prospect."

Campanis had come up to the Bay Area to see Burke; they were scheduled to meet at Campanis's hotel in Oakland, a conversation Burke expected to include an assessment of the 1977 season, when Burke had earned his first significant playing time, and an elaboration on Campanis's expectations for him in '78. Burke figured the meeting would be so brief that he told the friend who gave him a ride to the hotel just to wait in the car; he'd be right back.

What Burke didn't realize, as he walked into that room, was that Campanis knew that he was gay. And he had a plan to cover it up.

"Everybody on the team is married but you, Glenn," Campanis told Burke. "When players get married on the Dodgers, we help them out financially. We can help you so you can go out and have a real nice honeymoon."

On the surface, what Campanis said was true. The Dodger

Dodgers General Manager Al Campanis, shown here signing Willie Crawford to a contract, had been a part of the Dodger organization since the 1940s, when he was a Minor League roommate of Jackie Robinson. When Campanis offered Glenn Burke cash to get married and cover up his sexuality, Burke refused. (*Los Angeles Times* Archives / UCLA Special Collections)

organization did prefer their players to be married, believing it settled them down, allowed them to concentrate more on baseball and less on chasing women. And they did occasionally help out with expenses; even Tommy Lasorda had been given a $500 loan from the Dodgers to go on his honeymoon back in 1950. The whole premise was faulty, however: even the married players chased women, and the stress of wives, kids, and constant travel was at least as demanding as anything the single players experienced. And Burke understood that in his case, there was a more significant reason Campanis asked him to get married.

"You mean to a woman?" he replied.

Campanis said yes, adding that the organization was prepared to pay him a $75,000 bonus to do it, an amount equivalent to the average annual Major League salary at the time.

"Al," Burke replied, "I have no plans of marrying anyone anytime soon."

The meeting lasted for hours. "Al was making his bid with me to find a woman and get married," Burke recalled. "He also began to make it clear that my career with the Dodgers was in jeopardy if I didn't follow through with his wishes."

Burke had entered the meeting practically "hopping and skipping" with anticipation, expecting to be hearing about a pay raise. Instead, a man he liked and respected had essentially attempted to bribe him into joining a conspiracy to spare the Dodgers bad publicity by diving deep into the closet and bringing an unsuspecting woman with him.

He wouldn't do it.

He walked out of the hotel and into the parking lot. His friend was still waiting in the car, reading the newspaper. "I'm ready to go now," Burke said. "You don't mind if I don't want to talk, do you?"

They drove all the way back into San Francisco in complete silence.

Burke got out of the car at the corner of 18th and Castro, half a block from Harvey Milk's camera store.

In his own way, he had taken a stand for gay rights by refusing to accede to Campanis's plan.[1] He was proud of the man he'd become and he wasn't going to deny it, even if it meant his days with the Dodgers were numbered.

CHAPTER 19

BLACKBALLED

What we want—bottom line—is to be left alone. We're not asking for any special treatment. We're just asking to be allowed to express affection like any heterosexual would without fear of losing our livelihoods.

—Peter Scott, New Alliance for Gay Equality, Los Angeles,
March 19, 1978

With 1978 spring training underway in Vero Beach, Dodger management made two things clear.

One, ticket prices would escalate in the wake of the team's run to the World Series, only the second increase since the team had moved to Los Angeles. Reserved seats would rise to $3.50, parking to $2, while box seats would remain $4.50, general admission $2, and children's general admission $1.

Two, Glenn Burke would not be a member of the team much

longer. Which was curious considering the Los Angeles–Anaheim chapter of the Baseball Writers' Association of America had just named him Dodger Rookie of the Year in recognition of his contributions in '77.

By March 4, Ross Newhan of the *Los Angeles Times* was already reporting that Burke had fallen out of favor with management. Campanis and Lasorda, who had been so high on Burke in previous camps, pointed to his deficiencies.

"Glenn can run, field, and throw. He hasn't proved to us that he can hit," said Lasorda.

Campanis explained that Burke was out of options, meaning the Dodgers could not send him to the minor leagues without his permission. Since they didn't want him on the roster, they'd have to trade him. "I expect there will be interest in him when other clubs see him play later this spring," he said.

Burke forcefully objected to the criticism, pointing out that he had hit a respectable .274 while playing full time during the second half of the '77 season, and had hit .300 five times in the minors.

"What happens if Rick Monday can't play again, if his back won't let him play again?" he countered. "Who do they put out there in center field? Willie Crawford? That's a joke. Vic Davalillo? That's a joke. What can I say? What am I supposed to think? I start two games in the [NL Championship] Series. I play most of the season out there. And now I guess I'm not even going to make the club. Well, I'm trying to put it out of my head and get in shape on behalf of Glenn Burke. I'm going to be ready to play for some team somewhere because it doesn't look like it will be for the Dodgers, and I can assure you it won't be Triple-A since I have nothing to prove by going back to the minors."

Burke's assessment of his competition in center field was dead-on. Crawford played so poorly in camp that the Dodgers cut him before the season began and he never played another game in the major leagues. The thirty-eight-year-old Davalillo would start just four games all season. Monday's injuries caused him to miss as many games as he had the year before. And Burke also knew the real reason the Dodgers wanted him gone, even if they wouldn't admit it publicly. It had very little to do with his bat and everything to do with his sexuality, particularly his friendship with Spunky and his refusal to go along with Campanis's version of a marriage proposal.

Even before the 1978 season began, Glenn Burke knew his days with the Dodgers were numbered. (Topps)

Even before they could trade him, the Dodgers were already taking steps to punish him, Burke believed. Spunky wouldn't talk to him anymore, and Burke suspected the Dodgers had paid him to break off the relationship; he considered Spunky's new apartment in West Hollywood "evidence" of the deal.

Campanis was unable to trade Burke in spring training, so when the team flew to Atlanta to begin the regular season, Burke remained on the roster. When he got to play as a defensive replacement or pinch hitter he performed well, collecting four hits in eleven at-bats through May 5, committing no errors on seven chances in the field. But Lasorda mostly confined him to the bench, giving him just one start in the month of April. Burke fumed over the inactivity, pacing the dugout, glaring at

Lasorda. The manager took offense. "Burke!" he yelled. "If I was your age, I'd take you in the bathroom right now and kick your ass."

Burke never soured on his teammates; he was still the same clubhouse cutup, still the director of fun. "He was so alive and so fully engaged with people and life," recalled Lyle Spencer, a sportswriter who traveled with the team. "He was just a joy to be around. Dusty Baker had this great expression at the time, and it was 'all the way live' [rhymes with *five*]. And it applied to Glenn; he was 'all the way live.' He was turned on at all times, no matter where: in the clubhouse, in the back of the plane where all the wild guys would hang out and play cards. He would be back there entertaining everybody."

Burke's teammates appreciated his unifying presence more than ever; otherwise, the Dodgers appeared to be devolving into a Yankee-like mess. With the competition fierce in the NL West, players were openly hostile with one another, Lasorda's act wearing thin.

The irony of the closeted gay player being singled out as the "troublemaker," a characterization Dodger management leaked to the press, was the fact that while the Dodger players loved Burke, it was the player with the squeaky clean, heterosexual heartthrob image, first baseman Steve Garvey, who was the source of the most clubhouse friction.[1]

Everything about Garvey seemed too good to be true, from his square jaw and perfectly coiffed hair to his upright batting stance to his perky blond wife, Cyndy. Garvey happily granted interviews to reporters, signed autographs for fans, even hit a home run for a little girl in a wheelchair on Nuns' Day at Dodger Stadium. He didn't go out drinking with teammates, didn't curse, sat in the front of the team plane with management rather than in the back with the ballplayers.

Newspaper and magazine reporters called Steve and Cyndy Garvey the Ken and Barbie of baseball, marveling at their good looks and squeaky-clean image. Many teammates resented the portrayal and believed it was too good to be true, leading to greater tensions aimed at Garvey than anything Glenn Burke experienced with the Dodgers. (*Los Angeles Times* Archives / UCLA Special Collections)

The image he portrayed, and that was eagerly pushed by the Dodger PR machine, was so pristine that the national media called him Mr. Clean. "If he ever came to date my daughter," Lasorda told reporters, "I'd lock the door and not let him out." It was all too much for many of the Dodgers to take. Some resented his success, his "perfect" life. Others thought he was a phony, intentionally trying to make them look bad. In retaliation, some players refused to shake his hand after home runs, laugh at his jokes, or even speak to him. Pitcher Don Sutton punched him in the face in one clubhouse scuffle. Garvey felt so ostracized he used his teammates' negativity as motivation. As he stood in the batter's box waiting for a pitch, he told himself, "Fight it. Fight it. Fight it."

Not everyone disliked Garvey. Burke found him to be generous and friendly, and Dusty Baker remained his biggest supporter. A scene in the Dodger trainer's room told Baker all he needed to know about Garvey's decency.

While the Dodgers worked together as a team to win games, Baker said fans would have been surprised to know how much they competed among themselves, comparing everything from their cars to the size of their wives' diamond rings to their batting averages. But that day in the training room, Baker was in the midst of a slump, his average having dropped from .320 to .305. Garvey, meanwhile, was hitting .285 and smoking line drives every game; it was clear he was on the rise. "So Garve[y] told me, 'Hey man, don't come down to see me,'" Baker recalled. "'Let me come up to see you.' That's a pretty good teammate right there."

Still, tensions escalated as the calendar turned to May, intensifying as the club lost six of eight games between May 6 and May 14, falling from first place to third. Lasorda held a team meeting in the midst of the slide, unleashing an avalanche of profanities. The nadir came on May 14, when the Dodgers dropped a five-hour, fifteen-inning game to the Chicago Cubs in which Cub left fielder Dave Kingman destroyed Dodger pitchers with three home runs and eight RBI.

After the game, Associated Press reporter Paul Olden asked Lasorda for his opinion of Kingman's performance, inspiring a rant for the ages.

"What's my opinion of Kingman's performance?!" Lasorda replied. "What the *BLEEP* do you think is my opinion of it? I think it was *BLEEPING BLEEP*. Put that in, I don't *BLEEP*. Opinion of his performance?! *BLEEP*, he beat us with three *BLEEPING* home runs! What the *BLEEP* do you mean what is my opinion of his performance? How could you ask me a question like that, what is my opinion of his performance? *BLEEP*, he hit three home runs! *BLEEP*. I'm *BLEEPING* pissed off to lose that *BLEEPING* game. And you ask me my opinion of his performance! *BLEEP*."[2]

The Dodgers reversed the skid the next night, beating the Pittsburgh Pirates 7–6, and Burke earned a rare start the following game, a 3–2 Dodger victory on May 16. After the game, Lasorda called him into his office. Burke had been traded; his days with the Dodgers were over.

"We're tired of you walking back and forth in the dugout like a mad tiger in a cage," Lasorda said to Burke. "We're sending you to Oakland, where you can play more."

Meanwhile, Campanis entered the clubhouse to tell the rest of the guys about the deal. Lopes and Baker confronted him; there was no doubt in their minds that Burke had been traded because of his sexuality, but they wanted to see if Campanis would admit it. "Glenn? Why? What?" Lopes pleaded. "You traded our best prospect. Not to mention the life of the team."

Baker viewed the trade as a case of a public relations–obsessed organization "pushing dirt to the side" before it blemished the team's reputation. Lopes knew that management was onto Burke's secret, having gone as far as to spread a rumor that Glenn was "having personal problems off the field." A team executive had approached Lopes, asking, "Do you know what Glenn is?" Lopes was offended by the intent and the phrasing of the question. People had asked similar questions about him, not in reference to his sexuality but to his ethnicity. "What the hell kind of a question is that?" he responded, refusing to take the bait. "He's Glenn Burke, he makes us go."

As reporters entered the clubhouse to collect their postgame quotes, they were stunned by the sight of multiple players, including Don Sutton and Steve Garvey, sitting at their lockers crying. One by one, Burke's teammates came over to him to pay their respects and wish him well.

Lasorda and Campanis answered the sportswriters' questions about the trade. The Dodgers had obtained thirty-year-old outfielder Billy North in return from the A's. North was a speedy switch-hitter who had been a member of Oakland's World Series teams of the early seventies and would provide the Dodgers a proven veteran on the bench.

"We're playing for today," Campanis said. "Burke has potential, but it's in the future. We've obtained a player who can help us immediately with his experience and ability, who can help us more than Burke."

Lasorda claimed the trade was in Burke's best interests. "Well," he said, "this should give him a chance to play. We've got a hell of an outfield and it's hard for anyone to break into it."

While he knew there was more to the trade, Burke agreed that he'd get to play more in Oakland. But when sportswriters asked for his thoughts on the move, he also took a shot at Lasorda. "I never got a chance here," he told the reporters. "Every time I went to the plate I was looking over my shoulder, thinking that if I made an out they'd take me out. I felt I was supposed to kiss ass here and I didn't. I wouldn't. I wasn't brought up that way. I just wanted to play. As far as getting along with Lasorda, that didn't work out too well."

When sportswriters entered the Dodger clubhouse the next after-noon, the place was eerily quiet. No music, no joking. If any of the players had doubts why Burke was traded, they were put to rest when Dusty Baker posed a question to the team's trainer, Bill Buhler. Baker was fishing to see what Buhler might reveal. "Bill, why'd they trade Glenn?" he asked. "He was one of our top prospects." "They don't want any gays on the team," Buhler replied. "The organization knows?" Baker asked. "Everybody knows," Buhler said.

The general public and the sportswriters didn't know, but the writers still doubted the merits of the trade. Ross Newhan believed that it had been unfair for Dodger management to label Burke a menace simply because he wanted to play more. "It may be that the conservative people who held this view failed to take the elevator from the fifth-floor offices to the basement clubhouse as often as they should have," he wrote, alluding to Burke's popularity with his teammates. Yes, Burke was frustrated and angry sometimes. "But a troublemaker? An attitude spoiler? A bad seed? Anything but."

In the *Los Angeles Examiner*, Lyle Spencer made similar points—"about what a sense of loss it was for these guys who really cared about [Glenn]"—and he also made the argument that Burke had never really gotten a chance to play for an extended period of time and "find a groove, settle in, and show what an extraordinary talent he really was." Spencer's column irritated Lasorda, who pulled the columnist aside to complain that Burke wasn't nearly as good as Spencer had made him out to be. "Jesus," he said. "I didn't realize until I read your column we had traded Joe DiMaggio."

Just about everybody but Campanis and Lasorda, it seemed, mourned the trade as if there had been a death in the family. There was one member of the Dodgers' staff, malted ice cream salesman Bill Frishette, who took the news particularly hard. He had finished his shift at the Pirates game, turned on his car radio on the way home, and heard Dodger announcer Vin Scully break the news that his friend had been traded. Burke had been such a nice person, so down-to-earth, so easy to be around.

To hear that Glenn had been dealt to Oakland?

To Bill Frishette, it felt like he'd been stabbed right in the gut.

CHAPTER 20
SUPERFREAKY

Getting traded to the Oakland A's in 1978 was like being given a room on the *Titanic* as it was sinking, boarding the *Hindenburg* as it burst into flames.

Billy North had begged to be traded for years. When he finally received the news he was headed to the Dodgers, he had just one question for the A's: "How quickly can I get out of here?"

While the Dodgers were the very model of stability, consistency, and success, the franchise Glenn Burke joined on May 17 existed in a constant state of uncertainty, bending to the whims of absentee owner Charlie Finley, a man who was already eccentric and cheap and had doubled down on those qualities as he tried to sell the team to an investor in Denver. Everyone assumed it was just a matter of time until that announcement was made and the team relocated to Colorado.[1]

The A's in 1978 looked nothing like the team that had dominated all of baseball as recently as the early seventies, when they won five straight division crowns between 1971 and '75 and World Series titles in '72, '73, and '74. The A's had struggled to draw more than a million fans even in those successful seasons (while the Dodgers, for example, drew nearly three million in '77), and as Finley dismantled the franchise in the mid-seventies, trading the team's stars to avoid paying high salaries, attendance plummeted further as the losses piled up. The Dodgers had operated under the philosophy that "contented cows give sweeter milk," constructing the luxurious Dodgertown and buying their own plane. Finley served his players and staff sour milk and charged them double for it.

Finley was an outcast among Major League owners, an outsider, visionary, and cheapskate unbound by the traditions of the game. He had purchased the team in 1960 when the A's still played in Kansas City, earning a reputation as the "P. T. Barnum of baseball," bringing a circus promoter's colorful sensibility to a game that had long lived comfortably in gray-and-white flannel. "Baseball owners," he said, "don't seem to realize they are in the entertainment business."

Finley bought a live mule to serve as Kansas City's mascot and encouraged his players to ride it. He had his staff build a mechanical rabbit to deliver baseballs to the home plate umpire. When the rabbit repeatedly malfunctioned, he threw a funeral and buried it in a wooden casket.

Oakland A's owner Charlie Finley was a notorious cheapskate, but also a baseball visionary. Many of the ideas his critics laughed at in the 1960s and '70s—colorful uniforms, interleague play, the designated hitter—have become standard parts of the game. (National Baseball Hall of Fame)

After moving the team to Oakland in 1968, Finley continued to experiment, even as the team amassed talent and championships. He offered small cash incentives for players to grow mustaches and adopt nicknames—Rollie Fingers grew his famous handlebar 'stache, and pitcher Jim Hunter became "Catfish."

He advocated for bright orange baseballs; red, white, and blue bases; interleague play; three-ball walks; shorter games; shorter seasons; designated hitters; designated runners; and night games in the World Series. His teams didn't just wear white jerseys and pants at home and gray on the road: sometimes they wore white on white, other times gold on gold, green on white, gold on white, or white on gold. The possibilities were numerous and at times Finley called the clubhouse from his office in Chicago to demand the team change uniform combos right before game time. They tied white shoes with green laces and called themselves the A's rather than their official name, Athletics, because Finley thought there was value in having the shortest nickname in baseball.

Most of his ideas were considered bizarre by baseball traditionalists at the time, and some of them (a mechanical rabbit?) no doubt were. But more than a few—the DH, interleague play, colorful uniforms, postseason night games, dumping high-priced players to rebuild, a yearning to speed up the game—have become part of the fabric of modern baseball.

Still, Finley's impatient and demanding approach grated on players and front office staff. He once ran through five ticket managers in a single year. His public relations director quit three weeks into one season, while his entire switchboard staff quit in another. He preferred young employees, knowing they'd work hard for little pay. The franchise had no professional scouts, no Minor League pitching or hitting instructors, and no left-handed batting practice pitcher. Finley wouldn't pay for any video equipment, so outfielder Mitchell Page resorted to watching his swing at a restaurant called Ricky's that happened to record A's games.

Finley was the worst kind of micromanager, phoning players, managers, and sportswriters at all hours, for any reason. "All hours" is no hyperbole—he woke up his managers in the middle of the night and had a phone installed in the A's dugout so he could offer advice during games. When that method proved inefficient, he suggested that his manager wear headphones so he could communicate with him constantly.

He was so cheap, players were limited to a maximum of two towels in the clubhouse. The A's didn't even charter flights, let alone have their own plane. The team traveled coach with the general public at the mercy of the airlines' schedules; often they flew on game day, arriving in a new city just hours before first pitch.

Veteran pitcher Dock Ellis, who had been a member of a world championship team in Pittsburgh and helped lead the Yankees to the

World Series in '76, so badly wanted off the sinking A's in 1977 he engineered his exit on a flight from Oakland to Toronto. Turning to sportswriter Tom Weir, he announced his plans. "Newspaperman," he said. "Watch me. I'm getting out of here tonight." Ellis proceeded to get bombed on cognac, going on a drunken rampage for the five-hour flight through three time zones. By noon the next day, he'd been traded to Texas.

Finley's most endearing quality was his willingness to listen to kids and provide them opportunities beyond their years. The idea for red, white, and blue bases came from a fifteen-year-old boy; Finley later invited the kid to join him in his special seats at the Coliseum. When he was unable to reach a deal with a local radio station to carry A's games in '78, he gave broadcasting rights to a couple of students at Cal Berkeley. For the first few weeks of the season, Larry Baer and Bob Kozbert called the games on KALX FM, a student-run station with a ten-watt signal hardly anybody could hear. Baer's introduction to baseball set him on a path that eventually led him to become CEO of the San Francisco Giants. In 1969, Finley hired a middle schooler named Debbi Sivyer as the Major League's first ball girl; her specialty was baking, and delivering, homemade chocolate-chip cookies to umpires. In less than a decade, she started a business, Mrs. Fields cookies (using her married name), which became a $450 million enterprise.

Then there was the case of Stanley Burrell, a young African American kid Finley "discovered" one afternoon dancing for quarters in the Oakland Coliseum parking lot. Finley was impressed by the kid's skills and the crowd he had managed to attract. "Young man, you're quite a dancer," Finley told him. When Burrell thanked him by name,

Finley was impressed he knew who he was. Turned out, the boy's brothers already worked as clubhouse attendants, and everyone around the organization called him "Hammer" after a visiting member of the Milwaukee Brewers told him he looked a lot like legendary slugger "Hammerin'" Hank Aaron.

Hammer asked Finley if he and his friends could be guests at the game; Finley agreed, giving them seats next to the owner's box. When some of Finley's guests got hungry, he tapped on the glass and asked Hammer to go get them some hamburgers. From that day forward, Hammer became Finley's trusted sidekick, gofer, and personal broadcaster, relaying the pitch-by-pitch action over the phone to Finley when he was home in Chicago. One time Finley asked him to go run an errand in the middle of one of these broadcasts, so Hammer handed the phone to Jack McKeon, a former A's manager sitting beside him. McKeon's play-by-play skills paled in comparison to the kid's. "Dammit," Finley yelled into his phone. "You don't know how to broadcast the game! When Hammer gets back, I want you to sit there and listen to him and see how he does it. He checks the runners and he checks the signs!"

Finley even gave Hammer the title of Executive Vice President, paying him $7.50 an hour and giving him a special A's cap with the letters *VP* sewn on. Heady stuff for a sixteen-year-old student at Oakland's McClymonds High School, but it turns out this was just the beginning of a remarkable career for Stanley Burrell, not in baseball, but in music. Burrell's rapid-fire play-by-play skills came in handy, and in 1990, under the stage name MC Hammer, his *Please Hammer Don't Hurt 'Em*, featuring the hit song "U Can't Touch This," became the bestselling rap album of all time.

Stanley Burrell was the teenage "vice president" of the Oakland A's in the 1970s and a favorite of eccentric owner Charlie Finley. He went on to achieve fame as the iconic rap artist MC Hammer. (National Baseball Hall of Fame)

All told, when Glenn Burke joined the A's, there was reason to believe he'd landed in a good place, even with—or perhaps because of—the team's embrace of the unorthodox. He was back in his hometown, playing for a team that didn't mind being different from the rest, where young players were given a chance.

Could Oakland be the ideal spot to resurrect his career?

CHAPTER 21
SIGNATURE MOMENT

The split-level home at 27 Adams Court in Westwood, New Jersey, looked pleasant enough from the outside, a typical suburban home on a tree-lined street about thirty miles north of New York City.

But for twelve-year-old Erik Sherman, the house wasn't a happy place. His parents fought through an ugly divorce when he was six, and now he shared this home with his mother, Jo Ann, and his stepfather, John, a stern disciplinarian who was possessive of his time with Erik's mother. The air at 27 Adams was so thick with stress that Erik, a skinny and sensitive kid, developed a stutter.

His escape was baseball. He was a good ballplayer, a Little League All-Star who spent his summers at baseball camps and long hours in the backyard hitting off a tee. He collected baseball cards and autographs, knew every major leaguer's statistics. Every night, he'd listen to a game on the radio, spreading his cards out on the floor in front of him and moving them around imaginary basepaths. He hung a poster of his favorite Yankee, Graig Nettles, on his bedroom wall and imitated Nettles in Little League games, intentionally waiting on ground balls so he could make a diving stab like the Yankee third baseman. At the plate, he mimicked another big leaguer, Dodger Steve Garvey—stiff posture, twirling fingers.

Growing up in New Jersey, Erik Sherman loved everything about baseball—he played the game himself, listened to MLB games on the radio, and loved attending Yankees and Mets games with his father. (Erik Sherman)

Every other weekend he stayed at his father Frank's house, seven miles south in Bergenfield. Those were the happy times, an oasis from the tension at his mom's house. This is where his subscriptions to *Sports Illustrated*, *The Sporting News*, and *Baseball Digest* arrived, where he spent weekends playing catch with his dad, visiting museums, and going to ballgames, Yankees or Mets, depending on the schedule.

In 1977, his father received tickets to Game 6 of the World Series, great seats just a few rows behind home plate. He invited Erik to come along. But the game was played on a Tuesday, an October school night, and not one of the days his dad had custody. Jo Ann told Erik he couldn't go. When he protested, she became angry, telling him he couldn't watch the game on TV, either. Erik hid his radio under his covers and listened to the whole game in bed. To this day, every time Sherman is reminded of Reggie Jackson's legendary three-home-run performance, it brings back bittersweet memories. He knows he should have been there, six rows behind the plate, celebrating a moment in baseball history with his father.

But their every-other-weekend routine resumed in the summer of 1978, and on Saturday, August 26, Frank took Erik to see the Yankees play the Oakland A's. The game would start at eight p.m., and every fan would receive a Yankee photo album, complete with pictures of all the ballplayers. Erik loved to arrive at the stadium early so he could stand along the rail by the field and collect autographs, especially from players on the visiting teams. The A's weren't very good, Erik knew, but that didn't matter. Nothing was better than nine innings at the ballpark with his dad.

By late August of 1978, the A's were in the midst of a dreadful slide, winning just seven of twenty-eight games that month, a dismal feat they repeated in September. That the A's were losing three of every four games was hardly a surprise. When the *Washington Post* ran a headline back in spring training declaring that "1978 Could Be Disaster for Finley, A's," the choice of the word *could* was generous.

But to the shock of everyone in baseball, the A's had actually started the season on a tear, winning nineteen of their first twenty-four games. When Burke arrived on May 17, his new team still led the American

League West, and he contributed to the winning ways, collecting three hits in his first game as an A and hitting .346 over the course of his first week with the club. The fact that he had come up through the Dodgers' system gave Burke a measure of instant credibility, and he sought opportunities to counsel young players the way Baker had done with him in Los Angeles. When twenty-three-year-old outfielder Miguel Dilone neglected to congratulate a teammate after a home run, Burke scolded him.

When Glenn Burke was traded from the Dodgers to the A's, he returned home to the Bay Area, where he had grown up—and where the Castro was just a short ride away. (National Baseball Hall of Fame)

But things began to fall apart quickly, both for Burke and the team. On May 22, manager Bobby Winkles quit, fed up with Finley's late-night, early-morning, and in-game rants and the last-minute lineup changes dictated from Chicago via the sixteen-year-old team vice president. In his place, Finley rehired Jack McKeon, the manager he had fired the previous season and replaced with Winkles.

The Oakland A's were a clown show, but at least Burke had a chance to play every day. On May 20, he made a great diving catch to end a White Sox rally in the seventh inning. "I've got a lot of that in me," he told reporters after the game. But on June 1, the A's placed Burke on the disabled list with a pinched nerve in his neck. He sat out for three weeks and lost his opportunity to gain a foothold as an everyday starter. For all his faults, Finley proved to be a capable scout of young talent, and the A's were loaded with prospects, especially in the outfield.

Burke continued to travel with the team while he was injured, carrying his huge boom box on the plane, on the bus, into the locker room. "You could hear him coming before you even saw him," pitcher Mike Norris recalled. "He loved his music; it kept him sane. Glenn and his Funkadelic."

Even confined to the bench, Burke relished opportunities to keep his teammates laughing, reminiscent of the hoorah battles he'd dominated as a kid in Berkeley. "He was the funniest son-of-a-bitch," Norris said. "You're talking about people sitting on the bench in stitches laughing at stuff he came up with off the top of his head." In one game, Burke turned his needling on teammate Mike Edwards. "Mike!" Burke called out. "You were so poor when your mama sent you to the store to get a loaf of bread and a half gallon of milk, you pulled two rocks out your pocket to pay for it."

During a game in Chicago, Norris watched from the bench as Burke stepped to the plate.

"The White Sox catcher was Bill Nahorodny," Norris recalled. "He was huge, like six-four. It's unbearably hot and humid. At Comiskey Park, the dugouts were so close to home plate you could spit on it, so you could hear everything. The pitcher throws the ball and Nahorodny says 'strike' before the umpire does. Glenn's standing there with his bat on his shoulder. Then it happens again, Nahordony says 'strike' before the umpire. Glenn backs out of the batter's box, Nahorodny stands up, and Glenn says, 'Shut up, you ain't the umpire.' Nahorodny says, 'You ain't telling me to shut up.' Glenn looks at this six-four dude and says, 'You're lucky it's so hot out here, because if it wasn't so hot out here, I'd kick your ass.' We all hear this from the dugout, and we're dying laughing. I was on the floor, rolling around in tobacco spit. He was really going to kick this big mother's ass."

One of Glenn's closest confidants on the Oakland A's was Mike Norris, a talented young pitcher who had also grown up in the Bay Area. (Topps)

In mid-June, the A's traveled to Boston for a quick two-game series on the eve of the MLB trade deadline. The A's had grown accustomed to uncertainty—Finley loved to make trades, and anyone was subject to be cut loose. Following a 7–3 loss to the Red Sox on June 15, with the deadline approaching at three a.m. eastern time, a wave of gallows humor took over the visitors' clubhouse at Fenway Park, observed by the *Boston Globe*'s Leigh Montville.

Burke was at his playful best, smiling and snaking his way through the cramped locker room, mocking the here-today, gone-tomorrow nature of the franchise. He'd sneak up behind a teammate and shout, "Hello!" When they turned around, he'd yell, "Goodbye!"

Other players got in on the act. Larry Murray yelled over to Mitchell Page: "There's been a trade! They're sending you for a McDonald's burger, an order of fries and a large shake!"

Page: "Oh, yeah, they're sending you for a bucket of Kentucky Fried Chicken."

Taylor Duncan: "No, they're sending you for a jar of Afro Sheen."

First baseman Dave Revering joined in. "Two sportswriters just went. Two sportswriters, a waste basket, an equipment man."

In the midst of the banter, players found out that catcher Gary Thomasson had been traded to the Cleveland Indians.

"You've got to wear an iron uniform in Cleveland. Bullet-proof," Burke joked. "They'll get you on the streets of Cleveland. They have knives in Cleveland, and I don't mean the grown-ups, either. I mean the little kids. The girls!"

By the time the A's arrived in New York for a three-game series in late August, Burke was batting a pitiful .221, had yet to appear in a game for a week, and hadn't been used as more than a pinch runner or defensive replacement since August 10.

More than fifty-three thousand people showed up for the August 26 night game, including Erik Sherman and his dad. Sherman's hero, Graig Nettles, homered in the eighth inning to break a tie and lead the Yankees to a 5–4 win. But that's not what Sherman remembers more than forty years later.

The Shermans had arrived at the stadium two hours early, giving Erik time to scamper down to the railing along the left-field line before the game started. He waited patiently, clutching the Yankee photo album he'd been given at the turnstiles, hoping one of the Oakland A's would come over to sign autographs. Finally, one of them did. And when he handed Glenn Burke a photo album and a pen, neither could have guessed they'd meet again someday, when Erik Sherman would arrive on Glenn's doorstep to tell his story to the world.

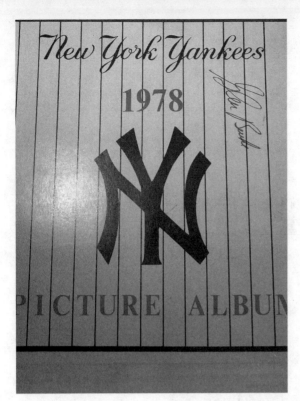

Glenn Burke was the only ballplayer to sign twelve-year-old Erik Sherman's Yankee photo album on **August 26, 1978.** (Erik Sherman)

CHAPTER 22
UNRAVELING

Dan White climbed through a basement window at San Francisco's City Hall, allowing him to evade the metal detector in the lobby. Concealing a .38 caliber pistol and ten extra rounds of ammunition, he walked calmly to Mayor George Moscone's office.

The mayor's secretary recognized him; until abruptly quitting the position just two weeks earlier, White had been a city supervisor. But White had held a press conference to announce he was resigning his post, choosing instead to run a baked-potato stand at Fisherman's Wharf, the popular tourist destination. But after his conservative political backers convinced him to change his mind, he had gone to Moscone to ask to be reinstated. The mayor had initially been sympathetic to White's plea, but then reversed course, in part due to pressure from Harvey Milk to appoint a liberal commissioner in his place. White wasn't getting his city job back.

Now White was back in Moscone's office, looking for revenge. He shot the mayor four times in the head, reloaded, walked down the hall to the other side of the building, found Milk, and shot him five times. The murder of his political adversaries complete, White met his wife at St. Mary's Cathedral a few blocks north, confessed to what he'd done, and turned himself in to a friend on the police force. By noon, the word was out in San Francisco: Milk and the mayor were dead, and White, a former police officer who had run for supervisor on a "Law and Order" and "Stop the Deviants" anti-gay platform, was the killer.

Even before the lifeless bodies of Moscone and Milk had been placed under white sheets and carried out of City Hall, bartenders at the Bear Hollow bar in the Castro tied black bands of fabric around their arms in memory of Milk, the gay crusader who had been elected to office just a year earlier. Word passed through the neighborhood: there would be a peaceful march to City Hall that evening. People flooded the Star Pharmacy on Castro to purchase long candles for forty-five cents apiece. At eight thirty p.m., a solitary drummer led thousands of men and women, connected arm in arm, on the otherwise silent march to the steps of City Hall. By ten p.m., more than forty thousand mourners gathered there, their tearstained faces illuminated by candlelight. The hero of their movement assassinated, they sang the anthem of the civil rights movement, "We Shall Overcome," and listened to speeches urging patience and strength.

All across the nation in the months leading up to White's murder- ous rampage, and particularly in California, where John Briggs's anti-gay initiative was on the ballot, the steady drumbeat of a "culture war" had pitted the hopes of equality for gay men and women against the increasingly fiery rhetoric of conservative Christians.

Outside a March 1978 Revival Fires event featuring Anita Bryant in Decatur, Illinois, a group of protestors holding signs reading "Gay Rights Are Human Rights" stood opposite a group of Ku Klux Klansmen and military veterans holding pro-Bryant posters.

The next month, Bryant said she favored prosecuting gays as felons, with prison terms of up to twenty years, adding that gays, Jews, Muslims, and "anyone else who does not accept Jesus" would go to hell.

In May, Briggs called San Francisco "the moral garbage dump of homosexuality in this country."

In June, twenty thousand Southern Baptists gathered at Atlanta's World Congress Center for their annual convention, greeted by two thousand gay rights demonstrators outside. One group held signs reading "Gay Rights Now," the other "Praise God for Anita." A reporter from the *Los Angeles Times* observed the scene. "The sneers, the stares, the glances, the homemade signs and the strong words spoke loudest for the rival groups who warily eyed—and even photographed—each other like species from two different planets." One teenage girl from Missouri whispered to her friends, "What do you think about all these f---s out here?" Another young woman from North Carolina responded, "Every one of those guys is going to burn in hell."

In October, a sixth-grade teacher in Los Angeles came out in support of the Briggs Initiative, claiming that words such as *deviant, perverse,* and *weird* were not slurs but accurate descriptions of gay people. But on November 4, California voters overwhelmingly rejected the Briggs bill, an enormous victory for gay rights. On November 27, an aggrieved Dan White shot Milk and Moscone dead.

Three months later, Glenn Burke reported to the 1979 Oakland A's spring training camp in Scottsdale, Arizona. He had spent the off-season socializing in the thriving gay bars of the Castro, earning admiration from patrons for living an "out" life. In spring camp, he did little to conceal his sexuality. Steve Vucinich, the team's longtime equipment manager, remembered a five-hour road trip to Palm Springs to face the California Angels. As the A's players got off the bus in front of the team's hotel, an expensive-looking convertible with its top down pulled up. The two men in the front seat, Vucinich recalled, looked "flamboyantly" gay. "I hate to label anybody like that," he said, "but they looked as gay as gay could look." Burke approached the team's traveling secretary, announced that he would not be staying in the hotel and would meet the team at the ballpark the next morning, jumped into the convertible, and waved at his teammates as he sped away. "If there was any doubt [that Glenn was gay]," Vucinich recalled, "it was then that we thought it even more. Everybody saw that and said, 'Ah, maybe he is.'"

As bad as the 1978 A's had been, the '79 club was even worse, eventually losing a team-record 108 games while attracting fewer than four thousand fans per game at the Coliseum. Still trying to sell the team, Finley showed no interest in the ball club. He didn't attend a game all season and didn't appear to care if anyone else did, either. At times, fans had to bang on box office windows to get someone's attention to sell them a ticket; other times they just walked in the stadium for free, no attendants at the gates to stop them. Only a few concession stands were open for business.[1]

No single game captured the essence of the '79 season better than an April 17 contest against the visiting Seattle Mariners. On a bitterly cold and windy Tuesday night at the Coliseum, the A's sold only 653 tickets; 250 diehards actually showed up. With the wind chill hovering around fifteen degrees, the teams played as poorly as the weather, committing a combined nine errors. When A's catcher Jim Essian singled with two out in the bottom of the ninth to win the game, third baseman Wayne Gross walked around the edge of the field, personally thanking the fans for sticking around to the bitter end. "This win is dedicated to those fans," A's pitcher Dave Heaverlo said. "Their enthusiasm was terrific. Their loyalty was terrific."

Glenn Burke never got off the bench, spending the night freezing in the drafty Oakland dugout, a fairly accurate representation of his predicament in this new season: uncomfortable, alone, frozen out by an increasing number of teammates as they learned of—and objected to—his sexuality.

Some A's resented Burke's presence in the clubhouse and showers to such an obvious degree that Burke felt he was treated as if his sexuality was "contagious." In response, he developed a predictable postgame routine, quickly showering and leaving the stadium before any of his teammates.

Pitcher Mike Norris, a fellow African American native of the Bay Area, said he and Burke remained close friends as it became increasingly

The Oakland A's were a franchise in turmoil the entirety of Glenn Burke's stint with the team. The team was losing games, owner Charlie Finley didn't seem to care, and fans stayed away in droves. Meanwhile, many teammates shunned Burke over his sexuality. Here he argues with umpire Larry Barnett during a 16–5 loss to the Angels. (AP Photo/Jim Palmer)

obvious that Glenn was gay. Norris, like many other big leaguers, had a girl waiting for him in every town. On road trips, Burke would often join him in his hotel room to listen to his boom box and smoke a joint. But whenever the phone rang to let Norris know his girl had arrived, Burke would leave. "It would happen every road trip," Norris recalled, "and it became so predictable it was quite comical, actually." So one night in Arlington, Texas, Norris came up with a plan. He had two women waiting in the room when Burke got there. "He comes in and spends about five minutes, and then he said, 'Oh, I forgot, I have to go back to my room to call my mama,'" Norris said. "I told him, 'Oh, you could have come up with something better than that.' That was pretty much enough proof for me."

While Norris got a laugh from Burke's obvious attempts to avoid women, he also understood there was nothing funny about it for Burke. He could see how few of his teammates, especially the white guys, went out of their way to befriend Glenn. He knew how lonely a long Major League season can be without a confidant. "I'm not being judgmental," Norris told him. "I just want to know the truth. I'm all right with you, brother. But everybody is wondering if you're gay."

Even the sportswriters covering the team were in on the secret. During one road trip, Tom Weir of the *Oakland Tribune* sat down for breakfast with A's outfielder Mitchell Page. Burke's name came up in the conversation. "He looked at me like, 'Oh, shit, how do you know?'" Weir recalled. "He asked if I was going to write about it, and I told him I wasn't. But I said, 'Look, if you're having a heart-to-heart with Glenn, tell him if he ever wants to tell the story, I'll work with him to present it properly, I never heard back from him. I'm sure there were other reporters who made the same pitch."

Page did let Burke know the subject had come up. Years later, he recalled telling Burke about his conversation with Weir. Burke remembered the story slightly differently, claiming that Page told him that it was a scout for the Pittsburgh Pirates who had inquired about his sexuality. Regardless, Page's motivation for telling Burke, and the effect on Burke, was the same. Page said he felt he should let Glenn know "instead of talking about it behind his back like other players." Burke said the conversation with Page caused his world to "screech to a stop." He had always maintained that his sexuality was irrelevant to baseball and none of anyone's business. Now it seemed to be everyone's. "I realized it had all come to an end," he said. "They'd stripped me of my inner-most thoughts."

As the calendar turned to May, all eyes in the Bay Area turned to the trial of Dan White, who had been charged with first-degree murder and faced a possible death sentence. His attorneys never made the claim that White hadn't killed Moscone and Milk; that was indisputable. But they argued that he shouldn't be found guilty of murder, that under California's "diminished capacity" defense, jurors should consider that he was not capable of the "premeditation, deliberation and malice necessary for being found guilty of first- or second-degree murder." Their rationale? That in the days before the killings, White had been severely depressed, betrayed by the mayor who had reneged on his word to give him his job back. A "good man," they argued, had simply snapped in the heat of the moment.

The all-white, mostly female, conservative jury (all jurors had to be willing to administer the death penalty, and all prospective non-white, gay, and gay-friendly jurors were dismissed) returned its verdict on May 21. White, they said, was guilty only of unpremeditated voluntary manslaughter, sentencing him to less than eight years in prison and eligibility for parole in just five.[2]

The light sentence was perceived by many observers, including San Francisco TV reporter Jeannine Yeomens, as a miscarriage of justice. "I remember facing the camera after the verdict was announced," she remembered, "and thinking, 'Try not to look too shocked.'" Henry Der, a Chinese American community leader, told reporters the verdict demonstrated that "if you're white, you don't have to be civil in this society," while gay citizens viewed it as further evidence that their lives did not matter to the heterosexual majority.

Gay men and women had marched peacefully on the night of the murders, silently carrying candles to City Hall. But on the night of the verdict they responded with fury on what became known as White Night, reacting to the crime and the verdict, but also, as gay journalist Ray Comeau noted at the time, to more than that, to an outcome that symbolized an "utter disregard for American justice." Hundreds and then thousands of people converged on the streets surrounding City Hall, and the scene turned violent as gay citizens confronted cops in riot gear and unleashed their frustrations by throwing garbage cans through windows, setting dumpsters on fire, destroying parked police cars, and slashing tires with jackknives.

San Francisco police, many of whom considered White one of their own, retaliated with attacks on Castro Street, in one case entering the Elephant Bar, police badges turned inside out, and clubbing patrons to the ground.

Many people felt it was a miscarriage of justice when a jury found Dan White guilty only of voluntary manslaughter after he shot George Moscone and Harvey Milk dead in their offices. Distraught and angry gay residents took to the streets of San Francisco, destroying property to protest a justice system that did not appear to value their lives. (AP Photo/Paul Sakuma)

By the next morning, 175 windows had been broken, 10 police cars burned, 120 civilians and 59 police officers injured, and 23 people arrested. Comeau, the journalist, later wrote he felt a strange mixture of emotions as he assessed the verdict and the resulting riot: rage at the jury's decision; renewed feelings of loss for the murders of two good men; and "feelings of utterly ecstatic joy at seeing gay men and women finally—finally!—fighting back, expressing their anguish and frustration openly, directly, against the warped system that still—still!—can and does oppress many. Bitterness and wonder, anxiety and joy."

For Burke, any sensations of wonder and joy were overcome by the bitterness and anxiety. His world was collapsing in senseless ways: the murders, the verdict, the riots, the ostracism, the whispers, the futility of his team.

Then things got worse. His old lover, Michael Smith, was still trying to convince Burke to publicly come out of the closet, going as far as to invite *San Francisco Chronicle* columnist Herb Caen to meet Burke for an interview. When Burke declined, Caen wrote a column anyway, sharing the provocative news that an unnamed professional baseball player could be found walking the streets of the Castro.

Burke felt betrayed by Smith and Caen, but that wasn't the worst of it.

To understand the worst of it, you've got to know about a kid named Bobby Glasser.

Bobby was thirteen years old in '79 and had been following the A's as long as he could remember. His whole family loved everything about the A's. Other people might call the Coliseum a dump or make fun of the small crowds or rip the owner for making so many trades, but those weren't real fans, as far as Glasser was concerned. He showed up at the stadium early to catch baseballs hit into the bleachers during batting practice and stayed until the last pitch, no matter the weather, no matter the score, no matter the hour. It was the number one rule his grandmother had taught him: never leave early. Once he turned eleven, his parents let him go to games by himself once a week, even on school nights. With five or six bucks in his pocket and a replica A's cap on his head, he'd take the bus from his house in Pleasanton to the BART station in Hayward, then board the train to the Coliseum. He didn't care if the team stank; it just made him more of a fan, pulling for the underdog when nobody else seemed to care. On weekends he'd go to the games with his grandmother, and they'd sit in the $2 outfield bleacher seats, coming to recognize the other die-hards who continued to show up to cheer for a dreadful team.

There was one group of guys who always sat in the left-center-field bleachers, blue-collar white men in their thirties or forties. They usually heckled the other team's center fielder—nothing too vulgar or mean-spirited, usually just the basic "You suck!" or "You're horrible!" or a dumb joke about the guy's last name.

But one day, Glasser heard something that offended his sensibilities as a loyal fan. One of the guys in the bleachers started harassing an A's player.

"Hey Burrrrrke," he bellowed. "You're a f--!" The slur seemed to stretch across the field.

"Burrrrrke, you're a f--!" Again, the man's voice echoed in the

A devoted fan of the Oakland A's, Bobby Glasser was a regular in the outfield bleachers at the Oakland Coliseum, often attending night games by himself after school. When he heard fellow A's fans heckling Glenn Burke, he was disgusted—and never forgot it. (Bobby Glasser)

cavernous, nearly empty stadium.

Glasser loved to stretch out over three rows in the wooden bleachers, but these highly offensive slurs made him sit up straight. If you're going to be one of the two thousand people showing up to support the home team, you do not turn against it; you do not taunt one of your own guys. Glasser didn't know why this bushy-haired man was saying this about Glenn Burke, but the very thought of yelling at one of the A's made him seethe.

After the game, Bobby and his grandmother exited the stadium into the Coliseum parking lot. Up ahead, there was a commotion, a dozen people gathered around two men fighting. As they walked closer, Bobby recognized one of the men as the heckler; the other guy was a muscular Black man. The men were locked in a violent embrace, the Black man grabbing the white man by the throat, the white guy pulling on the Black man's shirt. Then Glasser realized the Black man was Glenn Burke, dressed in a baseball undershirt and sweatpants. The telltale sign was his feet. He wasn't wearing shoes, just yellow socks and green stirrups, part of the A's uniform. He must have quickly changed into his sweats as soon as the game was over and run out to the parking lot to confront the heckler. People shouted as Burke squeezed his hands around the other man's neck, "Glenn, don't do it! Glenn, don't do it!" As confident as the bushy-haired man acted in the safety of the bleachers, he now looked like a scared little puppy, Bobby thought. Burke could kill him if he wanted to.

Finally, Glenn let the man go. Bobby's grandmother pulled Bobby along, but as he looked back, he could see Burke down on the ground, looking for something that must have been important, a necklace that must have come off during the fight, Bobby believed. Maybe the peace medallion Glenn used to wear back in Berkeley?

Over the ensuing decades, Bobby Glasser has returned to this fight in his mind, over and over. Might this have been the moment, he wonders, when Glenn Burke decided he'd had enough, when he decided that playing Major League Baseball simply wasn't worth it anymore? Was the fight in the parking lot rock bottom?[3]

On June 4, 1979, the Oakland A's hosted the Cleveland Indians in the first game of a four-game series at the Coliseum. The A's had lost sixteen of their previous twenty-two games and were firmly rooted in last place in the AL West. The Indians led 4–1 entering the bottom of the ninth, but the A's rallied for three runs to tie the game, no thanks to Burke, who had grounded out with the tying run on second. In the bottom of the thirteenth, with the score still tied, Glenn came up with runners on first and third; a base hit or a sacrifice fly or even a grounder in the right spot in the infield would win the game. But Glenn struck out, the A's never scored, and the Indians won the game in the fourteenth.

After the game, around midnight, Glenn's mother met him outside the clubhouse. She was surprised to see him carrying all his gear in his equipment bag. He never brought that stuff home; it always stayed with him at the ballpark.

"Mama," he said. "I quit."

CHAPTER 23

DISCO INFERNO

Less than a month after Glenn Burke decided he could no longer tolerate the homophobia in professional baseball, the sport played a major role in another manifestation of the culture war.

At Chicago's Comiskey Park on July 12, vinyl records flew out of the bleachers like Frisbees, spinning past ballplayers like razor blades.

Even after fifty thousand people filled the stadium to capacity, thousands more continued to pile into it, climbing walls, storming through gates, overpowering ushers, drawn by the clarion call of twenty-four-year-old radio deejay Steve Dahl.

The White Sox had hoped their Disco Demolition Night promotion would draw twenty-five thousand fans to a doubleheader against the Detroit Tigers, but more than twice as many people showed up, mostly white teenagers carrying disco records. Dahl, with the assistance of a blond model named Lorelei, collected the records and planned to detonate them between games. Admission was just ninety-eight cents, corresponding to the frequency of Dahl's rock station, WLUP-98 FM, a station that built its loyal following on a simple declaration: "DISCO SUCKS."

The disco movement that had existed under the radar in gay clubs and house parties before expanding to chic discotheques in major cities in the mid-seventies had exploded into the mainstream in 1977 and '78 thanks to the wildly popular movie *Saturday Night Fever*. While the roots of disco were built in Black, Latinx, and gay culture, with Black female artists recording many of the biggest hits, the movie portrayed a straight, white protagonist, a dancing machine played by popular actor John Travolta, and the soundtrack featured the music of the Bee Gees, a straight, white group of brothers from England. The movie fueled mainstream acceptance and oversaturation, with radio stations, dance clubs, and concert venues going all disco, all the time.

Predictably, a corresponding backlash against disco culture came next. On the surface, anti-disco fever had its merits: even disco admirers acknowledged the genre's preference for overproduced, mindless, sound-alike tracks. But there were more significant social forces at play, some of the same elements of the social and political divide that had produced the likes of Anita Bryant and John Briggs and had led to the nullification, whether through physical violence or verbal intimidation or jury verdicts, of prominent gay men like Harvey Milk and Glenn Burke. If the disco scene gave a measure of power, freedom, and cultural influence to gays and racial minorities, the anti-disco movement could be seen as an attempt by traditional majorities to seize back control.

Instead of handing their records to Dahl at the stadium turnstiles, thousands of fans chose to hang on to them and began flinging them onto the field during the first game of the doubleheader, which had to be delayed several times in the name of player safety. With records slicing through the air and landing in the dirt like darts, Tiger first baseman Rusty Staub urged his fellow infielders to don batting helmets. When Tiger reliever Aurelio Lopez got up in the bullpen to start warming up in the eighth inning, fans pelted him with a barrage of flying discs.

July 12, 1979, lives on in baseball lore as one of the most bizarre nights in Major League history. Led by Chicago radio deejay Steve Dahl (center), Disco Demolition Night at Chicago's Comiskey Park turned into a nightmarish mix of smoke, fire, flying discs, rampaging teenagers—and underlying backlash against social change. (Paul Natkin via Getty Images)

It was clear things were getting out of hand, but the between-games ritual proceeded as planned, with the fire goddess Lorelei joining Dahl on the field to ignite a crate of disco records in a thirty-minute orgy of smoke, fire, and explosion. That was supposed to be the end—Game 2 of the doubleheader was set to start in fifteen minutes. But as fumes from the blast swirled with clouds of marijuana to create a white haze over the stadium, seven thousand fans stormed the field, ripping up handfuls of grass, carrying homemade signs with obscene messages, and burning anti-disco banners. "This is our generation's cause," declared one seventeen-year-old reveler.

White Sox owner Bill Veeck tried to calm the chaos, grabbing a microphone and asking fans to return to their seats. "Please clear the field," he begged. "Please clear the field." Nobody listened. Finally, forty police officers arrived in riot gear, swinging clubs and handcuffing the kids they could chase down. Thirty-nine arrests later, the riot was over, but so was the doubleheader. After groundskeepers spent an hour clearing debris and trying to get the field in playing shape, umpires canceled the second game and awarded the Tigers a forfeit victory. The field was unsafe, the scene too unpredictable.

The spectacle drew national attention, an embarrassment for the White Sox, a publicity boon for Dahl and his radio station. But it wasn't long before Disco Demolition Night took on greater cultural significance, perceived to represent more than just a bunch of drunk and stoned teenagers losing control in a spasm of mindless hooliganism. For many, the eruption at Comiskey marked the symbolic end of the disco era and illuminated the cultural forces—anti-gay, anti-Black—behind the disco backlash. In that light, setting a ballpark aflame with disco records was the pop-culture equivalent of ridding baseball of a gay outfielder.

When the season began, Glenn Burke was a starting outfielder in the major leagues. By June, he was out of the game and never again held a steady job.

In July '79, the top six albums on the pop charts were all disco. By late September, there were none in the top ten.

CHAPTER 24

DON'T CALL IT A COMEBACK

The San Francisco Bay Area Pro-Am Basketball League game at the Potrero Hill Rec Center had just ended. Little girls chased boys around the court, while other kids tossed yellow tennis balls toward the hoops. Some older kids swept the floor with tall brooms, and Glenn Burke changed out of his red jersey and shorts into his street clothes.

The building was plastered with photos of the most famous person from the neighborhood, the star running back O. J. Simpson, soon to retire after eleven years in the NFL, his final two seasons with the hometown San Francisco 49ers. Simpson had proclaimed that he would never be one of those athletes who had no life after sports. He was prepared for the transition, ready to thrive as an actor and sports broadcaster. But first he planned to jump into an RV with his childhood friend A. C. Cowlings and drive wherever the road might take them. "Who knows where we will end up?" Simpson confessed. "Wherever it is, we'll just say that is where we are headed."[1]

After the basketball game, televised by Channel Six, a reporter wondered what was next for Glenn Burke. What was he going to do now?

Burke hesitated. The truth was, he had no plan. Sports had always been his only passion.

Was he really done with baseball?

"For the time being," he said, and then he was out the door, alone in the San Francisco night.

Burke had quit baseball a month earlier, vanishing for days in the Castro without returning phone calls. Eventually he told people that he had needed a mental break, time to get his head right. He didn't go into details with the press, but years later said his decision had as much to do with empathy for his teammates as for his own mental health. While it hurt him to see his teammates avoiding him, talking behind his back, he also believed his presence had become a burden. "I didn't want them to feel uncomfortable," he said. "Didn't want their families to be uneasy."

But the pull of baseball was strong. He missed the game, missed the paychecks. As fall turned to winter, he talked to A's owner Charlie Finley about a comeback. And then came the news that clinched his

When Billy Martin returned home to the East Bay to manage the Oakland A's in 1980, Glenn Burke was initially excited to play for a fellow Berkeley High School graduate. But Martin had other plans for Burke. (National Baseball Hall of Fame)

decision: the A's had hired a new manager, Billy Martin.

Martin was a hometown boy made good, an Italian kid from the East Bay who'd achieved success as a big league player and manager, most recently as manager of the Yankees. For Burke, Martin sounded like an ideal boss. Martin had grown up dirt-poor in Berkeley, a scrawny kid who earned respect with his fists. Like Burke, he was raised by a single mom in a racially mixed neighborhood, and learned to play baseball and basketball at the park. He never dated any girls at Berkeley High School, not because he was gay, but because he was self-conscious: he had big ears and bad clothes that didn't fit.

On March 4, the news of Burke's return became official. "Happy Burke Returns to A's Camp," read the headline in the *San Francisco Examiner*. "Billy's style will help me," Burke beamed. "I like to fight, too." But things immediately turned sour. Burke's left knee still bothered him from an injury the previous spring, and he underwent surgery to repair cartilage later that week, a surgery from which he was expected to take three months to rehabilitate.

Meanwhile, Martin had his eyes on a young center-field prospect named Rickey Henderson, a highly touted product of Oakland Technical

High School. More important for Burke's future, Martin had already written him off, regardless of his skills or the competition. Martin was a hard drinker who starred in a beer commercial. In spring training, he loved to hold court with scouts, baseball writers, and his coaching staff at a Scottsdale bar called the Pink Pony. One night over cocktails, he told his tablemates there was no way he was going to let Glenn Burke "contaminate" his team. When Burke returned from his knee surgery in only three weeks, Martin didn't compliment him or cite his remarkably speedy recovery as motivation for his other players. Instead, out of earshot of Burke, he "warned" players about the outfielder's return. "That's Glenn Burke," teammate Claudell Washington recalled Martin saying. "And he's a f-----."

Martin's homophobia was so severe that pitcher Mike Norris says it even cost another player a job. When Derek Bryant, an African American outfielder who was around the same age, height, and weight as Burke, appeared in left field in a spring training game, Martin mistook him for Burke and flew into a rage. "Get that fucking sonofabitch out of there!" Martin bellowed, sending another player onto the field to replace him. Bryant had no idea what was happening; he never appeared in another Major League game. "That was the end of Derek's career right there," Norris said. "Yes, sir."

Martin assigned Burke to Oakland's Triple-A affiliate in Ogden, Utah, the same town where Burke had begun his Minor League career when Ogden was home to a Dodger farm team. The Minor League demotion was touted as a way for Burke to continue working back from his knee injury, but Martin had no plans ever to promote him.[2]

Burke understood that Ogden was no place for a gay Black man to try to live anonymously, so he found an apartment thirty miles away in Salt Lake City, a marginally better spot for him. Support came in the form of Black teammate Shooty Babitt, an infielder who had also grown up in Berkeley and knew Burke from his days as a Bushrod Park legend. Babitt said Burke's sexuality was hardly a secret. When Glenn danced around the clubhouse in his red jockstrap, teammates couldn't help but notice—but they dared not say anything, revealing the ballplayers' mindset. "If you did, somebody else would say, 'What are you looking at him for, anyway?'" Babitt recalled. "So we didn't say shit. Plus, Glenn knew nobody was going to say anything to him. He was gorilla-strong, and the worst thing in the world would be to get beat up by a gay dude."

Mack "Shooty" Babitt grew up in Oakland and knew the playground legend of Glenn Burke before they ever became Minor League teammates. (Topps)

Babitt remembered an incident in a road game in Honolulu that cemented his friendship with Burke. Ogden's catcher was a grizzled veteran named Tom Hosley, an African American player who had grown up in South Carolina. Hosley was having a rough day behind the plate, continually bouncing throws down to Babitt at second base. In the dugout between innings, Babitt sniped at Hosley, scolding him for his bad throws. Hosley took offense at the young player's criticism and lunged for Babitt. But before he could get ahold of him, Burke jumped in between his teammates. "If you're going to fight somebody, you're going to fight me," he said to Hosley. "You're not going to jump my homeboy."

Babitt admits Burke's words gave him pause. Was he going to "owe" Glenn something sexual in return for his protection? Should he just take the beating from Hosley? "That's how shallow we were," he recalled decades later. After the game, Burke invited Babitt and Hosley up to his hotel room, intent on teaching both men a lesson, looking out for their best interests as Black men and professional baseball players. "Two African American men should not be fighting like that," he told them. In time, Hosley and Babitt became the best of friends.

Even before the incident in Hawaii, Burke had taken a stand on behalf of all of his teammates when he first reported to Ogden, even though many of those same homophobic teammates "kept their distance from him," Babitt recalled. The team's owner was a deadbeat, always a few weeks late with paychecks, refusing to hand over meal money. The man operated out of a trailer with a Doberman by his side. But Burke acted fearlessly, grabbing a baseball bat and heading into the trailer. Thirty minutes later, he was back in the clubhouse, handing out paychecks. "That's the kind of cat Glenn was," Babitt said. "Never mind what people felt about him, he was a stand-up dude."

While Burke fought Dobermans for paychecks in Utah trailer parks, his influence on Major League Baseball gained steam. The Dodgers had gone all in on the "high five" in 1980, adopting the gesture as the team's trademark form of celebration even after they'd run off the man who created it. The team sold high-five T-shirts, printed high-five promotional posters, and placed messages on their score-board encouraging fans to high-five one another if they answered trivia questions correctly. When a *New York Times* reporter asked him how the craze began and who invented it, Lasorda said he didn't know. A purposeful slight of Burke? Others in the organization credited Baker, but Dusty set the record straight with a nod to the progressive Black neighborhoods in which Burke grew up. "Glenn gets the credit for that one," he said. "He was from the Bay Area, and everything starts there before it gets to the rest of the world. It was a moment of jubilation. If he had slapped me across the head, I would have done the same."

Though the Dodgers had run off the inventor of the high five, they capitalized on his invention in marketing and publicity materials for years to come. (Los Angeles Dodgers)

Burke's contribution to pop culture went largely unacknowledged, but he gained attention in a way he would have preferred not to—from boyfriend Michael Smith. When Ogden played a road game in San Jose, Smith showed up at the game with a busload of gay friends from San Francisco. As Glenn ran off the field after the game, Smith and his entourage noisily ran toward the dugout to greet him. "I tried to be polite, but I had no control over the situation," Burke recalled many years later. "There must have been twenty-five of those

[guys], some of whom behaved poorly, running down to see me. None of them cared what I had just been through with Tom Lasorda or Billy Martin. None of them cared that I was trying to get back up to the Big Leagues." To Burke, the spectacle was just another example of Smith selfishly trying to force Burke to publicly acknowledge his sexuality.

After twenty-five games with the Ogden A's, Burke was hitting just .226; he'd struck out twice as many times as he'd walked; been caught stealing more times than he'd been successful. He drove sixty long miles every day to and from the ballpark, most of his teammates avoided him, Billy Martin hated him. His knee hurt. The Castro beckoned.

He decided to leave baseball again, this time for good.

"I didn't know what I'd do for work," he said. "But I had been able to put some money away from playing ball. I figured I would amount to little more than a freak. But at least this freak, me, Glenn Burke, was finally going to live his own life. I'd never have to look over my shoulder again."

Finally, he realized, it was more important to be himself than to be a baseball player.

CHAPTER 25
TOP DOG

Whenever Glenn Burke walked into the bars on Castro Street in 1980, men stared.

They weren't just impressed that a former Major League baseball player had entered their orbit, weren't just awed by his seventeen-inch biceps out of respect for his athleticism. They were sexually attracted to him. "His physique was unbelievable," one friend recalled. "He had an aura about him. Glenn knew he was the king of the hill."

For Burke, freeing himself from the confines of professional sports and diving into the Castro scene was the most liberating experience of his life. No longer did he have to look over his shoulder to see who might be following him or lie to teammates about where he was going or what he was doing. "I just started living my life," he recalled, "being me."

For Burke, the Castro felt like "a planet for gays," a safe space in a hostile world where people knew one another, looked out for one another—and partied constantly. Thousands of gay men flocked to the neighborhood from all corners of the country, embracing a community where they could explore a new sexual freedom. "It was the shimmering youth and attractiveness that astounded nearly as much as the sheer numbers of men," wrote one observer. "Here were the real beauties of San Francisco, flaunting every childhood taunt of 'sissy' with . . . athletic grace." By day, these young men dressed in three-piece suits and carried briefcases to jobs in downtown skyscrapers. By night, they donned the "official uniform" of the Castro—tight jeans, combat boots, T-shirt or Izod polo, mustache—a look so ubiquitous the men were dubbed Castro Clones and the neighborhood Clone Canyon. They congregated in bathhouses and bars including Toad Hall, Uncle Bert's, the Pendulum, Sutter's Mill, and Twin Peaks Tavern, the first to install clear plate-glass windows, sending a powerful statement that customers were not ashamed to be seen inside a gay establishment. "We had more than ten gay bars in a two-block radius," recalled Mark Brown, who moved to the neighborhood in the 1970s. "The gay life in San Francisco was awesome at that time. Everybody was friendly, you could do anything you wanted." In baseball, Burke never knew whom he could trust, and there was no one he could talk to about his most intimate feelings. In the Castro, everyone was a potential friend or lover.[1]

"To Glenn, the Castro was the diametrical opposite of the emotional prison he had been living in all his life," recalled close friend Cloy Jenkins. "To love and be loved—his soul was starving for that fundamental human drive. [In the Castro] it was safe to finally explore all those little things that are gigantic if they are denied to you. To openly tease and flirt, actually touch, hold hands, even kiss in public without fear of all hell breaking loose around you. The pervasive disguise you'd constructed all around your life now belonged in the dumpster. Glenn's appearance at this particular time and place in the gay movement could not have been more apropos."

Men admired him not only for his physique, but for the respect with which he had always treated them, even when he was playing professional ball. "He was the gay celebrity in town in the late seventies and early eighties," said Jack McGowan, who worked as a manager at the Pendulum bar and as a sportswriter for the *San Francisco Sentinel*. "He treated us like he was one of us. He didn't treat us like we were dirt. That was so thrilling for us in the gay community. He was great for our egos."

At the Pendulum, which had a more racially diverse clientele than most of the other bars, Burke helped many Black men work through a difficult period of transition. Even as they enjoyed life in the Castro, many still dealt with conflicted feelings about coming out, with strained family relationships, with the racism of gay white men, and with their place in the world. "Glenn was a basically a hero, the top dog, but he would take on the friendships of these guys and try to show them how to accept their sexuality," recalled Jenkins, a white gay friend who moved to San Francisco after college at Brigham Young University. "This was still very early in the movement and a lot of gay people were still struggling with that whole identity thing, and they responded to Glenn in such a positive way as a role model, somebody they could really look up to. He had quite a following in the city, particularly in the Black community."

Jenkins said the conversations weren't just one-sided; Burke, too, sought counsel as he adjusted to life out of the closet. "Now that they had dumped him from the Oakland A's, he felt free to find out what it was all about, being gay," he said. "He was still just going through that huge transition of figuring out what to do with his life."

Ever since the long summer days he spent playing strikeout and shooting hoops at Bushrod Park as a kid, Burke's identity had revolved around sports. At his core, he was an athlete before he was anything else. Which made him a hot commodity in San Francisco's gay softball league. It wasn't every day a Major League center fielder signed up to play.

Jack McGowan had founded the Gay Community Softball League in 1973, walking door-to-door to encourage neighborhood bars to sponsor teams. The league held its games on Sundays, and tradition called for the players to gather at the sponsoring bars of the losing teams immediately after the games, then move on to the winners' bars after an hour. Crowds of several hundred people turned out to watch the games, and players on championship teams rode in convertible parades down Market Street.

In the late 1970s, the infrastructure of San Francisco's burgeoning gay community was still forming, with the softball league joined by new professional associations for gay doctors and lawyers, a gay tennis federation, and a gay chamber of commerce, Harvey Milk's credo of "gay for gay" coming to fruition even after his death.

"All of us who were participating in it were doing so with an awareness that what we were doing had never been done before," gay activist Cleve Jones told a reporter from PBS. "So many of the things that
people take for granted now, like gay marching bands and pride parades
and gay churches and gay synagogues and gay newspapers and gay film
festivals—I remember when the first of each of those happened. It was
a political revolution; it was a social revolution; it was a sexual revolution. For those of us who were part of it, there was a wonderful sense
of self-discovery."

The softball league was important not only for the athletic opportunities it provided, but also for the social safety net it created. Former
high school and collegiate baseball players felt a freedom they'd never
experienced on the diamond, and young gay men who never would
have dared to play varsity sports for fear of being outed or harassed by
schoolmates finally had an opportunity to play. But most important,
the league functioned as one big family in ball caps and raglan shirts,
a welcome and poignant development for the many men whose parents had cut them out of their lives after they revealed their sexuality.
The league also helped build bridges with elements of society hostile
to the gay community, including the San Francisco police force. More
than five thousand people would show up to watch the annual game
between the gay league champions and the cops.

McGowan had convinced Burke to join his team, the Pendulum
Pirates, bonding over a shared desire to buck the stereotype that gay
men couldn't excel at sports. "We can be just as athletic as straight
people," McGowan would say. "It doesn't matter what your orientation
is on the field."

Run out of Major League Baseball by homophobic management of the Dodgers and A's, Glenn Burke (back row, middle, with hand raised) found happiness, acceptance, and success with another team far from the spotlight—the Pendulum Pirates of San Francisco's gay softball league. (Cloy Jenkins)

But like many baseball players accustomed to hitting ninety-mile-an-hour fastballs making the transition to slow-pitch softball, Burke struggled at the plate when he first joined the league. More than thirty years later, opposing pitchers remembered striking Burke out on numerous occasions, whiffing him with tantalizing knuckleballs. In the field it was another story; with his speed and reflexes, Burke could handle the entire left side of the infield all by himself. As he adjusted to the slow-pitch style, he started crushing home runs, and his "cult-hero" status in the neighborhood reached new heights. He began playing on five teams in two different leagues, one that allowed straight players and one just for gay men. He never had to pay for a drink—teammates, sponsors, and admirers took care of that. Bars would even slip him cash to play for their teams in certain games or tournaments. He'd party all night on Saturdays, crash in somebody's house, show up smiling and bleary-eyed at the ballfields each Sunday morning, clothes stuffed in a brown paper bag. And then he'd go out and dominate the game. When admiring fans called out his new nickname, Queenie, he'd acknowledge them with a playful limp wrist before sending a softball orbiting into the San Francisco sky.

"I think everybody looked at him as a star, and he was," recalled Mike Gray, a softball teammate. "He was the best gay softball player I've ever seen. He could do whatever he wanted to do."

He was a long way from Dodger Stadium, but Burke enjoyed the camaraderie, the chance to flash his athletic ability in front of hundreds of admirers, and the prestige that came with being the best at something. He took special pride in his teams' winning performances against the police department. "That was satisfying because I got some people to come together and realize how good athletes we were," he said. "We woke them up. That's all I wanted to do."

And yet Gray, Jenkins, and other friends couldn't help but notice an underlying anxiety as Burke began to better understand that his athletic abilities, the skills he'd spent his entire life developing, might gain him applause and a few free drinks—but nothing more. His career as a professional athlete was over, and he had no other real job skills, no work experience, and no résumé. For many former athletes, coaching is the logical career move, and Burke thought about coaching high school basketball, but he'd need a college degree first, and, regardless, there weren't many schools hiring openly gay men. So he found work here and there, such as temporary jobs behind a desk and handyman gigs in the neighborhood. Nothing lasted long.

"He'd start one of those jobs and just go nuts," Jenkins recalled. "It would drive him batty and he'd throw in the towel after a week or two. He couldn't handle being ordinary. He needed to be out there as the top dog. He'd gotten a taste of that celebrity, that money, that life in the major leagues, and he could not get over that. Sitting behind a desk or standing behind a counter in a retail store was not at all what he could handle."

In a self-destructive effort to gain a temporary high and to mask his worries, Burke increasingly turned to cocaine, a habit he had picked up in 1978 with the Dodgers at a time when the drug was becoming commonplace in many big league clubhouses. But coke was an expensive companion, and Burke had quickly burned through the money he'd earned in baseball—he'd bought cars and houses for his family, and paid for his estranged father's funeral. Michael Smith had spent Burke's money renovating the condo they shared, but never put Burke's name on the deed. With an expensive addiction and dim job prospects, Burke's survival became ever more dependent on his charm, charisma, and sociability. Men in the Castro were still impressed with his fame, admired his body, and enjoyed his stories and his sense of humor. They wanted to buy him a drink, they were eager to have him spend the night, and they gladly shared drugs just for the opportunity to be in his company.

Through it all, even as he struggled with anxieties about his future, Burke put on a happy face.

For many former residents of the Castro, a memory immediately comes to mind when they think back to those days.

Out in front of the Star Pharmacy on Castro Street, seated on the hood of a car, smiling ear to ear, it's Glenn Burke, greeting men as they walk by.

To friends and strangers alike, he lifts his right hand and offers a high five.

CHAPTER 26
RUSSIAN RIVER

Cloy Jenkins will never forget the afternoon in 1982 when Glenn Burke came into his life. Jenkins owned the Willows, a rustic resort catering to gay men along the Russian River sixty miles north of San Francisco.

Every other week, Jenkins drove down to the Castro to pass out coupons at the gay bars and restaurants, hoping to entice customers with $5 or $10 discounts. Burke had attempted to introduce himself a few of those times at the Pendulum, but Jenkins brushed him off: he didn't know Burke, he was working, and he had more coupons to distribute before driving back to his guesthouse in Guerneville.

But one time, as Jenkins exited the Pendulum, Burke beat him outside, blocking his path along the sidewalk.

"Hey, man, stop, I want to meet you," Burke said.

Jenkins was "stunned and amused" by Burke's boldness. "Who are you?" he asked.

"I'm Glenn Burke! You don't know who I am, huh? Who are you?"

"I'm Cloy and I own the resort up on the river."

"I want to get to know you."

Jenkins relented.

"Okay," he said. "I have to hand out more coupons, but I can meet you back here later on."

True to his word, Jenkins returned to the Pendulum later that night. Burke shared his life story, and Jenkins found him charming. "I was taken by who he was as a person," Jenkins recalled. "He just seemed very extraordinary in so many ways. It was fascinating." Jenkins told Burke about growing up Mormon in rural Idaho, and a groundbreaking manifesto he had written refuting the church's ultraconservative teachings on homosexuality.[1] "Both of us were amazed at the tremendous difference in our backgrounds and yet our strongly shared views of the gay liberation thing and the very diverse roles each of us were playing in it," Jenkins recalled. "Our connection was very powerful." He invited Burke to come up and see his place on the Russian River sometime. "How about now? I'll come with you tonight!" Burke replied, much to Jenkins's surprise.

All along the ninety-minute drive to the river and over the next several weeks, as he returned to the river to spend time with Jenkins, Burke opened up about his greatest fears and the difficulty of pulling his life together after baseball. "He had gotten used to the big bucks, and now he was back to trying to find an ordinary job paying $5 or $10 an hour,"

Cloy Jenkins will never forget the first time Glenn Burke accompanied him to the Willows. "He exuded happiness. Joy? It was one of the central schematics of how Glenn was wired emotionally. I could sense this big powerful man finally relaxing, laughing, and joking. It was like watching a lost puppy finding a home." (Cloy Jenkins)

Jenkins recalled. "He was out of money, he had no income. He hadn't broken into anything that was lucrative at all, and he couldn't see that on the horizon other than getting back into sports. But he couldn't really see that happening, either. So he was floundering. On the one hand, in the Castro he was held up to be this hero, this big celebrity. But on the other hand, he was forbidden [to play Major League Baseball]. It was a real dilemma for him."

Jenkins's country inn sat on five wooded acres overlooking the Russian River near the town of Guerneville, a rural lumber community that had become fashionable with gay vacationers seeking an escape from the city in the late 1970s. "At The Willows you'll find a relaxed, intimate and friendly atmosphere where you can get away from it all," Jenkins's advertisements promised.

Burke enjoyed relaxing in the hot tub and on the sundeck at the

Willows and partying at a gay bar on Guerneville's Main Street called Rainbow Cattle Company. The popularity of the Willows and other hotels, cabins, and bars catering to gay men from San Francisco had created tensions in the town of ten thousand. Some local business owners welcomed the influx of new customers and rising property values, while other locals violently resisted their presence—roughing up gay men on the street outside Rainbow Cattle Company and setting fire to a stretch of gay businesses on the block.

With its sloping hills, lazy river, tall trees, large party deck, hot tub, and comfortable rooms, the Willows resort appealed to gay customers seeking refuge from the busy streets of San Francisco. (Cloy Jenkins)

Burke's arrival, however, had a transformative effect on the community. After a local newspaper ran a story about Burke's presence in Guerneville, some of the regulars at Pat's Bar, an establishment that catered to the same locals who had assaulted gay men in the past, expressed an interest in meeting him. These guys were sports fans, and the idea that a former major leaguer was partying just down the block meant more to them than the fact Glenn was gay. For the first time, the local regulars from Pat's entered Rainbow Cattle Company.

"Glenn came back to the Willows and said he met so-and-so from Pat's Bar," Jenkins recalled. "He said they had invited him to come to

Pat's. I told him, 'Don't do that. Don't go in there, you're asking for trouble.'"

Glenn went anyway, but soon after he entered the bar, somebody purposely stepped on his foot. Glenn flinched, but resisted striking back. His new buddy, the guy who had invited him to Pat's, saw what had happened. "And some guys from Pat's took the redneck that stepped on Glenn's foot outside the bar and beat the shit out of him," Jenkins said. "Then they came back in the bar and said, 'Don't anybody mess with this guy.' It was an interesting turn of events."

Glenn's new friends at Pat's played on a softball team, and they challenged Glenn to bring his Pendulum team up to Guerneville for a game. Jenkins hosted the gay players from San Francisco at the Willows for a weekend of partying, and then came time for the game at the ballfield at Berry's Saw Mill. "Pendulum beat the shit out of Pat's, and Glenn knocked a number of home runs," Jenkins recalled. "They just skunked them."

And then the most unexpected thing happened. Players from both teams drove back into town and mingled together at both bars, bonding over a shared love of sports. Jenkins said there was no doubt that Burke's magnetic personality had changed attitudes. "Glenn was very charismatic without knowing he was," he said. "He had an ability to attract both straights and gays. The guys at Pat's Bar were as taken with him as anyone in the gay world."

Burke's influence on the town had a lasting effect. Where previously the Pat's Bar crew acted in "mean and underhanded" ways toward gays in the community, the environment began to change after the summer of '82, Jenkins said. "The fact that Glenn came to town helped move things along. It was much more acceptable to be openly gay, even in that little town. Usually when you grow up in a small town, you have to move to the big city or you're going to get so much crap from your family, your church, your school. But all of a sudden, local gays started to come out of the closet. And straight guys opened up to the idea that maybe gays aren't that bad after all."[2]

CHAPTER 27
GOT TO LET IT SHOW

Ever since the 1977 World Series, Glenn Burke's on-again, off-again lover Michael Smith had wanted to make Burke's sexuality public to shock the sports world into acknowledging the gay men in its midst. Burke had resisted, believing that coming out would doom his career.

But now that he was out of pro sports, struggling to make money while simultaneously gaining social acceptance and admiration from gays and straights alike, he gave Smith's idea a second thought. Maybe coming forward would open doors. But, even if not, he had nothing to lose.

Burke had reason to feel a sense of rising confidence in the summer of '82. In addition to breaking down barriers in Guerneville, he had led the Pendulum Pirates to a championship in the gay softball World Series and had earned gold medals in both basketball and softball at the first-ever Gay Games, an Olympic-style festival that attracted more than 1,300 gay athletes from around the world for a week of friendly competition in San Francisco.

As had always been the case, Smith had his own reasons for pushing Burke to publicly acknowledge his sexuality. On top of the political shock value the story was sure to create, Smith also believed that by helping Burke regain a moment in the national spotlight, he'd earn back his affections. When Burke had begun exerting greater independence and spending less time with him, Smith had tried various ways to capture Burke's attention, at one point dating so many other Black men in the Castro it became clear to everyone he was just trying to make Burke jealous. There was also financial motivation—Smith had pitched the idea of a story on Burke to *Inside Sports*, a national monthly magazine that would pay handsomely for such a bombshell.[1]

Burke decided to go along with Smith's plan. Surely, the story would do some good, either creating an opportunity for a second chance with a team accepting of his sexuality, or providing inspiration for other gay athletes by sending a powerful message that they were not alone.

Smith began working on the article, calling some of Burke's former teammates to fill in the gaps of a story he knew fairly well already. Dusty Baker received a call from Smith asking to talk about Burke. "I said, 'What about him?'" Baker recalled. "He said, 'He's coming out of the closet.' I said, 'What closet? I don't know what you're talking about.'" Baker knew Burke's secret but played coy, unwilling to betray Glenn's confidence. He asked for Burke's phone number and gave his old teammate a call.

Burke confirmed the story. "I'm coming out of the closet, homeboy. You can tell them anything you want. I'm trying to get paid."

With the article set to appear in the October issue of *Inside Sports*, which would hit newsstands in late September, the magazine's editors set out to gain advance publicity. Relaxing with Jenkins at the Willows one day, Burke received a phone call from Bryant Gumbel, the thirty-three-year-old African American former sportscaster in his first year hosting NBC's *The Today Show*, a popular program millions of Americans watched as they readied for work each morning.[2]

Gumbel, who knew Burke from his days as a reporter in Los Angeles, invited Glenn to New York to tell his story in a live interview. Jenkins listened as Burke told Gumbel he hoped the exposure might help him get back into baseball. Would a team take a chance on him as an openly gay player, Burke wondered aloud, or would they pretend he simply didn't exist? As they wrapped up their phone conversation, Burke told Gumbel he'd come to New York and that Jenkins would be coming with him, Cloy's first trip to the Big Apple.

Glenn Burke on the set of *The Today Show* in New York City, September 13, 1982. Speaking with Bryant Gumbel, the first-year host of the popular show, Burke revealed his sexuality to a national television audience. He hoped his honesty might earn him another shot in the major leagues. (AP Photo/ David Bookstaver)

When Jenkins and Burke arrived at NBC Studios together days later, some of the NBC staffers assumed Jenkins was the ballplayer's agent.

Dressed casually in a short-sleeve Lacoste shirt with thin purple-and-white stripes, Burke sat across from Gumbel in a gray wool suit and yellow tie. The conversation was straightforward and comfortable, with Burke appearing increasingly at ease as the interview unfolded.

Gumbel looked into the camera and spoke calmly as he introduced a guest who was about to become the first Major League baseball player ever to come out as gay.

"It is not uncommon these days for someone who is in the public eye to come forth and admit that he or she is a homosexual. But it is fairly uncommon when that person is a Major League baseball player. I'd like you to meet Glenn Burke right now. Glenn Burke is now retired from baseball, but was a member of the Los Angeles Dodgers and Oakland A's. Appeared in the World Series in 1977. What did you go, one-for-five?"

"One-for-five," Burke confirmed.

"In the current issue of *Inside Sports*, the one just hitting newsstands today, his story is told in 'The Double Life of a Gay Dodger.' Glenn, why did you decide to tell the story?"

The camera panned to Burke, his broad chest and biceps giving him the look of an athlete in top form.

"Well, it came to the point where I was uncomfortable. I thought the world should know how I felt. So, when I got fed up with the situation, I thought I would tell people about it."

"How long had you been keeping it all to yourself?"

"Hmm. Maybe around four or five years?"

"When you were in the major leagues . . ."

"Uh, yes."

"Why is it particularly difficult to be gay and be in the major leagues? Why is that arena so uncompromising?"

"It's not real difficult. It's just the problem that the people that you like and live with and work with might not understand, you know, the problem of being gay and a professional baseball player."

"Did you ever give them a chance to understand?"

"No, I was to myself pretty much of the time. So it really didn't matter."

"How and when did people in baseball come to learn that you were gay?"

"I guess from hearsay, because I hadn't said a thing. I was just working and playing ball and living a regular life, I thought."

"Was it difficult for you to hide? I know in the article the guys always wanted you to go out drinking with them and you had your own places you wanted to go to, and guys were always wondering why you weren't with somebody they had tried to set you up with . . ."

"I was sort of more considerate of them instead of myself. I didn't want to embarrass nobody or make them ill at ease. So I thought if I just kept to myself for a while, until I was ready to tell them, that they might understand, if they got to like me first instead of what I'd done, you know, sexually, or something like that."

"There had to be, and there has to be, other major leaguers who are gay. Why didn't you try to talk to anybody about your problem?"

"Well, it was kind of hard because you don't know who to talk to. And if you confront somebody, they might not want to talk about it. And at that time, I felt like it wasn't necessary. I was trying to accomplish something, and I didn't really have time to talk about my sexual life, because I think it should be private."

"Did the officials on the ball clubs you were with also think it should be private?"

"Um. I'm not really sure."

"Any of them ever give you a bad time about it?"

"No, I'm a little bit too big for that, for somebody to give me a bad time."

Burke smiled at his own comment, and Gumbel laughed.

"You said that, but you even make note in your article that you even had a tough problem in your own mind balancing out this big macho Glenn Burke with your idea of what a gay person should have been, that was a sissy."

"Yeah, so like stereotyping myself."

"So you were anxious to use your body to show them you weren't what they thought?"

"That's right. I'm just human like everybody else. And I'm a man. If I'm gay, I'm still a man. And that's the way I carry myself."

"Did the Dodgers trade you because you were gay?"

"I'm not quite sure. I'm still wondering about that, but in due time I guess it will all come out in the end."

"You told a story in the article that a Dodger official in fact called you in and offered you money if you'd get married, in a roundabout way. Is that right?"

"Well, in a roundabout way he said, 'Usually when the ballplayers make the major leagues, if they're married, they're more responsible and we usually give them a little bit of money to have a good honeymoon,' or something like that. But I told him out front, 'I don't think I'll be getting married for a while.' So they dropped the subject after that."

"Were you traded from the Dodgers to the A's because you were gay?"

"Uh, I'm not sure."

"What do you think?"

Burke looked offstage and smiled.

"Yeah."

"How about your teammates? I knew you when you were in LA. You were among the most popular guys on the ball club. You were a little bit rowdy. You had a lot of fun."

Burke smiled again.

"I was from Oakland!"

"Yeah, you were from Oakland. You were probably the loudest guy on the club, but you were good people. And everybody said that. Did their attitudes change after they found out?"

"I don't think so. There were a few people who made some snide remarks on the side. Basically the good people, they treated me real well. Which was Davey Lopes, Dusty Baker. Steve Garvey, Don Sutton. Lee Lacy, Tommy John. They respected me and I think they still do."

"You're thirty years old, baseball is behind you now. What are you doing?"

"I'm working towards another lifestyle I guess. Eventually I want to be a coach, if it's possible. I really have to go back to school and get my education."

"Do you think that's even possible with people knowing?"

"Anything is possible."

Gumbel asked about a blue-and-orange baseball cap Burke had brought with him on set.

"What's the hat for?"

"This is from the softball team I played for during this summer, which we won the Gay World Series, and they wanted me to give you this hat. That's from San Francisco, the Pendulum."

Gumbel leaned over as Burke handed him the cap.

"Thank you very much. It's a long way from the Los Angeles Dodgers in more ways than one."

"But I'm having more fun now."

With the interview complete, Jenkins wanted to explore Manhattan, but Burke said he preferred to go back to their room and watch TV. Later that night, Burke took Jenkins to a party at a high-rise condominium where Jenkins felt out of place. Men in black leather jackets walked around carrying guns while others snorted lines of cocaine. "I could tell this was another world that Glenn moved in, and he was comfortable with," Jenkins recalled.[3] Next they moved on to a gay bar. When Jenkins said he was going downstairs to the bathroom, Burke pulled him aside. "You can't go down there yourself," he warned. "It's too dangerous. You might not come back alive." For Jenkins, his first trip to New York was not nearly as enjoyable as he had imagined. "It was kind of a strange experience for me," he said. "For a country boy from Idaho, that world of guns and cocaine in New York was quite different."

For Burke, the publicity tour continued. Joined by reporter Randy Harvey from the *Los Angeles Times*, he rode an Amtrak train from New York to Philadelphia, where the plan called for him to attend a Phillies game at Veterans Stadium, the venue where he had celebrated the Dodgers' NLCS victory in 1977.

After arriving in Philadelphia, Burke and Harvey sat down to eat at a nice restaurant. Burke ordered a salad with Thousand Island dressing. "I'd like to go to a thousand islands with you," the waitress replied. Burke was visibly embarrassed by her comment, and as the waitress walked away, he turned to Harvey. "Not everyone," he said, "should try to be a comedian."

Harvey asked Burke a simple question. Why tell his story now?

"It's not an easy subject to talk about," Burke admitted. "But I thought it might help some other people. I can be a plus for gay people by going out and talking about it and being a good representative. I might help where others can't. People admire and look up to athletes. Here I am, an athlete. This might be my mission on Earth as far as God is concerned. I'm real religious in certain ways. I know I'm here for a reason."

Later that evening, Harvey accompanied Burke to the Phillies' game against the St. Louis Cardinals. Burke had been given a field pass so he could meet reporters prior to the game. As he stood on the turf, Phillies infielder Iván DeJesús, a former minor league teammate, spotted him. "What are you doing here?" he called. "Are you with the press now?"

"*Inside Sports* brought me here for an interview," Burke replied. DeJesús looked confused, but Burke didn't elaborate.

As the game started, Phillies fans began razzing Cardinal right

Standing by the field at Philadelphia's Veterans Stadium, Burke chats with former Minor League teammate Iván DeJesús. Burke traveled to Philadelphia to speak to sports writers and publicize the *Inside Sports* article that detailed his experience as a gay Dodger. (Cloy Jenkins)

fielder George Hendrick. "Hendrick!" one man yelled. "You're a queer!"

Burke turned to Harvey and laughed. "They say that to everybody, huh? How about that? I always thought it was just me."

Meanwhile, the October issue of *Inside Sports* landed in subscribers' mailboxes around the country. On the cover, beneath an action shot of Pittsburgh Steelers linebacker Jack Lambert, there was the tantalizing headline "The Dodger Who Was Gay," and on page 57, Smith's article: "The Double Life of a Gay Dodger." In New Jersey, Erik Sherman, now sixteen years old, read the story and recalled asking for Burke's autograph at Yankee Stadium. As a kid who lived for baseball, he agonized over how devastating it must have been for Burke to be "blackballed from a sport he loved." In California, when Bobby Glasser read the article, the fight in the Oakland Coliseum parking lot made a made more sense. In Des Moines, Iowa, editors at the *Register* praised Burke's courage. "Maybe a great deal of good could come from confessions by our heroes," they wrote. "Maybe if we got used to the idea of a homosexual hitting a major league home run, we'd be more willing to accept him in less heroic roles as well. Or maybe not. The public has never shown any great capacity for understanding before, so there's really no reason for any gay player to trust us now."

When football player Dave Kopay had come out of the closet in Lynn Rosellini's *Washington Star* series seven years earlier, the reaction was harsh, even within his own family. His mother shunned him, his father threatened to kill him, and his brother blamed Kopay's admission for costing him a head coaching job in college football. Nobody would hire Kopay, either, and a columnist in Milwaukee wrote that she wanted to tear up the autograph Kopay had once given her son. Letters to the *Star* were overwhelmingly negative. Lefty Driesell, the basketball coach at the University of Maryland, wrote Rosellini's editor to complain. "What about the kids who read this stuff? They're easily influenced by what they read. What are they supposed to think? That to get publicity playing sports you have to be queer?"

By contrast, the reaction to Burke's story was one of deafening silence. The big splash he had anticipated never materialized. No Major League teams contacted him, and he made no money off the article—Smith kept it all. "I think everyone just pretended not to hear me," he said. "It just wasn't a story they were ready to hear."

Burke was likely right about that. But his story was also overshadowed by other news originating in gay America.

In San Francisco, the carefree days in the Castro were over.

Young gay men were dying from a new disease, and no one knew why.

CHAPTER 28

GROUND ZERO FOR THE PLAGUE

The man's high fever and weight loss were alarming, but for Michael Gottlieb, an assistant professor of medicine at the UCLA Medical Center, his thirty-one-year-old patient's other symptoms were absolutely baffling: severe yeast infections in his mouth and throat, a lethal form of pneumonia, and an absence of the white blood cells that trigger the body's immune system. Gottlieb had never seen this combination of conditions before, let alone in a man so young. He figured it was a one-of-a-kind case.

But then another young man checked into the hospital with similar symptoms. Then another. Curiously, all three men were gay.

Gottlieb alerted other doctors, describing the unusual cases in a June 1981 publication of the Centers for Disease Control. Immediately, physicians in New York and San Francisco responded to his report—they'd seen the pneumonia strain, too, as well as highly unusual occurrences of Kaposi's sarcoma, a rare skin cancer. Within days, the Associated Press picked up on the story, and for the first time, Americans learned that gay men were dying of a mysterious illness.

For Glenn Burke and the other gay men who had transformed the Castro in the 1970s, their slice of heaven on earth was about to descend into an unimaginable hellscape of pain and suffering. The young men with the uncommon symptoms were dying from a disease that would come to be known as AIDS.

Researchers would later discover that AIDS (acquired immuno-deficiency syndrome) is a sexually transmitted infection caused by the human immunodeficiency virus (HIV), a virus that destroys the white blood cells that protect the body from disease. For a person to become infected with HIV, infected blood, semen, or vaginal secretions must enter their body, most often through sex without condoms or through intravenous drug use with a contaminated needle. Someone can have an HIV infection for several years, living symptom-free, before developing AIDS. When HIV/AIDS first appeared in the United States, it mainly affected men who had sex with men. With the causes of AIDS still unknown, gay men were initially at particular risk for a number of reasons: with no potential for pregnancy, they often had sex without condoms; the disease spreads more easily through anal than vaginal sex; many gay men had more than one sexual partner, increasing their potential exposure.

In 1981, this understanding of AIDS was still years away; all anyone knew for sure was that an ever-increasing number of gay men were sick and dying. In October of that year, twenty-nine-year-old Bobbi Campbell placed a poster on a window at the Star Pharmacy, the same spot on Castro Street where Glenn Burke frequently high-fived his neighbors. Campbell's poster featured photos of the purple lesions on his feet, the telltale sign of Kaposi's sarcoma. He encouraged anyone with similar symptoms to immediately see a doctor. On August 5, 1982, the *Bay Area Reporter*, a San Francisco gay newspaper, ran a cover story on AIDS (which it called "AID"), sharing what was known about risks of transmission, symptoms, and treatments. "Behind the mystery of the unaccountable appearance of KS [Kaposi's sarcoma], another of equal perplexity has surfaced," the paper warned. "The latest acronym is AID, which stands for an immune system gone haywire. . . . [AID] is now recognized as a totally new syndrome with no precedent in history." While the article illustrated a rising consciousness of the disease, some of the information it contained was wildly inaccurate, including suggestions that marijuana use could be a cause and that the disease might not be contagious.

Around the same time, an overflow crowd gathered at the city's Metropolitan Community Church for a public forum on the outbreak of Kaposi's sarcoma. With HIV yet to be discovered, a dermatologist told the men who crowded the church that they needed to focus on maintaining a healthy immune system. He recommended getting plenty of sleep and eating a well-balanced diet, as well as limiting recreational drug use. None of this advice was helpful in preventing the spread of AIDS.

For gay men, the disease carried a social and political significance beyond the physical suffering. Ever since the Stonewall uprising of 1969, gay men had made great strides toward self- and societal acceptance, resisting the oppressive attitudes of those who claimed that gay people were perverted and depraved. Now, it appeared, a medical stigma had replaced the old social one: with the arrival of AIDS, gay people could once again be portrayed as sick and untouchable, carriers of a "gay plague," and "worthy" of persecution. "The epidemic is straining relationships between heterosexuals and homosexuals," wrote the *Boston Globe* in 1983, "reviving dormant prejudices and appearing to justify existing ones."

By 1984, *Time* magazine labeled San Francisco "Ground Zero for the Plague," and visitors to the Castro described the neighborhood as a surreal ghost town where the sidewalks were crowded with young, zombie-like men walking with canes. The physical appearance of the

AIDS victim was unmistakable: thin, pale, and delicate, eyes hollow and expressionless. Bathhouses went out of business; crowds thinned at bars. Young men made plans for their own funerals; a travel agency specialized in "last trips" for the dying.

At San Francisco General Hospital, AIDS patients filled an entire ward, 5B. These men spent their final weeks living in excruciating pain, with meningitis inflaming tissues around their brains and cancer spreading throughout their bodies. Suffering from seizures, dementia, and coughing fits, skin drawn tightly against bone, they lay in pools of their own urine and stool as they lost control of their bowels and bladders, constant diarrhea causing them to lose ten quarts of fluids each day.

The pain was compounded by the fact that many of these men were completely alone in the world. They'd either left their families to live free in San Francisco, or had been disowned by disapproving parents and siblings. Either way, they experienced the terror of a painful death all by themselves.

For the social workers and doctors who interacted with AIDS patients every day, the psychological toll was devastating. One doctor told a journalist he was living through the most depressing, frustrating, and demoralizing experience of his career, unable to offer his AIDS patients a sliver of hope. "The helplessness that I feel in dealing with it is overwhelming," he said. "We're dealing with productive, otherwise healthy, happy, young patients. To see them dying—lawyers, doctors, teachers, bankers, contributors to society—to watch this is devastating. I have never before seen young people die like this."[1]

While one might expect that with thousands of people suffering from a mysterious, deadly, and incurable new disease, government action would be swift and public reaction nothing but compassionate, that wasn't the case. Many Americans felt little sympathy for the sick and dying if the sick and dying happened to be gay. Valuable time and countless lives were lost due to both cruelty and apathy.

In 1982, President Ronald Reagan vetoed legislation that would have earmarked $500,000 for AIDS research. He refused to even utter the word *AIDS* in public until 1985, and that was only in response to a reporter's question. When a journalist asked Reagan's press secretary Larry Speakes to comment on the president's lack of interest, Speakes mocked the newsman, insinuating he must have AIDS himself for even caring to ask about the epidemic. Meanwhile, many of the leaders of the Christian-conservative movement that fueled Reagan's 1980 victory outrageously called the pain and suffering of gay AIDS victims God's punishment for their sexuality.

"If we violate certain moral and physical laws," said Cal Thomas, vice president of communications for a Christian, right-wing political organization called the Moral Majority, "we reap what we sow." Newspaper columnist Pat Buchanan mocked gay men suffering from AIDS. "The poor homosexuals—they have declared war upon nature and now nature is exacting an awful retribution." Moral Majority vice president Ronald Goodwin complained that insufficient money was being spent—not to cure the disease but to prevent straight men and women from catching it. "I'm upset that the government is not spending more money to protect the general public from the gay plague," he said. "What I see is a commitment to spend our tax dollars on research to allow these diseased homosexuals to go back to their perverted practices without any standards of accountability."

Goodwin's comments played into the fears of Americans of all political persuasions. With so little known about the causes of AIDS, even people in no danger of contracting the disease took extraordinary steps to avoid it—often dehumanizing friends and family in the process.

In Denver, a woman contacted health authorities asking if she should fumigate an apartment she had just bought from a gay man. In Houston, an increasing number of people refused to donate blood, concerned they might get AIDS from even the single-use needles used at the blood bank. When a New York man with AIDS boarded a plane so he could die in his hometown of Phoenix, the pilot attempted to throw him off the flight. When the man checked into a Phoenix hospital, nurses refused to touch or bathe him. When he died, hospital staff wrapped the man in sheets and placed him in a plastic bag. At the funeral home, staff poured embalming fluid on the sheets, closed the plastic bag, and threw the body bag in a casket. In San Francisco, some landlords evicted gay tenants who weren't even sick, and the police chief issued gloves and masks to officers fearful of working in the Castro. When one healthy gay man called his mother to say he was coming home to visit, she phoned the health department to ask if it was safe to allow him in her home.

A gay man in San Francisco scheduled a doctor appointment, worried about the purple bumps on his tongue. Were they evidence of Kaposi's sarcoma? The doctor had to show his patient a medical textbook to convince him the bumps were merely taste buds. When a clubhouse attendant set out a catered pregame meal for the Oakland A's on one road trip, several players refused to eat the food—simply because the attendant "looked" like he might be gay.

While some people in no danger of contracting AIDS lived in fear of implausible scenarios, for Glenn Burke, the impact of AIDS was real and immediate. In 1982, the same year he revealed his sexuality on *The Today Show* and in *Inside Sports*, he lost a friend to the disease, a softball teammate named Bob Thomas. Thomas had complained of a persistent cold, then constant stomachaches and diarrhea. He checked himself into a hospital and died just days later. Burke's friend Wes Jackson, who had been his guest at the '77 World Series, also contracted AIDS. Jackson's lover, Bob Linquist, struggled to pay his medical bills, selling his home and most valuable possessions to raise cash, but it still wasn't enough. Soon after Jackson died, a despondent and broke Linquist died by suicide. When Burke spent time with Cloy Jenkins at the Willows, the conversation inevitably turned to the new "gay cancer"—questions about how it spread, who was in danger, how to avoid it, and which friends already had it. The dying wish of one of Jenkins's employees had been to have his ashes spread in the Russian River; Jenkins wondered if even a dead man's remains could spread the disease. Jenkins had a guest whose check bounced for insufficient funds. When he tried to contact the man, he received no response. Finally, Jenkins ventured into the city to collect the money he was owed. When the man answered Jenkins's knock at the door, he was covered with purple lesions. "Okay," Jenkins said. "Never mind. Never mind."

For Burke, Jenkins, and their Castro neighbors, life had devolved into a web of perpetual misfortune, hundreds and then thousands of personal tragedies playing out on the streets, in bedrooms, and in hospital wards of San Francisco. Their address books became page after page of scratched-out names and numbers; and it wasn't just friends who disappeared, but the familiar faces of the city—mailmen, bus drivers, and store clerks.

Life had fallen apart so quickly for Chuck Morris, a forty-year-old former newspaper editor, that he hadn't even realized he'd hit rock bottom until the day he stood alone at the corner of 18th and Castro, taking stock of his surroundings. In his right hand, he clutched a small plastic bag containing all of his belongings. Just a year earlier, he'd considered himself a successful man, a business owner with numerous friends living in a thriving city. Now, suffering from the effects of AIDS, he'd endured three brain seizures and was unable to hold a job. His old friends shunned him, using his hospital stays as opportunities to evict him from shared apartments. One roommate told Morris he'd kill him if he tried to move back in. And now Morris stood in the middle of the Castro, homeless and broke, uncertain where he'd spend the night. The horrifying reality overcame him—his world had crumbled, and he knew things would only get worse.

Burke didn't have AIDS, at least not yet, but his world was crumbling, too. His drug addiction was intensifying, friends were dying, and in 1983, he received the shocking news that his sister Elona, a former track star and the mother of five children, had been stabbed to death during a robbery. Glenn was crushed to lose Elona, devastated that his nieces and nephews would grow up without their mother. Very little, it seemed, was going right in his life. "Here he had all this talent and charisma, this wonderful personality, and all these horrible things were going on," Jenkins said. "Things were not working out. It was heartbreaking to see him come to the realization that he was never going to get that call [from another Major League team]. He had beaten his brains out to be the very best, and it was not going well. The stark contrast was tragically a rude and haunting reality to someone otherwise absolutely hellbent on having fun."

And, it turned out, more tragedy was just around the corner. The best days of Glenn Burke's life were behind him.

CHAPTER 29
THE CRUSHING BLOW

On the northeastern edge of the Castro District, there's an intersection so wide a baseball field could fit inside. Noe Street, running north-south, and 16th Street, crossing from west to east, are dissected diagonally by Market Street, a four-lane behemoth with a light-rail track running down its center. All told, it's a massive patch of concrete, with cars, trains, and pedestrians crossing in six directions.

One night in 1987, as Glenn Burke walked across this intersection, a teenage girl driving her mother's car ran a red light as she made a sharp right turn, slamming into Burke and sending him flying through the air more than seventy feet down the road.

Glenn remained conscious as horrified onlookers called for an ambulance, but his legs burned in excruciating pain, broken in three places. By the time his mother and sisters arrived to see him at the hospital, doctors had already placed a temporary rod in one leg to help stabilize it; he'd need to return for more surgery later. Lutha wasn't surprised Glenn had been hit—it seemed like people were always getting struck by cars in the city—but her sister Joyce was taken aback by an inscription she saw on Glenn's hospital chart. She'd discuss it with her family later.

For Burke, the accident was a defining moment, more profound than being driven out of baseball. His greatest joys had come on the fields of play, his self-esteem directly linked to his identity as an athlete. As she comforted Glenn in his hospital bed, Lutha sensed that her brother's spirit was broken as badly as his legs. "He had to come to terms with the fact that he wouldn't be able to play sports the way he used to," she recalled. "That was the crushing blow. Glenn had lived and breathed sports ever since he was a kid. Even after he wasn't playing professional ball, the love of the game was still within him." But as he lay in the hospital, Burke was overcome by anxiety. "Other than sports," he said, "I really didn't have another life. I had no other serious career aspirations. Being an athlete was my life." And now that life was over.[1]

Before the accident, Glenn had taken odd jobs here and there, working briefly as a chauffeur, as a handyman at the Willows, and as a doorman. But after the accident, he spent even less time looking for work and more time looking for drugs. He and Jenkins began to drift apart. "He kept getting involved with guys I didn't think were good for him," Jenkins recalled. "My cautions and advice were no longer appreciated. He seemed determined to just continue 'the party.'" In the months following the accident, with his legs still in pain, his drug dependency intensified, progressing from occasionally snorting lines of cocaine to constantly smoking crack. A cheaper, highly addictive form of cocaine that began appearing on the streets of major American cities in the early 1980s, crack gave Burke and other users brief feelings of euphoria followed by long periods of intense depression and paranoia, a vicious and all-consuming cycle of ever-shorter highs and deeper lows.[2]

By 1988, as both of his former teams, the Dodgers and the A's, advanced to the World Series without him and Jenkins sold the Willows and moved to Hawaii, Glenn was addicted to crack, out of work, and limping on broken legs. Surrounded by men dying of AIDS in the Castro, including his former lover Michael Smith, who passed away that year, Burke was hardly alone in his misery. But his predicament came with a special dose of betrayal, revealing the shallow depths of the celebrity worship that had once sustained him. The bars that never charged him for a drink while he was at the top of his game wouldn't dare give him a free one now that he had no money. The establishments that threw him parties when he played for the Dodgers now turned him away, embarrassed by his condition. The people who had gladly shared a joint with him when it was cool to be in his presence were now offended by his addiction. The men who slapped his open palm when he high-fived them on Castro Street walked right past that hand when it sought loose change. "You're a hero one day," Burke reflected years later, "and the next day you ain't crap."

The fact that Glenn was Black and most of the men in the neighborhood were white fed the dynamic. The Castro, for all its promises of equality and acceptance, was no safe haven from racism. The neighborhood had its very roots in gentrification. When gay white men began buying the Victorian homes there in the 1970s and painting them in candy colors, the people they displaced were typically Black and Latinx. While many of these newcomers claimed that they were sensitive to racism because of the discrimination they had encountered as gay men, their empathy typically didn't amount to much.

Bouncers asked Black men for IDs but didn't demand the same of white customers; Black men might wait for lengthy periods of time to get a bartender's attention while a line of white men were served right away; some white men felt no shame in declaring they'd "never date a Black man," while others fetishized African Americans, the darker and bigger their date the better. Burke and other gay Black men faced a daunting challenge in their quest for liberation—integrating two marginalized identities in a society hostile to both.[3]

And while Burke's celebrity status had once granted him a special waiver of social acceptance from the white men of the Castro, he discovered those relationships were built on a paper-thin foundation. "With all athletes and celebrities," said Vincent Fuqua, a gay Black softball player in the city, "there comes a time when it's 'What have you done for me lately? Now that you're having a hard time, we don't want anything to do with you.' And that's magnified when you're Black. We're something when we're able to benefit [white people], but the minute we can't benefit them, we're nothing. Glenn was a star, but the minute he had a hard time, they forgot who he was."

Burke had no job, no car, no phone, and no permanent home. Occasionally he'd stay with family in Oakland, but more often he bounced from couch to couch in San Francisco. He wandered the Castro shirtless, sometimes wearing jean overalls, other times nothing but basketball shoes and shorts. One night, his childhood friend Vincent Trahan was driving down Van Ness Avenue with his wife just after midnight. Trahan stopped at a red light and watched a group of people crossing the street in a light rain. A thin, disheveled man walked by with a limp. "Hey," Trahan called to his wife, "that's Glenn!" "That guy?" she replied. "You know him? No way. He looks homeless." Trahan, who is African American, leaned out his window. "Hey, Mr. Monkey!" he shouted, a term of endearment from their childhood days. Burke peered through the rain into Trahan's car, and tears came to his eyes. "Vince!" He approached the car, Trahan got out, and the men hugged.

Burke's free fall was evident even to those who hadn't seen him. One night, Jerry Pritikin, an eccentric local photographer and softball player, walked into a pawn shop near the historic Curran Theatre on Geary Street to peruse the store's jewelry selection. Pritikin scanned a row of rings when one caught his eye—Burke's runner-up ring from the 1977 World Series. "It was shocking to see it there," Pritikin recalled. "And it was a telltale sign that he had gotten heavily into drugs."

Even while experiencing homelessness and living in pain, Glenn Burke continued to find moments of joy on the softball field. Here, wearing an Oakland A's cap, he offers a high-five to teammates at home plate during a game in San Francisco. (Nancy Andrews)

How had things turned out so badly for a man who had once brought so much joy to his world?

Who is to blame?

While it's too simplistic to say Burke brought on his own troubles by making bad choices, it's also untrue to say he was merely a victim of circumstances, an unwilling participant in his own demise. Rather, he suffered from a toxic mixture of adverse experiences large and small, some well beyond his control, some of his own making. In baseball terms, while he may have swung at some bad pitches, he often came to the plate with two strikes already against him.

He was Black and gay in a racist and homophobic society, growing up poor without the privilege of a family safety net. He came of age in the wrong places at the wrong time, with the introduction of cocaine in baseball, AIDS in the Castro, and crack in the inner city just at the moments he entered those spaces. He was struck by uncommon personal tragedy, his sister murdered, his legs crushed in a freak accident that shattered his identity as an athlete. His father abused his mother, left his family, and was likely an alcoholic. The athletic feats of his adolescence propelled him to the major leagues but also encouraged misplaced priorities as he channeled all his energies toward sports and away from school, while enablers overlooked his academic deficiencies. As soon as he arrived at the top of his chosen profession as one of the best baseball players in the world, homophobic executives pushed him out, the road to homelessness initially paved by employment discrimination. His brief taste of celebrity made him impatient with the realities of ordinary life outside the spotlight, and a stubborn independence prevented him from accepting the help he needed. He began using drugs at a young age, and then suffered from addiction in a society whose first instinct is to punish rather than rehabilitate. A lover took advantage of him financially and belittled him psychologically. He spiraled into deeper and deeper levels of despair.

With nowhere else to turn, he maintained his friendship with Doug Goldman, the fabulously wealthy Levi Strauss heir, asking for small sums of money to buy crack. Goldman typically obliged, often on the condition that Burke check himself into a drug treatment program. Burke occasionally complied, but he never stayed in rehab long. One night, he showed up at Goldman's office as Goldman was preparing to head out for a swanky awards dinner honoring his father's long career in the insurance business. Burke asked Goldman for money and a ride, directing Goldman into an alley off Van Ness. Burke got out of the car, leaving a tuxedoed Goldman alone in his beige BMW, a conspicuous vehicle for a dark San Francisco alley. Fifteen minutes later, Burke reappeared with some crack, lighting up in Goldman's car. "I was constantly looking in my mirror to make sure a cop wasn't rolling down the alley," Goldman recalled. "This was not exactly where I would have chosen to be. I was supposed to be at this black-tie affair honoring my father. In fact, I showed up late and had to explain to my mother that I had connected with Glenn."[4]

While there were no flashing police lights in the alley that night, Burke's drug use eventually did attract the attention of law enforcement. He was arrested for drug possession at a party in early 1991 and served six months of a sixteen-month sentence at San Quentin, a notorious Bay Area prison. When he failed to report to his parole officer after his release, he was sent back to San Quentin for another month a year later. Burke felt out of place in the penitentiary, not only because he had not committed a violent crime like the murderers and rapists in the cells next to him, but also because he was forced to take sides between white and Black inmates when he just wanted to get along with everyone. And when some inmates learned he was gay, they attempted to force him to perform sexual acts by stealing his food. "Prison," Burke said, "was hell."[5]

When he returned to the streets of the Castro, he faced a new stigma, ex-con, which made it even harder to get a job, and harder to gain sympathy. "People didn't connect the dots to addiction, which is a medical condition," said Roger Brigham, a longtime San Francisco sportswriter. "We vilified people who were addicts back then. And he was also vilified by homophobes. He had a lot of things working against him when he needed support the most." Even with the few remaining friends who might have helped him by providing a place to stay, Burke resisted, ashamed to reveal the depths of his addiction. "I didn't stay with anyone because I didn't want people to know what I was doing," he later admitted. "I needed total freedom in my life, even if it meant living on the streets."

On November 7, 1991, as Burke readjusted to street life following his first stint in prison, the worlds of sports and AIDS collided in Los Angeles, arguably the single most important day in the history of the epidemic. Members of the Lakers NBA basketball team were stretching before practice at a local college when coach Mike Dunleavy told his guys to grab their belongings; the team would be driving over to the Forum, their home arena, for a mandatory meeting.

Players cracked jokes as they entered their locker room, but the room grew quiet as the team's charismatic star player, one of the most famous athletes in the world, Earvin "Magic" Johnson, began to speak.

"I want to talk to you guys first," he said. "And let you know what's going on first. I've contracted the HIV virus, and for right now I know I'm going to have to stop playing. I might have to retire. We're trying to find out more."

Johnson's teammates wept. The HIV diagnosis was presumed to be a death sentence.[6]

Moments later, Johnson appeared in the Lakers' press room, standing behind a microphone in front of dozens of television cameras and reporters. Smiling, he broke the shocking news to the world. "Here I am saying it can happen to anyone, even me, Magic Johnson."

The next night, millions of people watched Johnson's interview on *The Arsenio Hall Show*, a popular late-night television program. Because most Americans believed HIV to be a disease that afflicted only gay men, Johnson sought to silence rumors that he must be gay. After the live audience greeted him with a nearly three-minute standing ovation, the thirty-two-year-old Johnson encouraged viewers to practice safer sex. Then Hall allowed him to make one thing clear: "I'm far from being a homosexual," Johnson said to the crowd's delight, implying he'd slept with scores of women.

In the Castro, reaction to Johnson's comments was mixed. Many were quick to see the hypocrisy on display—there had never been any

Just a day after his press conference in which he revealed that he was HIV positive, Magic Johnson of the Los Angeles Lakers appeared on the popular *Arsenio Hall Show* to discuss his diagnosis. It was a landmark moment in raising awareness that anyone, not just gay men, could contract HIV/AIDS. (AP Photo/Nick Ut)

standing ovations for gay men with HIV, no wink-and-nod approval of promiscuity as there was for Johnson. But there was also an acknowledgment that the basketball star's disclosure lifted the disease out of the shadows and into the public consciousness like never before, potentially bringing desperately needed attention and resources toward treatment or a cure.

Johnson was just one of forty thousand people to learn they were HIV positive in 1991, but his diagnosis forever changed Americans' perceptions of the disease, forcing straight people to confront the fact that HIV/AIDS did not discriminate. At the Centers for Disease Control, fifty thousand calls came in to its AIDS hotline within the first seven hours after Johnson's announcement, more than ten times the previous daily average. The next day, there were 128,000 calls. By December, the number of people requesting tests for HIV increased by 60 percent nationwide. Public opinion began to shift, too, with more people starting to view those suffering from HIV/AIDS as sympathetic victims of an incurable disease rather than as deviants deserving of punishment.[7] Mike Norris said Johnson's revelation sent a shudder through Major League clubhouses. "That freaked the shit out of us," he said. "That led us to know that anybody could get it. That was scary, to the point that you didn't want to get the damn test but you knew you had to take it and worry about the results."

As he watched Johnson's press conference and the awareness it created about HIV, it's unclear what sort of connections Glenn Burke drew to his own life. At one time, Burke had been bound for stardom in Los Angeles; Johnson had achieved it. Some sportswriters had even credited Johnson with popularizing the high five as a college star at Michigan State in 1979, two years after Burke invented the move. Both men had been driven from pro sports; both could light up a locker room with their smiles.

And it turned out they had one more thing in common.

When Glenn's sister Joyce, a nurse, had glanced at his hospital records as he recovered from the accident that broke his legs, she noticed an alarming code on his chart.

"Immunocompromised."

Glenn Burke was HIV positive.

CHAPTER 30
THE TERROR OF KNOWING

When the Burke family gathered to celebrate Christmas in 1993, Glenn's sisters were worried about his health. He'd lost too much weight, he was coughing all the time, and he had a 105-degree fever.

Within weeks, he checked into the hospital and received the diagnosis that his HIV had progressed to AIDS. On May 5, he called Doug Goldman, asking for help. The homeless man's multimillionaire friend started pulling strings on Glenn's behalf, taking notes every step of the way.

First, Goldman contacted Visiting Nurses and Hospice, a program that provided basic health care for homeless people living with AIDS in the Tenderloin district of San Francisco. They found a place for Glenn to stay at the West Hotel, a crumbling structure at 141 Eddy Street. Next, Val Robb of the Tenderloin AIDS Resource Center contacted Bobby Haskell of the Tom Waddell Clinic, and it was Haskell who found Burke curled up in the fetal position on a mattress at the hotel, crying out in pain. Within days, Burke was transported to the AIDS ward at San Francisco General, where he was admitted by Richard Kelly, a young doctor just finishing his internship at the hospital serving the city's "poor and downtrodden."[1]

In the fifth-floor AIDS ward, sparsely furnished rooms lined two long hallways, each occupied by someone dying. People struggled to breathe and were covered with the telltale purple lesions of Kaposi's sarcoma. Some men were still able to walk; others were confined to their beds, gasping for air even with their faces covered with oxygen masks. "These people were all types," Dr. Kelly recalled. "Flamboyant, quiet, people who had been strung out on drugs. But they all shared the common affliction of having AIDS. People were dying on a daily basis." By 1994, fifty-seven thousand people had died of AIDS in San Francisco alone.

For a young doctor, the AIDS ward was "emotionally draining but highly instructive." Kelly observed the ways in which people died, some "with courage, with or without friends, those who died whimpering and those who died with stoicism." He remembered large groups of men showing up to throw elaborate farewell parties for their friends, and lovers climbing into hospital beds to cling to their mates as they drew their last breaths.

But Glenn Burke didn't stick around long enough for Kelly to remember much about his stay. Nearly as soon as he checked into the hospital he departed, hospital records noting that Burke "went against medical advice" by walking out on May 13.

He returned to the streets of the Castro, not wanting to "burden" family members by showing up on their doorstep. "Glenn was never the type to come to the family with any kind of problem," Lutha recalled. "We were a big family that had some tragedies, and he was just trying to deal with it on his own."

Over the course of the summer, he'd make several brief returns to San Francisco General, a combination of pride, resignation to his fate, and the unrelenting cruelty of addiction pulling him back to the Castro each time. "If I'm on the streets, I'm on the streets because I want to be, not because I have to be," he told a reporter. When a friend named Tommy Lee offered him a place to stay, Burke refused. "Tommy, just leave me alone," he said. "I'm going to die doing drugs."

By this time, his former Dodger teammate Dusty Baker had become manager of the San Francisco Giants. Baker often left tickets for Glenn, not knowing if Glenn ever used them (and he rarely did). Prior to one game at San Francisco's Candlestick Park, Baker stood just outside the Giants' dugout when he heard a man calling his name. "Hey, Dusty! Hey, Dusty!" To Baker, it sounded like an elderly fan. He kept his eyes trained on the field; he couldn't reply to every fan who shouted his name. But then the fan called out, "Hey, Johnny B!" (his real first name and middle initial), something only other ballplayers called him. Baker turned around and saw what appeared to be an eighty-year-old version of Glenn Burke walking down the steps toward the top of the dugout.

"Glenn?" Baker asked.

"Hey, man, I'm a little sick," the forty-year-old Burke replied in a whisper-soft voice. He looked worn, weathered, and frail. He looked like he was dying.

"That just killed me," Baker recalled decades later. "Goddammit, man. I think that was the last time I saw Glenn."

Burke continued to rapidly lose weight, dropping more than seventy-five pounds between February and August of 1994, his brown eyes cloudy, his teeth chipped, and his legs covered with large and painful lesions. He had the fidgety manner of an addict and couldn't keep any food down. His head throbbed with pain for months on end, he gulped for breaths of air when he talked, and he knew his condition would only get worse. "I hurt every day, every day, 24 hours a day," he told a *Los Angeles Times* reporter in August. "It's frightening, what's in store for me."

His mother, Alice, took pity on her son. "The poor boy. We all love him and we're all worried about him," she lamented. "But we feel like his time is near."

One of thousands of men dying of AIDS in the Castro, Burke received little sympathy in the neighborhood where he had once been king. "They say he's a panhandler and street thug, drug user and thief," wrote Jerry Crowe in the *Los Angeles Times*. "They say he is unwelcome in almost every nightspot in the Castro district."

Burke disputed the notion that he had stolen money from anyone. In his mind, he had merely asked for the support of the same neighbors he'd once assisted without condition. "If they gave me money, they gave me money, and put it in my hand," he said. "I've done a lot, too. I used to give parties every year, 300 people, 400 people. Folks forget."

One person who remained sympathetic to his plight was Jack McGowan, the bar manager and softball organizer. "You can't tell the truth about Glenn without saying bad things because he's gone through a hell of a 10-year period where he hit rock bottom and did many personal things that are bad," McGowan said. "It's a matter of being sympathetic, but being honest. Many, many gay people have tried to help him because they loved him and because he was a hero. He's still a hero."

Any disagreements Burke had with his detractors were the least of his concerns. The Kaposi's sarcoma lesions on his legs and feet burned at all hours; sores in his throat made swallowing nearly impossible. "It's worse than a sharp pain," Burke said. "It's a killing pain." The man who had once been the life of any party no longer saw a reason to live. "I'm ready," he said. "I'd rather go than to go through this pain much longer."

One afternoon, as McGowan stepped out of a cab on Castro Street, he looked up and saw Burke huddled against a wall, thin and shivering, his eyes foggy and distant. McGowan called Sandy Alderson, general manager of the Oakland A's, and told him the A's had a former player dying on the streets not too far from Oakland. "No one is helping him," McGowan told Alderson. "He is dying of AIDS, and baseball should be ashamed of itself."

Alderson listened with compassion to McGowan's plea and then acted on it, assigning one of the team's longtime employees, Pamela Pitts, to find sources of support for Burke. She called the Association of Professional Ball Players and the Baseball Assistance Team, two organizations supported by current and former players to assist low-income retirees. Both groups contributed $500, which Pitts used to establish a running tab at the Welcome Home restaurant in San Francisco. Burke could show up anytime and charge his meals to an account that Pitts paid every few weeks.

The first time they met, Pitts had arranged to meet Burke at the restaurant. She sat alone at a table when Burke came shuffling in. As he approached, Pitts's face lit up with a huge smile. "You must be Glenn!" she said as she got up from her seat to give him a hug. Glenn smiled back, then burst into tears.

"I can't believe you want to help me," he said. "I can't believe you want to help me."

"My God, Glenn," Pitts replied. "If I were in your predicament, I would hope to God someone would have the heart to help me, too."

Pitts understood that providing a place for Burke to eat met just one of his basic needs. She researched social services available to homeless people suffering from AIDS, and discovered Marty's Place, a shelter in San Francisco's Mission District just east of the Castro. The ministry was run by a priest named Richard Purcell, who had moved to San Francisco in 1989 to care for his dying brother, Marty. After Marty died of AIDS, Purcell continued to support others in his brother's memory, first out of Marty's old apartment and then a larger Victorian home. "The homeless, the sick, and the rejected among us deserve more than scraps, crumbs, and leftovers," he said. "They deserve choice and preferential treatment. All it takes is love."

After years on the streets, Burke finally found peace at Marty's Place. Purcell looked past Burke's rough exterior, and his drug addiction, to see the essence of a good man who'd been dealt a series of bad breaks. "He was talented as well as magnetic and articulate," Purcell said. "He was an extraordinary individual." Purcell treated Glenn with compassion and grace, listening and acting without judgment. If Burke had spent a lifetime chasing acceptance, love, and understanding, it was here that he finally found it. "Burke's time in the Mission was a game-changer," recalled Sean Maddison, a Bay Area television producer. "I truly believe that his stay at Marty's Place allowed him to come to terms with his life, to regain the dignity he had lost to the streets."[2]

With that dignity restored, Glenn was ready to return home and spend his final days back where it all began, in the East Bay with his family. Doctors expected him to die by Christmas 1994.

His sister Lutha was busy with a life and family of her own, raising two kids as a single mother and working a long shift in the kitchen at the Claremont Hotel. But she welcomed her brother without hesitation, opening her home to a series of visitors intent on sharing one last moment with an unforgettable man.

Some guests came over from the Castro, gay men who had partied with Glenn back when the neighborhood was heaven on earth. There were the friends from Oakland and Berkeley, straight Black and white men who had once played baseball and basketball with Glenn at Bushrod Park. The phone rang with calls from former Major League ballplayers—men like Dusty Baker sharing laughs and memories from Glenn's too-short stay in the big leagues.

And then there was the twenty-eight-year-old stranger who arrived from New York, a writer and technology salesman with sandy blond hair and blue eyes. The man's name was Erik Sherman, and he'd only met Glenn Burke one time before, in 1978, when Erik had gone to a ballgame with his dad at Yankee Stadium, and Glenn was the only player to sign his photo album.

CHAPTER 31

NO BURDEN IS HE

Late at night, as Lutha sat at the end of the bed and rubbed her brother's feet, Glenn would often begin softly singing a song that provided comfort in the midst of debilitating pain.

Ooh-oo child, things are gonna get easier.

Ooh-oo child, things'll get brighter.

Lutha had arranged one of her children's bedrooms as Glenn's final hideaway. He spent day and night lying in a small twin bed, clutching at thin sheets printed with red-and-blue toy cars. Amber bottles of pills covered a small bedside table. Even when the weather was warm, Glenn turned up the heat and zipped a winter coat snugly over his shirt and long pajama pants. Still, he'd shiver with chills, drifting in and out of sleep as he watched cartoons and football.

Glenn's feet had swollen to three times their normal size, and the muscles that had once made him the envy of professional baseball players and an object of desire in the Castro had withered away to nothing. He could barely get out of bed; sometimes he had to crawl on the floor just to get to the bathroom. Other times Lutha changed his diaper when he couldn't muster the strength to get up.

And he knew that every day he lived would be more painful than the last. "It scares me," he said. "I'm afraid of when it gets worse. I don't want to be in a lot of pain. I can't stand pain."

Lutha tried to bring joy to her brother's life, cooking three pots of gumbo for his birthday and inviting dozens of friends to visit. Jack McGowan arrived one day with a group of softball players and other gay friends from the Castro, each carrying a covered dish for a potluck dinner. The group sat and talked with Glenn for hours, any animosity over his "panhandling" forgiven and forgotten. After a few national sportswriters discovered Glenn's plight and wrote articles about what had become of the man who invented the high five and had been the first Major League baseball player to come out as gay, letters began arriving in Lutha's mailbox and at Pam Pitts's office at the Oakland Coliseum. There were letters from parents who praised Glenn's kindness to their kids, letters from adults who had met Glenn as children, and letters from gay men who admired his sacrifices as a pioneer. He'd read the letters and weep. "They make me feel like I was sent to this earth to make certain people happier," he said. He was proud to have busted stereotypes, proving that a gay man could play Major League baseball. "No one can say I didn't make it," he said. "I played in the World Series. I'm in the [record] book, and they can't take that away from me. Not ever."

Lutha went to heroic lengths to bring her brother comfort. She'd wake up in darkness each morning and leave the house by five thirty a.m., taking the bus across town to her job at the swanky Claremont Hotel, where she cooked food for well-to-do guests. She'd work straight through her breaks so she could leave the hotel early, catching a bus home around four p.m. to make dinner for Glenn and her kids. Then after dinner, she'd sit up late with Glenn, laughing, talking, listening to music, dressing his wounds, sharing oatmeal and peanut butter, and sitting beside him as he slept, typically not going to bed until after midnight.

One night, Lutha was awakened by the sound of Glenn screaming out in agony. "I said, 'Glenn, you're going to wake the neighbors,'" Lutha recalled. "But he just hollered and hollered. He was sitting straight up in the bed, wild-eyed. I asked him what was the matter, but he said he didn't know. It was heartbreaking."

Even in the midst of terrible pain, Glenn retained his sense of humor and a love for Lutha's soul food. One night she was in the kitchen making dinner when she heard sirens in front of her house.

Next, there was a knock at the door.

"Does Glenn Burke live here?"

"Huh?" Lutha replied.

Glenn shouted from behind her. "Yeah, I'm right here!"

Unbeknownst to Lutha, Glenn had crawled out of bed and dragged himself to the living room to place a call for an ambulance.

As the medics prepared to take him out on a stretcher, Glenn smelled Lutha's cooking and called out to his sister.

"Give me some of those pigs' feet! It's going to be a long time before they feed me at the hospital."

Lutha ran back to the kitchen, took the food out of the pot, and wrapped it up for her brother.

"They put him on a stretcher and he's carrying his pigs' feet," she said. "I just stood there and had to laugh."

Lutha went to bed that night and was awakened by another knock at the door around three a.m.

She opened the door and there on her porch were the ambulance driver, Glenn, and a stretcher.

"I'm baaaaaack!" he shouted with a smile.

Erik Sherman lived on the Upper West Side of Manhattan in the fall of 1994. He worked for Sprint, selling data and voice services to large companies, and wrote freelance sports articles for a small newspaper in New Jersey. One day in early November 1994, he stopped at the newsstand at the 86th Street subway station and picked up a copy of the *New York Post*. He was shocked by an article in the sports section, a two-page feature on Glenn Burke's battle with AIDS.

Sherman had long wanted to write a book, and had once come close to authoring one on the 1986 Boston Red Sox. But in the story of Glenn Burke, he saw the opportunity to write something that transcended baseball. He called Pamela Pitts of the A's and told her he was interested in mailing her a book proposal for Glenn to review.

"Well," Pitts replied, "you're not alone. There are seventeen other writers and four movie producers interested in the story, too. But, if you want, send your proposal to me and I'll make sure Glenn gets it." Erik went to work immediately, drafting a proposal that promised to tell Glenn's story in his own words, a story "of a guy who loved playing baseball and how that was taken away from him just because of his sexual orientation." Sherman also pledged to split any proceeds from the book with Burke.

He doubted he'd hear from Pitts. But two weeks later, she gave Erik a call. Burke liked his letter and felt it was sincere. Burke wanted to work with him.

"But he's not well," Pitts said. "How quickly can you get out here?"

Three days later, Sherman caught an early-morning flight to San Francisco, arriving at Lutha's doorstep that afternoon. Lutha welcomed Erik into her kitchen, where they chatted for a few minutes. She warned Erik that Glenn was in bad shape, and then walked him back to Glenn's room, where he lay in bed.

"He was unrecognizable from the pictures I'd seen," Sherman said of Glenn's frail body. But Burke smiled, and the two men started to talk, beginning a routine that would last for the next seven days as Burke shared his life story, his voice barely louder than a whisper, with Sherman sitting at the foot of his bed holding a tape recorder. Every fifteen minutes or so they'd have to stop and take a break, Burke closing his eyes, clenching his fists, and crying in pain.

"Glenn," Sherman would tell him, "we don't have to go on. Don't worry about it. If you want to stop this, it's fine."

But Burke insisted they continue. "Let's keep going," he'd say. "I'll hang in there if you do."

Every afternoon when he left Lutha's home to return to his hotel, Sherman was worn out, physically and emotionally. "I was depressed," he said. "It was a very solemn experience."

But he'd return the next morning, Lutha making coffee and

Glenn spent his final months living at his sister Lutha's home in Oakland. At night, she'd sit beside his bed, rubbing his feet, and they'd talk about happier times. (John Storey, the *LIFE* Images Collection via Getty Images)

breakfast, sharing stories about her brother before Erik ventured into Glenn's room to continue their interviews. Sherman came to deeply admire the way Lutha sacrificed so much of her own life to care for her brother. "She's an angel," Sherman said. "She could very well be the finest person I've ever met in my life."

Finally, after a week of interviews, it was time for Sherman to head back to New York to begin writing the book. He and Glenn watched a bit of a Cowboys–49ers game on TV, and as Erik prepared to leave, Glenn told him to hang on. He had something to give him. "It's been so great having you here," Burke said. "The only thing I can give you is in the closet. Go ahead and open it up."

Sherman opened the door and looked inside. A brown wooden baseball bat leaned up against the wall, one of Glenn's bats from his days with the Dodgers.

"Glenn, are you sure?"

"Yes, I really want you to have it."

Sherman asked if Burke would sign a baseball for him. Glenn took the ball and scribbled with a pen:

Have a nice life. Glenn Burke

At the airport, Sherman called his mother from a pay phone. What did you learn? she asked. "Every student in high school should experience what I just did, so they would be careful with sex and drugs," he told her. When his flight landed in New York, he went straight to work writing the book, one that would be told in Glenn's voice, not his own. The story would be positioned as an autobiography "written with" Sherman. Erik understood the improbable nature of their relationship. Glenn had grown up in the city, Erik in the suburbs. Glenn was Black; Erik was white. Glenn was gay; Erik was straight. "We could not have been any more different," Erik recalled, "and yet we got along so well, and by transcribing the tapes of our interviews, I felt that I became him. I was writing just like I was Glenn Burke, with a little bit of his edge and his sweetness."

Doctors had told Burke that he likely would not live past Christmas '94, and Sherman had only started writing the book in late November. But Glenn told visitors he would survive to see the book published. It became his reason for living.

In the meantime, a group of his oldest friends in the East Bay came together to throw him one last party, to celebrate the remarkable life of one the funniest people they'd ever known, one of the greatest athletes they'd ever seen, to honor a man who had shattered stereotypes of what it meant to be gay in America. "We wanted to pick Glenn up above the circumstances he was going through and to let him see how many lives he'd touched and how many people loved him," his friend Vincent Trahan recalled.

Trahan and a friend named Rusty Jackson took the lead organizing the party, calling on friends to contribute $20 each to offset the costs of food, music, and the venue, an Oakland jazz club known as Geoffrey's Inner Circle.

On the night of the party, Trahan sent a limousine to Lutha's house to bring Glenn to the club in style. A printed program included a photo of the undefeated Berkeley High School starting five, and former A's teammate Shooty Babitt emceed a lineup of seven speakers. When the limo arrived at Geoffrey's, Glenn's friends placed him in a wheelchair and escorted him into a room packed with admirers. Tears welled in his eyes as person after person approached to give a hug and pay respects. When Mike Norris, the former A's pitcher, came over to see Glenn, he tapped his leg as a casual greeting.

"Aaaaaahhh! Aaaaaaahhhh!" Burke screamed in agony. Norris had unknowingly struck one of the lesions on Burke's leg, sending a piercing pain throughout his body.

The rest of the room fell silent as Burke wailed. Finally, friends wheeled him behind a curtain and let him smoke crack to ease the pain.

Then it was time for the program to begin, starting with a video tribute from former Berkeley High School and NBA star Phil Chenier.

"Hey, Glenn," Babitt said as someone popped the tape in a VCR, "Phil wants to say something to you."

As Chenier told stories about the great playground basketball battles he'd waged with Burke as a kid, praising Glenn's athleticism and toughness, Burke's eyes locked on the screen. A hint of a smile creased his lips.

And then, in a drug- and pain-induced hallucination, Burke began talking back and waving to the TV screen as if Chenier could see and hear him.

"Hey, Phil!" he called. "How are you doing? Hey, Phil, how are you doing?!"

As Burke continued to wave, Trahan and others wiped tears from their eyes.

Back in New York, Sherman continued to transcribe his interviews with Burke and turn his words into a manuscript, writing not only to beat the clock, to finish before Burke passed away, but also under a new pressure: his small publisher had dropped him. When a 1994 Major League Baseball players' strike continued without end in sight, Sherman's editor told him nobody would be interested in a baseball book when there was no baseball being played. Sherman had promised Burke he'd get his story out to the world. He began writing letters to other publishers, but received only rejections, a full array of condescending, maddening disinterest in the story of a pioneering figure in sports history. Random House: "I just don't see it as a book." Crown: "[It] won't work from a commercial point of view." St. Martin's Press: "Simply not enough here to sustain a book." Doubleday: "It's just not right for any of our lists, so we're going to have to pass." William Morrow: "Strikes me as exploitative and sensational. Also, hard to figure out who the audience is; not sure we can count on gay market. Thanks for trying me, though. And good luck with this." Dutton: "It seems to me that Burke's story should have been published in the early '80s, when it would have had more of a chance of getting major publicity." Sherman gave up on the New York publishers, but not on the project. He told his agent he'd spend his own money to publish the book himself when he finished writing it.[1]

In April, players and owners resolved their issues and the MLB sea-son got off to a belated start. Burke clung to life, desperate to see his story in print. With a balanced diet the least of his concerns, he feasted on junk food. "Leave that ice cream for me," he half-seriously berated one of his nephews. "I'm the one who's dying." Lutha administered greater doses of painkillers; Burke gave a few more interviews. He wished for peace—for himself and for humanity. "I don't have any strength," he told a writer from Philadelphia. "I get tired of life. I pray a lot. I'm lonesome a lot of the time. I think about all sorts of things. I think about people being violent, mostly. I hate that. I hate that more than anything."

There were more visitors. Doug Goldman came by with a young son. Roger Brigham, the gay San Francisco sportswriter, sat with Glenn and was overcome by the senselessness of it all. "It just seemed like such a tragic combination of events in his life where he could not have the strength of freely being who he was," Brigham recalled. "If ever anybody paid a price for his sexuality and prejudice against it, it was

Glenn Burke. God knows how he could have flourished as a pro athlete if he had been given a grain of support." When former Minor League teammate Larry Corrigan paid a visit, the conversation turned to basketball. Corrigan asked Burke to name the five greatest players of all time. "Magic, Jordan, Kareem, Larry Bird, and me!" Glenn replied, his sense of humor intact until the end. If he had one regret in life, he told Corrigan and others, it was not pursuing a basketball career.

And there were those who didn't come to visit, friends and family members who, like many others in the country, were afraid to be in the presence of someone with AIDS. "I was squeamish about it," Glenn's old playground pal Jon Nikcevich said decades later. "So I didn't go see him. That was one of the worst deeds of my life. Oh, if I could go back. You don't have that many friends who are always there for you. He always had my back."

When Lutha came home from work one evening in late May, a nurse who had been attending to Glenn told her she didn't want to go home that night; Glenn's readings were low, and she thought he might be about to die. That was troubling news, not only because her brother's death sounded imminent, but also because she had to go to work in the morning. If Glenn didn't pass away until the next day, Lutha didn't want her young children to be home without their mother when it happened.

In the morning, she called an AIDS hospice program at the Fairmont Hospital in San Leandro, just south of Oakland. But when a medic arrived to pick up Glenn, he didn't show up in a nice van or ambulance, but in an open-bed truck. Lutha and Glenn's nurse were mortified. "We turned the driver's ass around and asked them to send an ambulance instead," Lutha recalled. Already late for work, Lutha caught a bus to the Claremont. "I'm just trying to hold on to my job," she said. "I'm the only one my kids have."

After work, she hurried back to the hospital, where Glenn seemed to be feeling a little better, well enough that his appetite had returned. He requested some of Lutha's specialties, and she stayed up until one a.m. fixing ribs, collard greens, potato salad, and sweet potato pie.

"And he ate like a champ," Lutha recalled. "Every time he sat up the next day, he was eating. I told myself there was no way he was going to die after eating this food."

But the next day, May 30, at 2:34 p.m., while Lutha was working in the kitchen at the Claremont, Glenn passed on.[2]

He never got to see Erik Sherman's book.

CHAPTER 32
MONUMENTAL

On June 5, 1995, friends and family gathered at Fouche's Hudson Funeral Home on Telegraph Avenue in Oakland for Glenn's memorial service.

The eclectic, standing-room-only crowd included childhood buddies, teammates from Berkeley High School and the minor leagues, men from the Castro dressed in colorful drag, blue-jean heir Doug Goldman, Pamela Pitts from the A's, and biographer Erik Sherman. Glenn's siblings surrounded his open casket and sang a jaw-dropping a capella rendition of "He Ain't Heavy, He's My Brother," then high-fived one another before returning to their seats.

Father Richard Purcell, who had helped Glenn regain his self-respect at Marty's Place, delivered a eulogy praising the grace Burke displayed even in dire straits, his empathy for others, and his unwilling-ness to deny who he was to make intolerant people comfortable.

"He died in truth," he said. "He told the truth. He didn't live a lie, and I believe the truth sets people free."

And in that proclamation resides the paradox of Glenn Burke's life, and the lesson to us all. Allowed to be his authentic self, Glenn embodied achievement, innovation, love, humor, friendship, freedom, and compassion. But when powerful elements of society told him that was unacceptable, that he must somehow instead deny a fundamental aspect of his being, his life devolved into one of confusion, lies, ambiva-lence, anxiety, seclusion, and self-destruction. What clearer evidence do we need that homophobia, like other hatreds, not only deprives indi-viduals the ability to become their very best selves, but also robs the world of their gifts?

Nearly two decades after Glenn's death, on July 14, 2014, Lutha attended a press conference at Target Field, home of the Minnesota Twins. The occasion was the Major League Baseball All-Star Game, and baseball officials had invited her and her daughter Alice Rose to help MLB officially recognize Glenn's pioneering role for the first time.[1] Jason Collins had come out as the NBA's first openly gay player a year earlier, and linebacker Michael Sam had come out two months prior to the April 2014 NFL Draft. In contrast, baseball still appeared behind the times in its dealings with gay people inside and outside the game.

Lutha appreciated the gesture. Late as it was, it was not too late. Glenn, she said, would be proud. But as much as the reconciliation

Lutha Davis traveled to Minneapolis for the Major League All-Star Game in July 2014. MLB Commissioner Bud Selig (right) and the league's newly appointed ambassador for inclusion, Billy Bean, honored Glenn's legacy and vowed to provide support for gay players in the future. (AP Photo/Paul Sancya)

meant for her family, she understood the moment would only have true transformational power if "other little boys" in the future had the chance to live out their Major League dreams without fear of reprisal if they were gay. Inspiring a new generation of gay athletes would be one of two important measures of Burke's legacy.

As for Glenn Burke's other lasting contribution to the world?

One of his lifelong friends, Abdul-Jalil al-Hakim, said we're channeling Burke's spirit anytime we stop and appreciate the rare moments of exhilaration in our lives and in the lives of those around us.

"He was a joyous, gregarious person. He could high-five you without necessarily going through the motion with his hands," al-Hakim said. "The high five liberated everybody. It gave you permission to enjoy your high points."

On April 1, 2017, baseball fans gathered at the White Horse Inn, just a few blocks north of Oakland's Bushrod Park, where Glenn played as a kid. Patrons at the bar munched on popcorn, hot dogs, peanuts, and nachos, entered a raffle for A's tickets, and danced to music spun by a DJ.

Forty years earlier, when Glenn Burke took note of the Yankee Stadium monuments at the '77 World Series, he wondered aloud if someone might build a tribute to him one day.

It turned out they would. The White Horse was the oldest gay bar in the Bay Area, established in 1933. And on this spring day in 2017, people gathered there to celebrate Glenn's addition to the Rainbow Honor Walk, a series of bronze panels, embedded in sidewalks traversing the Castro District, recognizing some of the most significant lesbian, gay, bisexual, and transgender figures in history.[2]

Stretching down Castro and Market Streets, the plaques pay homage to the likes of astronaut Sally Ride; artist Frida Kahlo; writers James Baldwin, Tennessee Williams, and Virginia Woolf; mathematician Alan Turing; disco star Sylvester James; civil rights leaders Bayard Rustin and Barbara Jordan; and Queen lead singer Freddie Mercury.

In announcing the newest honoree, Honor Walk cofounder David Perry told the crowd at the White Horse that gay heroes and heroines can be found all around us.

Even, he said, at home plate.

Glenn Burke's plaque on the Rainbow Honor Walk in San Francisco's Castro District. Located on Market Street between Castro and Noe, the plaque reads: "First openly gay major league baseball player whose raised hand, after a home run, led to the invention of the high five." (Andrew Maraniss)

NOTES

CHAPTER 1

1. Bobby Haskell is not the real name of the social worker who found Burke in the West Hotel. After an on-the-record interview, Haskell preferred a pseudonym for HIPAA (patient privacy) reasons.

CHAPTER 5

1. Larry Green is serving a life sentence in California as one of four men convicted for a series of fourteen murders in San Francisco in 1973 to 1974. The string of grisly killings came to be known as the Zebra murders. I wrote Green a letter at San Quentin (where Burke had also served time), and he wrote back with a few thoughts on Glenn as a high school teammate.

CHAPTER 6

1. Merritt College was the meeting place of students Huey P. Newton and Bobby Seale, founders of the Black Panther Party, the legendary and controversial organization they founded in 1966 in response to police brutality against African Americans in Oakland.

CHAPTER 8

1. Actor/comedian Eddie Murphy portrayed Rudy Ray Moore in the 2019 Netflix film *Dolemite Is My Name*.

CHAPTER 9

1. A few weeks later, the Quebec Carnavals came to Waterbury for a series of games. League officials and the head umpire visited the Waterbury clubhouse before the first game to warn players against any retaliation from the fight in Canada. Pitcher Bob Lesslie takes it from there: "They said, 'If anything happens whatsoever, you'll be thrown out. No fighting.' Guess what? I was the starting pitcher and Tony Scott [the guy who'd knocked his teeth out] was the lead-off hitter. I hit him with the first pitch in the left ear with a 95-mile-per-hour fastball. He went to the hospital and I was thrown out of the game after one pitch."

CHAPTER 10

1. "Rocket Man" singer Elton John is gay; "We Are the Champions" was performed by Queen, whose lead singer, Freddie Mercury, was bisexual; Robert Reed, who played the father on *The Brady Bunch*, was gay; George Takei, who played Mr. Sulu on the original *Star Trek* TV series, is gay; James Whale, director of several classic horror films, including *Frankenstein*, was gay; fashion designers Christian Dior, Gianni Versace, and Yves Saint Laurent were all gay; poet Walt Whitman and authors James Baldwin and Truman Capote were gay; historians believe Leonardo da Vinci was almost certainly gay; *The Nutcracker* composter Pyotr Tchaikovsky was gay; many historians believe the artist Michelangelo was gay; inventor publisher Malcolm Forbes and civil rights icon Bayard Rustin, organizer of the famous March on Washington where Martin Luther King Jr. gave his "I Have a Dream" speech, were gay.

2. I learned the name of Burke's teacher while researching this book, but opted not to use it because Burke had used a pseudonym in his autobiography. I spoke to a colleague of the teacher who told me that the man, who is deceased, lived an openly gay life. Still, I saw no value in revealing his name if Burke had reason to keep it private.

3. The University of Nevada, Reno, is the alma mater of two other socially significant athletes: Colin Kaepernick, who was blackballed by the NFL for protesting police brutality, and Marion Motley, one of the first two African American professional football players.

CHAPTER 12

1. John Duran later became the mayor of West Hollywood.

2. San Francisco leaders weren't always supportive of the city's gay citizens or appreciative of their economic clout. In 1979, a journalist asked San Francisco Chamber of Commerce president Bill Dauer about the positive effects of the gay community. "There are no positive effects," he said.

CHAPTER 13

1. The term "cup of coffee" has long referred to a brief stint in the major leagues—just long enough for a sip of joe.

2. Dodger first-base coach Jim "Junior" Gilliam would have been another good choice for the job. Gilliam spent his entire MLB career in the Dodger organization after being signed out of the Negro Leagues. He succeeded Jackie Robinson as the Dodgers' second baseman in 1953 and rose to the challenge, winning National League Rookie of the Year honors. He became a player/coach for the Dodgers beginning in 1964 and a full-time coach in 1967. One of the few African American coaches in the game, he was a trusted advisor to the Dodgers' Black players. At age forty-nine, Gilliam died of a brain aneurysm in 1978. The Nashville Sounds' Triple-A ballpark is located on Junior Gilliam Way in honor of the Nashville native.

CHAPTER 15

1. Dusty Baker told me that Tommy Lasorda and Dodger GM Al Campanis once encouraged him to go dancing at a disco while the team was in Chicago to play the Cubs. "We were playing all-day games, and they told me to go out and dance after a game. I thought it was a trap," Baker said. "Most of the time they were telling me to stay in. I said, 'You're telling me to do what?' Al said, 'You go out dancing tonight because you don't have any rhythm [at the plate]. Go out and dance and find out where your feet are.' It worked. To this day, when I'm working with my son or somebody on hitting, I always have music on because of what Al told me."

2. Baker said Black and Latino players on opposing teams forged relationships in the minor leagues playing in small Southern or Midwestern towns

where they did not feel welcome. "You needed to know where to go," he said. "Whether it was a nightclub or a restaurant, if you end up on the wrong side of town after a game and they can tell you're not from there, you had some possible trouble." These relationships continued on into the major leagues. "When we'd go to Pittsburgh, one day we'd eat at Gene Clines's house and another day at Al Oliver's house and then end up at Willie Stargell's house." In Cincinnati, Baker enjoyed spending time with Joe Morgan, Ken Griffey, Tony Perez, and Pete Rose, who is white. When Baker was with the Braves, Rose drove Baker and teammate Ralph Garr to his house for lunch, with Baker crammed in the back seat of Rose's Porsche. "He gave Ralph like ten leisure suits, matching top and bottom," Baker said. "He made his whole wardrobe. He was going to give me some, but I put them on and looked like Li'l Abner. Highwaters weren't in then like they are now."

3. "My son wasn't gay," Lasorda told GQ's Peter Richmond. "No way. No way. I read that in a paper. I also read in that paper that a lady gave birth to a fuckin' monkey, too. That's not the fuckin' truth. That's not the truth. . . . I know what my son died of. I know what he died of. The doctor put out a report of how he died. He died of pneumonia."

CHAPTER 16

1. J. R. Richard's career ended suddenly at age thirty when he suffered a stroke prior to an Astros game. He later was the victim of a business scam and went through two divorces. Having lost all his money, he was homeless for a period in 1994 and 1995, living under a highway overpass in Houston. He has since become a minister.

2. If the name Tommy John rings a bell for younger fans, you may be familiar with the surgery that bears his name. In 1974, Dodger team doctor Frank Jobe replaced a torn ligament in John's left elbow with a tendon. Ever since, this procedure has been known as Tommy John surgery.

3. Dodger team photographer Rich Kee gives Fred Claire, the Dodgers' VP of public relations at the time, credit for coining the term "high five" and popularizing it as a marketing device for the team. National High Five Day is celebrated annually on the third Thursday in April.

CHAPTER 17

1. I had to find out if Lasorda's prediction came true. I found Anthony Darren and messaged him to see if he remembered this night in the Dodger clubhouse. He said that he did, and that he still has some of the items Lasorda gave him.

CHAPTER 18

1. Al Campanis's long career in baseball came to an end in April 1987 when he appeared on ABC's *Nightline* television program. On the fortieth anniversary of Jackie Robinson's historic Major League debut, host Ted Koppel asked Campanis why there were no Black managers or general managers in the majors. Campanis, seventy, said African Americans "may not have some of the necessities" and then compounded his troubles by continuing to dish out numerous ugly stereotypes. After public backlash to the comments, Campanis resigned and MLB executives were forced to confront the lack of diversity in the sport's leadership, hiring noted sports sociologist Dr. Harry Edwards to develop a strategy. One of the first people he heard from was Campanis. "He wanted to know how he could help and he said that if what he said on *Nightline* opened the door for him to help, then it was worth it," Edwards later told ESPN. "I was pleasantly surprised with the sincerity of his sentiment. . . . He didn't get a raw deal, he got the deal he ordered up, but he was one of the most honorable men in the whole process and he handled it with class, with conscientiousness and with courage."

CHAPTER 19

1. Many of the tired assumptions about the "disruptive" nature of an openly gay player in the major leagues are exposed for their hypocrisy in this story. Heterosexual heartthrob Steve Garvey was the biggest source of tension in the Dodger clubhouse, not Burke. Lasorda purposely invited distractions into the clubhouse mere minutes before playoff games while players on many teams were inviting cocaine dealers to their lockers (see Chapter 27 note below). Most Dodgers knew Burke was gay and loved him anyway. Distractions? The Oakland A's owner brought mechanical rabbits and

donkeys onto the field and telephoned his manager during games.

2. Search "Tommy Lasorda Kingman rant" for full audio of the profane tirade that has become a cult classic among baseball fans.

CHAPTER 20

1. While the A's never moved to Denver, the city did get a Major League team in 1993 when the expansion Colorado Rockies played their inaugural season. Finley sold the A's in 1980 to Walter Haas Jr., president of the Levi Strauss company and Doug Goldman's uncle.

CHAPTER 22

1. Sportswriter Kit Stier has a memorable story about how empty the Coliseum used to be in the late seventies. "I covered a game on a Friday night in 1979 and the press box was open. A foul ball came up and I reached for it, and the ball took my ring off my left hand. I got up, walked down to the second deck and picked it up off the ground. There was nobody there."

2. Dan White's attorneys mounted what has become known as the "Twinkie defense," arguing that White's mental state was impaired in part due to the sugar-laden diet he ate while feeling depressed in the wake of resigning his city position.

3. Bobby Glasser defended Glenn Burke's honor in 2017 when it was announced that Tommy Lasorda would serve as grand marshal of San Francisco's Italian Heritage Parade. Glasser contacted city officials to make them aware of Lasorda's treatment of Burke. In a city with a large gay population where Burke once lived, it made no sense for Lasorda to be honored, Glasser argued. His campaign was effective, and Lasorda ultimately withdrew from the event.

CHAPTER 24

1. When O. J. Simpson was accused of murdering his ex-wife Nicole Brown Simpson and her friend Ron Goldman and led police on a chase down Los Angeles freeways, it was lifelong friend A. C. Cowlings driving the infamous white Bronco. A copy of the book *The Secret Life of Cyndy Garvey*, about her

unhappy marriage to Steve Garvey, was found at Nicole's bedside.

2. Martin lasted three seasons in Oakland before returning to New York. The Yankees' 1977 championship was his only World Series title as a manager. He died in a drunk driving accident in 1989 at age sixty-one.

CHAPTER 25

1. The availability of sex in the Castro was hardly different from the atmosphere surrounding Major League players, where every road trip was an opportunity for many players, single or married, to hook up. Being a big leaguer, Tommy John wrote, "is a little like being a rock star. If you want cheap sex, it's yours for the asking."

CHAPTER 26

1. Jenkins's book is called *Prologue* and has been updated with new editions over the years. From Jenkins's website (prologuegaymormons.com): "There are still thousands of young gay and lesbian men and women in far flung areas that feel isolated and alone in their private struggles to come to terms with their sexuality. They clearly get the messages from their parents, preacher, bishop, teachers—and especially their peers—that to disclose their sexuality would be self-destructive. They have no support group, no sympathetic counselor or minister, not even a parent or sibling they can confide in. Today thanks to the internet, a resource library is just a few clicks away for a . . . frightened teenager trying to grasp the complex and powerful forces that seem to be taking over their life. That he or she can quickly access valuable information, gain an understanding, and find support can make a crucial difference almost instantaneously. This benefit is not only transformational, it can be life-saving. *Prologue* can still contribute in this way as it has in the past to both a better self-understanding, and additionally reveal valuable insight to LDS parents, friends, teachers, and Church leaders who are struggling themselves to understand a son or daughter, a friend or student, or a member of their ward."

2. Cloy Jenkins's business partner at the Willows, Alon Fish, offers an interesting perspective on Glenn. "I never saw him wash a single dish. Ruby worked

for us at the B&B and she didn't put up with his shit. 'You just put a dish in the sink, Glenn. You have been here long enough you are not a guest anymore, do something to contribute.' Ruby could get away with telling him off in a way I only dreamed of. He always thought of himself as a celebrity and above any domestic duty. I say this not out of spite but only as an observation. On the other end of the scale, he had little, but whatever he did have, he shared it with friends and people he did not know. What he did to bring the community together in Guerneville was legendary. That is the reason I didn't step in the way of the ultra-prima-donna. He was worth it. In himself, he had high esteem. He had a little bit of Muhamad Ali's attitude without doing the work. I never saw the insecure part of Glenn. Over the years I knew he was broken only because of what I heard from others. My take is his life became so tragic. I personally believe if he had stayed in the closet a while longer, life would have been better for him. Glenn was not emotionally stable enough to handle the repercussions of coming out at that time. Glenn was just a storm passing through and I knew it. No one can sustain that intensity. He was a star. I got that, and he burnt out. No, I don't want to be trite and say 'too soon.' He burnt so hot for enough time. As I write this I start to wonder if Glenn felt more comfortable as a big fish in a small pond. I understand now what that meant for him, with the amount of pride he had. Above all he needed to be admired."

CHAPTER 27

1. *Inside Sports* was a monthly competitor to *Sports Illustrated* from 1979 to 1998.

2. Bryant Gumbel, younger brother of CBS Sports broadcaster Greg Gumbel, was a sportscaster and host at NBC from 1975 to 1982 before serving as host of *The Today Show* from 1982 to 1997. He has hosted HBO's *Real Sports with Bryant Gumbel* since 1995.

3. Major League Baseball's cocaine problem came to light in 1985 when several players testified before a grand jury in Pittsburgh. Among other revelations, the Pirates' mascot, the Pirate Parrot, admitted to introducing players to drug dealers, and Tim Raines of the Montreal Expos stated that he only slid headfirst so as not to break a vial of cocaine he kept in his uniform pocket.

John Milner of the Pirates said he once purchased $200 of cocaine in a stadium restroom during a game. Glenn Burke said drug dealers were frequent visitors in Major League clubhouses, often posing as agents or vendors.

CHAPTER 28

1. By the end of 1995, the year Glenn Burke died, there had been 513,486 cases of AIDS reported in the US and 319,849 deaths. The first Major League baseball player to die of AIDS was not Burke but Alan Wiggins, who contracted the disease through intravenous drug use and passed away in 1991.

CHAPTER 29

1. Lutha Davis said Glenn settled out of court with the teenager who caused the accident, but the money did not last long.

2. A 2006 report by the American Civil Liberties Union on disparities in sentencing for crack-related offenses versus those for powder cocaine highlighted racial disparities: "Distribution of just 5 grams of crack carries a minimum 5-year federal prison sentence, while for powder cocaine, distribution of 500 grams—100 times the amount of crack cocaine—carries the same sentence. Because of its relative low cost, crack cocaine is more accessible for poor Americans, many of whom are African Americans. Conversely, powder cocaine is much more expensive and tends to be used by more affluent white Americans. Thus, the sentencing disparities punishing crack cocaine offenses more harshly than powder cocaine offenses unjustly and disproportionately penalize African American defendants for drug trafficking comparable to that of white defendants. Compounding the problem is the fact that whites are disproportionately less likely to be prosecuted for drug offenses in the first place; when prosecuted, are more likely to be acquitted; and even if convicted, are much less likely to be sent to prison."

3. Concept addressed in "Growing Up Gay in Black America," 2011 dissertation by DeMarcus Clarke, Syracuse University. "Lehoczky (2005) further found that these messages directly increase the risk for African American queer youth for devastating problems such as drug usage, family alienation, homelessness and suicide."

4. Douglas Goldman, founder of the software firm Certain, developed software to establish a genetic repository at the Museum of the Diaspora in Israel known as the Douglas E. Goldman Jewish Genealogy Center. He and his wife also created the Lisa and Douglas Goldman Fund, which supports democracy and civil liberties, education and literacy, and the environment. His Goldman Environmental Foundation awards the annual $150,000 Goldman Environmental Prize for grassroots environmental activism. The Lisa and Douglas Goldman Plaza outside the University of California, Berkeley, football stadium is named in the couple's honor after they made a $10 million gift to Cal Athletics.

5. Some well-known inmates at San Quentin over the years include Eldridge Cleaver, Merle Haggard, Charles Manson, and Sirhan Sirhan. Anyone interested in what it's like to be an inmate there now should listen to the fantastic *Ear Hustle* podcast. Thanks to Lt. Sam Robinson at the penitentiary (a familiar name to *Ear Hustle* listeners) for confirming the dates Glenn Burke spent at the prison.

6. Magic Johnson has lived with HIV ever since his 1991 diagnosis. He was a member of the US Olympic basketball Dream Team in 1992 and made an NBA comeback in 1996. He became a minority owner of the Los Angeles Dodgers in 2012. His son, E. J., is gay.

7. Magic Johnson's revelation had profound effects on people from all walks of life. Rubin Thomas was experiencing homelessness in Los Angeles, suffering from night sweats, diarrhea, and various infections, when he heard the news. "Before Magic, I felt very much alone," he told a reporter at the time. "Now it almost makes me stick my chest out a little bit. It just goes to prove we are all human beings. Magic Johnson, although he might be a famous basketball player, is a human being and makes mistakes like all of us do."

CHAPTER 30

1. The AIDS ward at San Francisco General is the subject of the 2018 documentary *5B*.

2. Sean Maddison worked on Doug Harris's 2010 documentary *OUT: The Glenn*

Burke Story. The film includes a remarkable bedside interview with Father Richard Purcell, who was dying of ALS at the time.

CHAPTER 31

1. After losing his publisher, Erik Sherman decided to self-publish his book, *Out at Home*. At $4 per copy, he spent $10,000 printing 2,500 copies, essentially all the money he had in the bank. He kept the thirty-six boxes of books in his basement and sold them at $14.95 apiece, donating $1 per copy to the Gay Men's Health Crisis. He spent around $5,000 advertising the book, including a $2,100 ad buy with *Baseball Weekly*. In the end, Sherman estimates he sold around a thousand copies; the Oakland A's bought fifty. The book was reissued by Penguin's Berkley imprint in 2015.

2. "Glenn had succumbed to the same vile enemy that had taken the party away from the Castro," Cloy Jenkins wrote me in an email. "It had lost one of its heroes. Although a tragic end to such a magnificent life, Glenn had made a lasting impact on many lives as well as the gay movement itself. His poignant story remains very much alive, possibly influencing the sports world since and in the future regarding the viability of openly gay pro players. This remains a serious issue that needs reckoning."

CHAPTER 32

1. When Glenn Burke was posthumously honored at the 2014 Major League Baseball All-Star Game, MLB also announced that former player Billy Bean had been named ambassador for inclusion. Bean had played six seasons (1987–89, 1993–95) in the Major League as a closeted gay man. When I interviewed him over the phone for this book, he told me it was hard to fathom that no Major League player has come out of the closet since he did in 1999. Yet given the brief window of opportunity major leaguers have to make enormous amounts of money, he can understand the reasons current gay players remain closeted. "You don't get into a big league clubhouse unless you are first and foremost a world-class athlete," he said. "That means you have found a way to eliminate distractions. And if one of those distractions happens to be that you are contemplating sharing your sexual orientation,

you've had to navigate around that and make a determination of when that will be the best decision for you. The desire to be a part of something bigger than yourself, the uncertainty of how you would be accepted, and the short time with an incredibly high ceiling of opportunity to realize your dreams and take care of yourself weigh into the decision now more than ever." (Bean is not to be confused with Oakland A's executive Billy Beane of *Moneyball* fame.)

2. On a family trip to California in the spring of 2019, my wife and two kids and I visited the Castro District to see the house Glenn lived in on Collingwood Street. We also walked by Harvey Milk's old camera store (now a gift shop run by the Human Rights Campaign) and found Glenn's plaque on the Rainbow Honor Walk.

INTERVIEWS

Shooty Babitt, Dusty Baker, Billy Bean, Bill Berrier, Steve Brener, Roger Brigham, Mark Brown, Pete Carlson, Ed Carroll Jr., Fred Claire, Jim Cody, Larry Corrigan, Lutha Davis, Chalmer Dillard, John Duran, Bill Frishette, Vincent Fuqua, Bobby Glasser, Doug Goldman, Larry Green, Rick Green, Robert Heywood, Paula Hunt, Cloy Jenkins, Ruppert Jones, Rich Kee, Richard Kelly, Shawn Kelly, John Lambert, Mike Lefkow, Bob Lesslie, Davey Lopes, David McFarland, Mickey Morabito, Jon Nikcevich, Mike Norris, Pete Padgett, Jerry Pritikin, Sam Robinson, Jim Riggleman, Glenn Schwarz, Jeff Sheppard, Erik Sherman, Joe Simpson, John Snider, Lyle Spencer, Kit Stier, Vincent Trahan, Steve Vucinich, Gary Warren, Ron Wayne, Marvin Webb, Tom Weir

BIBLIOGRAPHY

Anderson, Eric. *In the Game: Gay Athletes and the Cult of Masculinity.* New York: SUNY Press, 2005.

Boykin, Keith. *One More River to Cross: Black and Gay in America.* New York: Anchor, 1997.

Burke, Glenn, and Erik Sherman. *Out at Home: The True Story of Glenn Burke, Baseball's First Openly Gay Player.* New York: Berkley, 2015.

Claire, Fred, and Steve Springer. *My 30 Years in Dodger Blue.* Champaign, IL: Sports Publishing, LLC, 2004.

Coe, Roy M. *A Sense of Pride: The Story of Gay Games II.* San Francisco: Pride Publications, 1986.

Echols, Alice. *Hot Stuff: Disco and the Remaking of American Culture.* New York: W. W. Norton & Co., 2010.

Epstein, Dan. *Big Hair and Plastic Grass: A Funky Ride Through Baseball and America in the Swinging '70s.* New York: Thomas Dunne Books, 2010.

Fallon, Michael. *Dodgerland: Decadent Los Angeles and the 1977–78 Dodgers.* Lincoln: University of Nebraska Press, 2016.

Finley, Nancy. *Finley Ball: How Two Outsiders Turned the Oakland A's into a Dynasty and Changed the Game Forever.* Washington, DC: Regnery History, 2016.

Garvey, Steve, and Skip Rozin. *Garvey.* New York: Crown, 1986.

Hemphill, Essex. *Brother to Brother: New Writing by Black Gay Men.* New Orleans: RedBone Press, 2007.

John, Tommy, and Dan Valenti. *T.J.: My 26 Years in Baseball.* New York: Bantam Books, 1991.

Jones, Cleve. *When We Rise: My Life in the Movement.* New York: Hachette Books, 2016.

Jones, Cleve, and Jeff Dawson. *Stitching a Revolution: The Making of an Activist.*

New York: Harper Collins, 2000.

Kopay, David, and Perry Deane Young. *The David Kopay Story: An Extraordinary Self-Revelation*. New York: Arbor House, 1977.

Lasorda, Tommy, and David Fisher. *The Artful Dodger*. New York: Arbor House, 1985.

Mahler, Jonathan. *The Bronx Is Burning: Baseball, Politics and the Battle for the Soul of a City*. New York: Picador, 2006.

Monagan, Charles. *Greater Waterbury: A Region Reborn. A Contemporary Portrait*. Chatsworth, CA: Windsor Publications, 1989.

Pallone, Dave, and Alan Steinberg. *Behind the Mask: My Double Life in Baseball*. New York: Penguin, 1990.

Pepe, Phil. *Talkin' Baseball: An Oral History of Baseball in the 1970s*. New York: Ballantine Books, 1998.

Richard, J. R., and Lew Freedman. *Still Throwing Heat: Strikeouts, the Streets, and a Second Chance*. Chicago: Triumph Books, 2015.

Sanders, Prentice Earl, and Bennett Cohen. *The Zebra Murders: A Season of Killing, Racial Madness & Civil Rights*. New York: Arcade Publishing, 2006.

Seale, Bobby. *Seize the Time: The Story of the Black Panther Party and Huey P. Newton*. New York: Random House, 1970.

Shilts, Randy. *And the Band Played On: Politics, People and the AIDS Epidemic*. New York: St. Marin's Press, 1987.

Shilts, Randy. *The Mayor of Castro Street: The Life and Times of Harvey Milk*. New York: St. Martin's Griffin, 2008.

Turbow, Jason. *Dynastic, Bombastic, Fantastic: Reggie, Rollie, Catfish and Charlie Finley's Swingin' A's*. Boston: Houghton Mifflin Harcourt, 2017.

NEWSPAPERS, MAGAZINES, WEBSITES

Albuquerque Journal, Arizona Republic, Asbury Park Press, Associated Press, *Atlanta Constitution, Atlanta Daily World, Bakersfield Californian,* Baseball-reference.com, *Bay Area Gay Sports, Bay Area Reporter, Boston Globe, Burlington Free Press, Chicago Tribune, Christian Science Monitor,* CNN.com, *Delaware County Daily Times, Des Moines Register, Detroit Free Press,* ESPN.com, *ESPN The Magazine, Fremont Argus, GQ, Hartford Courant, Inside Sports, Long Beach Independent, Longview News, Los Angeles Daily News, Los Angeles Sentinel, Los Angeles Times, Los Angeles Examiner, Mansfield News-Journal,* National Baseball Hall of Fame, *New York Daily News, New York Times,* NPR.org, *Oakland Tribune, Owensboro Messenger-Inquirer, Ottawa Citizen,* Outsports.com, *Palm Springs Desert Sun, Pascack Valley Community Life,* PBS.com, *People, Philadelphia Daily News, Provo Daily Herald,* Rainbowhonorwalk.org, *Redlands Daily Facts, Reno Gazette-Journal, San Bernardino County Sun, San Francisco Bay Times, San Francisco Chronicle, San Francisco Examiner, San Francisco Sentinel, San Francisco Sun-Reporter, Santa Cruz Sentinel, The Sporting News, Sports Illustrated, St. Louis Post-Dispatch, Toronto Globe and Mail,* United Press International, *USA Today, Vanity Fair, Van Nuys Valley News, Village Voice, Virginian-Pilot, Washington Informer, Washington Post, Washington Star,* Wikipedia, *Wisconsin State Journal, Women's Review of Books,* YouTube

BASEBALL STATISTICS AND CHARTS

LOS ANGELES DODGERS FARM SYSTEM

	1972	1973	1974	1975	1976	1977
AAA	Albuquerque	Albuquerque	Albuquerque	Albuquerque	Albuquerque	Albuquerque
AA	El Paso	Waterbury	Waterbury	Waterbury	Waterbury	San Antonio
A	Bakersfield, Daytona Beach	Bakersfield, Daytona Beach	Bakersfield, Orangeburg	Bakersfield, Danville	Danville, Lodi	Lodi, Clinton
A-	Spokane	Bellingham	Bellingham	Bellingham	Bellingham	
Rookie	Ogden	Ogden				Lethbridge

1977 LOS ANGELES DODGERS WORLD SERIES ROSTER

No.	Pos.	Name	G	HR	RBI	SB	AVG	OPS	Ht	Wt	Age	Birthplace
3	CF	Glenn Burke	83	1	13	13	.254	.600	6'0	205	24	Oakland, CA
5	C	Johnny Oates	60	3	11	1	.269	.666	6'0	185	31	Sylva, NC
6	1B	Steve Garvey	162	33	115	9	.297	.834	5'10	190	28	Tampa, FL

No.	Pos.	Name	G	HR	RBI	SB	AVG	OPS	Ht	Wt	Age	Birthplace
7	C	Steve Yeager	125	16	55	1	.256	.779	6'0	190	28	Huntington, WV
8	RF	Reggie Smith	148	32	87	7	.307	1.003	6'0	195	32	Shreveport, LA
9	C	Jerry Grote	18	0	4	0	.259	.570	5'11	190	34	San Antonio, TX
10	3B	Ron Cey	153	30	110	3	.241	.797	5'10	185	29	Tacoma, WA

No.	Pos.	Name	G	HR	RBI	SB	AVG	OPS	Ht	Wt	Age	Birthplace
11	LF	Manny Mota	49	1	4	1	.395	1.021	5'11	168	39	Santo Domingo, D.R.
12	LF	Dusty Baker	153	30	86	2	.291	.876	6'2	187	28	Riverside, CA
15	2B	Davey Lopes	134	11	53	47	.283	.779	5'9	170	32	E. Providence, RI
16	CF	Rick Monday	118	15	48	1	.230	.713	6'3	200	31	Batesville, AR
18	SS	Bill Russell	153	4	51	16	.278	.664	6'0	175	28	Pittsburg, KS
21	1B/3B	Ed Goodson	61	1	5	0	.167	.430	6'2	185	29	Pulaski, VA
33	OF	Vic Davalillo	24	0	4	0	.313	.667	5'8	155	37	Cabima, VZ
34	OF	Lee Lacy	75	6	21	4	.266	.720	6'1	175	29	Longview, TX
56	SS/2B	Rafael Landestoy	15	0	0	2	.278	.659	5'10	163	24	Bani, D.R.

No.	R/L	Name	G	W-L	S	ERA	SO	BB	Ht	Wt	Age	Hometown
20	RHP	Don Sutton	33	14-8	0	3.18	150	69	6'1	185	32	Clio, AL
25	LHP	Tommy John	31	20-7	0	2.78	123	50	6'3	185	34	Terre Haute, IN
27	RHP	Elias Sosa	44	2-2	1	1.98	47	12	6'2	186	27	La Vega, D.R.

No.	R/L	Name	G	W-L	S	ERA	SO	BB	Ht	Wt	Age	Hometown
29	RHP	Mike Garman	49	4-4	12	2.73	29	22	6'3	200	27	Caldwell, ID
31	LHP	Doug Rau	32	14-8	0	3.43	126	49	6'2	175	28	Columbus, TX
36	RHP	Rick Rhoden	31	16-10	0	3.74	122	63	6'3	195	24	Boynton Beach, FL
38	LHP	Lance Rautzhan	25	4-1	2	4.35	13	7	6'1	203	24	Pottsville, PA
46	RHP	Burt Hooton	32	12-7	1	2.62	153	60	6'1	200	27	Greenville, TX
49	RHP	Charlie Hough	70	6-12	22	3.32	105	70	6'2	190	29	Honolulu, HI

Coaching Staff

Manager: Tommy Lasorda

Coaches: Red Adams (Pitching Coach), Monty Basgall (Bench Coach), Jim Gilliam (Batting, 1B Coach), Preston Gómez (3B Coach)

Trainer: Bill Buhler

Equipment Manager: Nobe Kawano

GLENN BURKE ALL-TIME MINOR LEAGUE STATISTICS

Year	Age	Team	G	AB	R	H	2B	3B	HR	RBI	SB/CS	BB	SO	BA	OPS
1972	19	SPO	41	141	31	48	9	1	2	16	8/3	9	27	.340	.841
1972	19	OGD	14	45	5	9	1	0	0	5	0/0	1	7	.200	.440
1973	20	DB	110	372	68	115	17	2	10	57	42/6	28	55	.309	.807
1973	20	BAK	11	34	6	6	1	1	1	3	2/0	2	6	.176	.569
1974	21	WAT	51	153	19	38	5	2	1	14	9/5	12	31	.248	.632
1974	21	BAK	66	263	46	89	17	0	7	26	20/2	19	45	.338	.868
1975	22	WAT	119	478	66	129	14	2	12	49	48/19	39	56	.270	.709
1976	23	ABQ	116	467	72	140	17	10	7	53	63/13	18	71	.300	.745
1977	24	ABQ	47	188	42	58	9	5	6	47	20/5	20	43	.309	.877
1980	27	OGD	25	84	7	19	3	1	2	12	2/3	7	15	.226	.640
TOT			**600**	**2225**	**362**	**651**	**93**	**24**	**48**	**302**	**214/56**	**155**	**355**	**.293**	**.759**

GLENN BURKE ALL-TIME MAJOR LEAGUE STATISTICS

Year	Age	Team	G	AB	R	H	2B	3B	HR	RBI	SB/CS	BB	SO	BA	OPS
1976	23	LAD	25	46	9	11	2	0	0	5	3/2	3	8	.239	.583
1977	24	LAD	83	169	16	43	8	0	1	13	13/5	5	22	.254	.600
1978	25	LAD	16	19	2	4	0	0	0	2	1/0	0	4	.211	.421
1978	25	OAK	78	200	19	47	6	1	1	14	15/8	10	26	.235	.560
1979	26	OAK	23	89	4	19	2	1	0	4	3/1	4	10	.213	.506
TOT			**225**	**523**	**50**	**124**	**18**	**2**	**2**	**38**	**35/16**	**22**	**70**	**.237**	**.561**

GLENN BURKE ALL-TIME MAJOR + MINOR LEAGUE STATISTICS

Year	Age	Team	G	AB	R	H	2B	3B	HR	RBI	SB/CS	BB	SO	BA	OPS
9 Seasons			825	2748	412	775	111	26	50	340	249/72	177	425	.282	.722

US GAY RIGHTS TIMELINE

Dec. 10, 1924   Society for Human Rights, the first US gay rights organization, founded in Chicago.

1933   White Horse Inn opens in Oakland, now considered the oldest continuously operated gay bar in the US.

1936   Mona's 440 Club opens in San Francisco, the first lesbian bar in the US.

Nov. 11, 1950   Mattachine Society founded in Los Angeles to change the public perception of homosexuality and to fight discrimination.

April 1952   American Psychiatric Association lists homosexuality as a "sociopathic personality disturbance." Many doctors and mental health professionals criticize the categorization.

Nov. 16, 1952   Glenn Burke is born in Oakland.

April 27, 1953   President Dwight Eisenhower signs an executive order banning gay citizens from working in the federal government.

Sept. 21, 1955   Daughters of Bilitis in San Francisco launched as the first lesbian rights organization in the US.

Jan. 13, 1958   US Supreme Court rules in favor of the First Amendment rights of the lesbian, gay, bisexual, and transgender magazine *One: The Homosexual Magazine*.

1961	Jose Sarria runs for San Francisco supervisor, becoming the first openly gay person to run for public office in the US.
Jan. 1, 1962	Illinois becomes the first state to decriminalize homosexuality.
June 1964	*LIFE* magazine runs an article titled "Homosexuality in America," the first time a mainstream national publication has reported on the topic.
April 21, 1966	Members of the Mattachine Society in New York stage a "sip-in" to challenge the city's laws that prevent gay people from being served alcohol. Following the protest, the New York City Commission on Human Rights states that gay people have the right to be served.
August 1966	Activists in San Francisco establish the National Transsexual Counseling Unit, the first support and advocacy organization of its kind in the world.
June 28, 1969	Customers at the Stonewall Inn bar in New York City rebel when police officers raid the bar to harass gay and transgender patrons. After three days of clashes with police, their resistance is credited with sparking the modern gay rights movement.
July 1969	The Gay Liberation Front is formed, becoming the first organization to use "gay" in its name.
April 1970	The *Los Angeles Advocate* becomes *The Advocate*, now considered the nation's longest-running LGBTQIA+ publication.
June 18, 1970	On the one-year anniversary of the Stonewall riots, members of New York's LGBTIA+ community march in what is considered the country's first gay pride parade.
1971	The University of Michigan becomes the first US college to open an LGBT office.

1973	Lambda Legal becomes the first dedicated legal organization to advocate for the rights of gay and lesbian citizens.
1973	Community Softball League formed in San Francisco, the first gay softball league in the world.
March 26, 1973	The organization that comes to be known as Parents, Families and Friends of Lesbians and Gays (PFLAG) holds its first meeting.
Dec. 15, 1973	The American Psychiatric Association removes homosexuality from its list of mental illnesses.
January 1974	In Ann Arbor, Michigan, Kathy Kozachenko becomes the first openly gay politician elected to office, winning a spot on the city council.
December 1975	The *Washington Star* publishes a four-part series on gays in sports; retired NFL player Dave Kopay comes out as gay.
April 9, 1976	Glenn Burke makes his MLB debut with the Los Angeles Dodgers.
1977	Billy Crystal, on the sitcom *Soap*, becomes the first actor to portray a gay character on a primetime US television show.
February 1977	First gay film festival in the US is held in San Francisco.
August 1977	Renee Richards, a transgender woman tennis player, wins a lawsuit against the US Tennis Association after she is prevented from competing in the 1976 US Open.
June 7, 1977	Anita Bryant leads a successful campaign to overturn a gay rights ordinance in Dade County, Florida.
Oct. 2, 1977	Glenn Burke invents the high five, congratulating Dusty Baker on his thirtieth home run of the season.
Nov. 8, 1977	Gay businessman and community leader Harvey Milk is elected to the San Francisco Board of Supervisors.

June 25, 1978 Gay pride (rainbow) flag, designed by Gilbert Baker, flies for the first time at the San Francisco Gay Freedom Day Parade.

Nov. 27, 1978 Harvey Milk and San Francisco Mayor George Moscone are assassinated by former San Francisco police officer and city supervisor Dan White.

May 21, 1979 Dan White is convicted only of voluntary manslaughter and receives a light seven-year sentence. The White Night riots ensue, with more than five thousand protestors setting police cars ablaze and damaging numerous buildings.

The following night, more than ten thousand people gather to peacefully demonstrate and to commemorate what would have been Milk's forty-ninth birthday.

June 4, 1979 Glenn Burke plays his final MLB game, with the Oakland A's.

Oct. 14, 1979 Around seventy-five thousand people participate in the National March on Washington for Lesbian and Gay Rights.

July 8, 1980 At their national convention Aug. 11–14, the Democrats become the first major political party to endorse a gay rights platform.

April 1981 Lesbian women's tennis star Billie Jean King is "outed" by her ex-lover in a lawsuit.

March 2, 1982 Wisconsin becomes the first state to ban discrimination on the basis of sexual orientation.

Aug.–Sept. 1982 The first Gay Games take place in San Francisco.

October 1982 Glenn Burke comes out as gay in *Inside Sports* and on *The Today Show*.

March 1987 The AIDS Coalition to Unleash Power (ACT UP), a grassroots political action group working to improve the lives of people living with AIDS, is founded in New York.

Oct. 11, 1987 Hundreds of thousands of activists descend on Washington,

DC to demand that President Ronald Reagan finally address the AIDS crisis. The AIDS Memorial Quilt is publicly displayed for the first time.

1991   The red ribbon is adopted as the visual symbol of awareness for those living with HIV.

Dec. 21, 1993   The Department of Defense adopts its "Don't Ask, Don't Tell" policy toward gay service members. Applicants are not to be asked about their sexuality, but neither are they to make any statements disclosing they are gay.

May 30, 1995   Glenn Burke dies at the age of forty-two.

March 1996   Muffin Spencer-Devlin comes out as the first openly gay LPGA golfer.

April 1997   Comedian and actress Ellen DeGeneres comes out as a lesbian on the cover of *Time* magazine.

July 1999   Former Major League baseball player Billy Bean reveals that he is gay.

1999   Outsports.com, the first website devoted to sports news for gay fans and athletes, is launched by Cyd Zeigler and Jim Buzinski.

1999   The pink, blue, and white transgender flag is created by transgender woman Monica Helms and debuts the next year at a gay pride parade in Phoenix.

April 26, 2000   Vermont becomes the first state to legalize same-sex civil unions.

Aug. 8, 2000   A lesbian couple is ejected from Dodger Stadium for kissing during a game.

June 26, 2003   US Supreme Court rules sodomy laws unconstitutional.

May 18, 2004   Massachusetts becomes the first state to legalize gay marriage.

Oct. 26, 2005	Sheryl Swoopes comes out, becoming the first openly lesbian player in the WNBA.
Nov. 4, 2008	Proposition 8 is passed by California voters, making same-sex marriage in the state illegal.
June 17, 2009	President Barack Obama signs a memorandum providing benefits to same-sex partners of federal employees.
August 12, 2009	Harvey Milk is posthumously awarded the Presidential Medal of Freedom by President Obama.
Oct. 28, 2009	The Matthew Shepard Act expands federal hate crime legislation to include crimes motivated by a victim's gender, sexual orientation, or gender identity.
Dec. 18, 2010	The US Senate votes to repeal the "Don't Ask, Don't Tell" policy, allowing gays and lesbians to serve openly in the US military.
2011	The NCAA adopts a transgender athlete inclusion policy and the NBA, MLB, NHL, and NFL adopt nondiscrimination policies that include sexual orientation.
Feb. 23, 2011	President Obama announces his administration will not enforce the Defense of Marriage Act that had banned same-sex marriage.
Sept. 4, 2012	The Democratic Party becomes the first major political party to support same-sex marriage on a national platform during the Democratic National Convention.
Nov. 6, 2012	Tammy Baldwin of Wisconsin becomes the first openly gay politician elected to the US Senate.
July 2012	Soccer star Megan Rapinoe comes out as a lesbian.
April 2013	NBA player Jason Collins comes out as gay in *Sports Illustrated*.

May 10, 2014	College football linebacker Michael Sam becomes the first openly gay player selected in the NFL Draft.
July 15, 2014	Major League Baseball honors the legacy of Glenn Burke and names Billy Bean its ambassador for social responsibility and inclusion prior to the All-Star Game in Minneapolis.
June 26, 2015	The US Supreme Court declares same-sex marriage legal in all fifty states.
June 24, 2016	President Obama announces the first national monument recognizing gay, lesbian, bisexual, and transgender rights, the Stonewall National Monument in New York.
May 17, 2016	When Eric Fanning is confirmed as secretary of the army, he becomes the first openly gay secretary of a branch of the US military.
June 30, 2016	The Pentagon lifts the ban on transgender people serving openly in the US military.
Nov. 9, 2016	Kate Brown is sworn in as Oregon governor, becoming the highest-ranking LGBTQIA+ person elected to office in the US.
June 27, 2017	Residents of the District of Columbia are given the ability to select a gender-neutral option on their driver's license, a first in US history.
Nov. 7, 2017	Danica Roem of Virginia becomes the first openly transgender person elected to a state legislature.
Nov. 6, 2018	Jared Polis is elected governor of Colorado, becoming the first openly gay male governor of a state.
February 2020	Democrat Pete Buttigieg becomes the first openly gay presidential candidate to win a primary or caucus.
June 15, 2020	US Supreme Court rules that a key provision of the 1964 Civil Rights Act protects LGBTQIA+ employees from workplace discrimination.

A SELECTION OF SIGNIFICANT BLACK AMERICAN LGBTQIA+ FIGURES FOR FURTHER STUDY

As long as there have been Black people, there have been Black LGBTQ and same-gender-loving people. Racism combined with the forces of stigma, phobia, discrimination and bias associated with gender and sexuality have too often erased the contributions of members of our community.

—David J. Johns, executive director of the National Black Justice Coalition

Alvin Ailey: Dancer, choreographer, and activist; recipient of Presidential Medal of Freedom.

Josephine Baker: Actress, dancer, singer, civil rights activist, French Resistance spy.

James Baldwin: Novelist, essayist (*Notes of a Native Son*), playwright, activist.

Simone Bell: First African American openly lesbian woman to serve in a US state legislature (Georgia).

Gladys Bentley: Lesbian cross-dressing performer during the Harlem Renaissance.

Jason Collins: First openly gay player in the NBA (Brooklyn Nets).

Alphonso David: First Black president of the Human Rights Campaign.

Angela Davis: Political activist, scholar, feminist, author.

Wade Davis: NFL quarterback who came out after his retirement; speaker, activist.

Stormé DeLarverie: Leader of Stonewall rebellion; entertainer, drag king, bouncer.

Alicia Garza: Activist, writer, co-founder of Black Lives Matter.

LZ Granderson: Sportswriter, ESPN commentator, sports radio host.

Lorraine Hansberry: First Black female playwright to have her work performed on Broadway (*A Raisin in the Sun*).

Elle Hearns: Transgender rights activist who co-founded the Black Lives Matter Global Network and founded the Marsha P. Johnson Institute.

Langston Hughes: Poet, civil rights activist, novelist, columnist, leader of Harlem Renaissance.

Sylvester James: Singer-songwriter known as the "Queen of Disco."

Andrea Jenkins: First Black openly transgender woman elected to public office (Minneapolis City Council).

Marsha P. Johnson: Drag performer, founding member of Gay Liberation Front, Stonewall rebellion leader, AIDS activist.

Barbara Jordan: Civil rights activist, first Southern Black woman elected to US House of Representatives (Texas).

Lil Nas X: His "Old Town Road" became the longest-running *Billboard* No. 1 song in history. First openly gay artist to win a Country Music Association award.

Audre Lorde: Poet, essayist, feminist, civil rights activist, educator.

Moms Mabley: Comedian, actress, vaudeville performer, first woman comedian featured at the Apollo Theater.

Pauli Murray: Writer, poet, civil rights activist, co-founder of CORE, first African American woman Episcopal priest.

Miss Major Griffin-Gracy: Transgender rights activist, feminist, Stonewall rebellion participant.

Frank Ocean: Singer, songwriter, record producer, photographer.

RuPaul: Drag queen, actor, model, singer, songwriter, Emmy Award winner.

Bayard Rustin: Civil rights activist who organized the Freedom Rides and March on Washington for Jobs and Freedom.

Michael Sam: First openly gay football player to be drafted in the NFL (St. Louis Rams).

Barbara Smith: Feminist leader, author, scholar, community organizer.

Bessie Smith: Regarded as the most popular female blues performer of the 1920s and '30s.

Billy Strayhorn: Jazz composer, pianist, lyricist, collaborator with Duke Ellington.

Sheryl Swoopes: Member of Naismith Memorial Basketball Hall of Fame and Women's Basketball Hall of Fame.

Wanda Sykes: Comedian, actress, gay rights and PETA activist, Emmy Award winner.

Alice Walker: Novelist (*The Color Purple*), poet, activist, feminist, womanist, Pulitzer Prize and National Book Award winner.

Phill Wilson: HIV/AIDS activist, writer, founder of Black AIDS Institute.

SELECT RESOURCES

LGBTQIA+

Family Equality Council (familyequality.org): Advances legal and lived equality for LGBTQIA+ families, and for those who wish to form them, through building community, changing hearts and minds, and driving policy change.

GLAAD (glaad.org): Rewrites the script for LGBTQIA+ acceptance. As a dynamic media force, GLAAD tackles tough issues to shape the narrative and provoke dialogue that leads to cultural change.

GLSEN (glsen.org): Works to ensure that LGBTQIA+ students are able to learn and grow in a school environment free from bullying and harassment.

Human Rights Campaign (hrc.org): America's largest civil rights organization working to achieve lesbian, gay, bisexual, transgender, and queer equality.

LGBT National Hotline (glbthotline.org): Provides vital peer-support, community connections, and resource information to people with questions regarding sexual orientation and/or gender identity.

National Black Justice Coalition (nbjc.org): Civil rights organization dedicated to empowering Black lesbian, gay, bisexual, and transgender people.

National Center for Transgender Equality (transequality.org): Founded in 2003 by transgender activists who recognized the urgent need for policy change to advance transgender equality.

PFLAG (pflag.org): The first and largest organization for lesbian, gay, bisexual, transgender, and queer (LGBTQIA+) people, their parents and families, and allies.

Rainbow Book List (glbtrt.ala.org/rainbowbooks): The American Library Association's Rainbow Book List presents an annual bibliography of quality books with significant and authentic LGBTQIA+ content, which are recommended for people from birth through eighteen years of age.

The Trevor Project (thetrevorproject.org): Leading national organization providing crisis intervention and suicide prevention services to lesbian, gay, bisexual, transgender, queer, and questioning (LGBTQIA+) young people under the age of twenty-five.

Zuna Institute (zunainstitute.org): National advocacy organization for Black lesbians that was created to address needs in the areas of health, public policy, economic development, and education.

LGBTQIA+ SPORTS

Athlete Ally (athleteally.org): Mission is to end the rampant homophobia and transphobia in sport and to activate the athletic community to exercise its leadership to champion LGBTQIA+ equality.

Outsports (outsports.com): Leading national LGBTQIA+ sports news source.

HIV/AIDS

Black AIDS Institute (blackaids.org): Mission is to stop the AIDS epidemic in Black communities by engaging and mobilizing Black institutions and individuals in efforts to confront HIV.

Centers for Disease Control and Prevention—HIV Resources (cdc.gov /hiv/library): Fact sheets discuss how HIV affects specific subpopulations and provide information about topics such as risk behaviors and prevention tools. Reports and slides share the latest data and research. Downloadable infographics and awareness day materials.

HOMELESSNESS

National Alliance to End Homelessness (endhomlessness.org): Non-partisan, nonprofit organization committed to preventing and ending homelessness in the United States.

National Coalition for the Homeless (nationalhomeless.org): National network of people who are currently experiencing or who have experienced homelessness, activists, and others committed to ending and prevent homelessness while ensuring the immediate needs of those experiencing homelessness are met and their civil rights are respected and protected.

BASEBALL

Baseball Almanac (baseball-almanac.com): Interactive baseball encyclopedia filled with 500,000+ pages of in-depth baseball facts, original research and statistics.

Baseball Reference (baseball-reference.com): Complete source for baseball history including complete Major League player, team, and league stats, awards, records, leaders, rookies, and scores.

Fangraphs (fangraphs.com): Statistics for Major and Minor League Baseball with analysis, graphs, and projections.

National Baseball Hall of Fame (baseballhall.org): Nonprofit committed to preserving the history of America's pastime and celebrating legendary players, managers, umpires, and executives.

RetroSheet (retrosheet.org): Founded in 1989 for the purpose of computerizing play-by-play accounts of as many pre-1984 major league games as possible.

ACKNOWLEDGMENTS

After writing *Strong Inside* and *Games of Deception,* I had a conversation with my literary agent, Alec Shane, about the fact that I wanted to continue writing sports-related nonfiction with a social justice bent. It was Alec who suggested a biography of Glenn Burke. I remembered Glenn's 1978 Topps baseball card, but not much else about him. Before Alec nudged me in his direction, I didn't know Glenn had invented the high five, or that he was considered the first openly gay Major League baseball player. I'm indebted to Alec for the terrific suggestion.

My first task in writing this book was to read *Out at Home*, the autobiography Glenn collaborated with Erik Sherman on as he was dying. I was apprehensive about contacting Erik to let him know I was working on this project, figuring he might be territorial about the story and reluctant to help another author. But Erik could not have been kinder. I spent a day with him at his home in New Rochelle, New York, where he shared not only memories but also documents, letters, and audio and video recordings.

Erik told me that Glenn's sister Lutha is an angel, and I cannot disagree. Lutha spent many hours on the phone helping me understand her brother, and was always quick to text back whenever I had a question about some minor point as I wrote the manuscript. Thank you also to Glenn's sister Paula Hunt, who was generous with her time and memories, and Glenn's good friends Vincent Trahan, Cloy Jenkins, Doug Harris, and Doug Goldman. I enjoyed getting to know Bobby Glasser, an A's fan who saw Glenn Burke play as a kid and has gone on to become a Burke memorabilia collector. Bobby, thank you so much for the jersey!

From the world of baseball, former Dodgers PR man Steve Brener helped me understand the vibe around the team in the 1970s and also introduced me to several former players. Among those, Dusty Baker was as cool, kind, and generous as advertised. We spent an enjoyable afternoon talking about Glenn Burke and the Big Blue Wrecking Crew in Asheville, North Carolina, where he was scouting for the Giants prior to being named Astros manager. My other most enjoyable interviews for the book were with Glenn's Minor League teammates; thank you to Larry Corrigan and Bob Lesslie for going above and beyond by providing connections to other players. Thank you to Fernando Alcalá of the Oakland A's, Billy Bean and Ethan Orlinsky of Major League Baseball, my former Tampa Bay Devil Rays boss Rick Vaughn, and my sportswriter buddies Tyler Kepner, Dave Sheinin, and Jesus Ortiz for their help and connections. At the National Baseball Hall of Fame, Bill Francis located valuable archival documents, and John Horne provided several of the photos in this book.

At Philomel, I am fortunate to work with wonderfully supportive and kind people, led by Ken Wright and Jill Santopolo. I'll always be grateful to Ruta Sepetys for making the connection. Kelsey Murphy was a fantastic editor on this project, providing just the right balance of encouragement and constructive criticism to make this a better book in so many ways. Thank you to artist Nigel Buchanan and designer Maria Fazio for amazing work on the cover, incredible copyeditor Marinda Valenti, and others who work so hard behind the scenes, including Cheryl Eissing, Monique Sterling, Gerard Mancini, Elise Poston, Krista Ahlberg, Nicole Wayland, and publicists Lathea Mondesir and Jennifer Dee.

I'm incredibly fortunate to work as a Visiting Author at Vanderbilt Athletics, surely the only position of its kind. Thank you, Candice Lee and Angie Bess, for putting up with me (most of the time). I'm also grateful for the assistance of Vanderbilt librarian Pam Morgan, as well as Chris Purcell of the university's LGBTQIA+ Center, who advised me at the outset of research, read the manuscript, provided invaluable feedback, and suggested further reading. Thank you also to filmmaker David McFarland, who helped educate me on the challenges and triumphs of gay athletes and vouched for me with a few interview subjects.

I completed this manuscript during the first month of the COVID-19 quarantine and the time spent with my family in Nashville and the multiple

FaceTime and Zoom conversations with my parents, David and Linda, in DC, and my in-laws, Doug and Cathy Williams, up the street, were constant reminders of what really matters in life. I could not write books without the sacrifices (and great edits!) of my wife, Alison, and the patience and enthusiasm of our two young children, sweet Eliza and Charlie. The best part of sheltering-at-home was growing even closer with the ones I love.

INDEX

and Burke's decline and death, 225–26, 269n2

and Burke's prospects after baseball, 195

Burke's relationship with, 190–92

and Burke's time in Guerneville, 197–201

and the HIV/AIDS crisis, 221–22

John, Tommy, 121, 209, 262n2, 265n1

Johnson, Earvin "Magic," 231–33, 232, 268n6, 268n7

Johnson, Lyndon B., 83

Jones, Cleve, 132, 193

Kee, Rich, 107–8, 262n3

Kelly, Richard, 236

Kingman, Dave, 142, 264n2

Knight, Phil, 114

Kopay, Dave, 81, 213

Koppel, Ted, 263n1

Korich, Stan, 29

Kozbert, Bob, 151

Lacy, Lee, 121, 209

Lambert, Jack, 212

Lambert, John, 18, 21, 24, 58

Lasorda, Tommy, *86*

background, 85–86

and Baker's batting, 261n1

and Burke's post-season starts, 4, 116–18, 121–22

and Burke's sexuality, 102–4

and Burke's trade, 138, 139–42, 143–45

coaching style and team dynamics,

81, 86–87, 91–93, 109, 111–12, 116–20, 263n1

criticisms and backlash for treatment of Burke, 145–46, 264n3

and Dodgers' promotion of marriages, 135

and invention of the high five, 187, 188

"Kingman rant," 142–43, 264n2

and NCLS victory, 121–22, 125

and son's sexuality, 103–4, 262n3

and World Series, 130

Lasorda, Tommy, Jr. ("Spunky"), 102–3, 139

Lavelle, Gary, 77

Lee, Tommy, 237

LeJohn, Don, 52, 53

Lesslie, Bob, 35, 53, 290n1

Linquist, Bob, 221

Lopes, Davey, *100*

and Burke's call up to majors, 75–76, 78

and Burke's coming-out interviews, 209

and Burke's gregarious nature, 93

and Burke's sexuality, 99–100

and Burke's trade, 143

and Dodgers winter basketball, 130

and home run record (1977), 111

and invention of the high five, 119

and Lasorda's coaching, 86

and mentorship in baseball, 105–6

Lopez, Aurelio, 178

Los Angeles Dodgers

Smith, Cleo, 31–32, 47–48, 100

Smith, Michael, 123–25, 171, 187–88, 196, 203–4, 226

Smith, Reggie, 100, 107–9, 109, 121–22, *122*, 130, 134

Snider, Jane, 62–63

Snider, John, 34, 51, 62–63

softball leagues, 70, 192–95, *194*, 201, 204, 210, 221, 227–28, 239, 243

Sosa, Elias, 126

Speakes, Larry, 219

Speier, Chris, 77

Spencer, Lyle, 93, 140, 145

Stargell, Willie, 29

Staub, Rusty, 178

Stevenson, Jack, 116–18

Stier, Kit, 264n1

Stonewall riots, 69, 217

Studio One (disco), 66–67

Sutton, Don, 92–93, 119, 130, 141–42, 144, 209

Tenderloin district (San Francisco), 1–2, 7, 236

Thomas, Bob, 221

Thomas, Cal, 219

Thomas, Rubin, 268n7

Thomasson, Gary, 160

Today Show, *205*, 205–10, 221

Tom Waddell Clinic, 1, 236

Tournament of Champions, *21*, 23, 28–29, 118

Trahan, Vince, 16–17, 228, 249–50

Valentine, Ellis, 43–44, 53

Veeck, Bill, 179

Vero Beach, Florida, 40–41, 73, 85, 103, 137

Voeller, Bruce, 95–96

Vucinich, Steve, 165

Warren, Gary "Burger," 24–25

Washington, Claudell, 184

Wasiak, Stan, 80

Webb, Marvin, 31–32, 41–43, 47, 48, 63–64, 100–101

Weir, Tom, 151, 168

White, Dan, 162–63, 165, 169, 264n2

Wiggins, Alan, 267n1

Williams, Gus, 58

Williams, Jimmy, 90

Willows resort, 197, *199*, 199–201, 200, 205, 221, 225–26, 265n2

Winkles, Bobby, 157

World Series (1977), 4–6, *5*, 123–27, 155–56, 226, 277–79

Yeager, Steve, 129, 130

Yeomens, Jeannine, 169

YMCA, 63–64